LANGUAGE AND LITER/

Dorothy S. Strickland, Fou
Celia Genishi and Donna E. Alverm
ADVISORY BOARD: *Richard Allington, Kathryn Au,*
Anne Haas Dyson, Carole Edelsky, Mary Juzwik, Susan L

MW01035878

Partnering with Immigrant Communities:
Action Through Literacy
GERALD CAMPANO, MARÍA PAULA GHISO, & BETHANY J. WELCH

Teaching Outside the Box but Inside the Standards:
Making Room for Dialogue
BOB FECHO, MICHELLE FALTER, & XIAOLI HONG, EDS.

Literacy Leadership in Changing Schools:
10 Keys to Successful Professional Development
SHELLEY B. WEPNER, DIANE W. GÓMEZ, KATIE EGAN CUNNINGHAM,
KRISTIN N. RAINVILLE, & COURTNEY KELLY

Literacy Theory as Practice:
Connecting Theory and Instruction in K–12 Classrooms
LARA J. HANDSFIELD

Literacy and History in Action: Immersive Approaches to
Disciplinary Thinking, Grades 5–12
THOMAS M. MCCANN, REBECCA D'ANGELO, NANCY GALAS, & MARY
GRESKA

Pose, Wobble, Flow:
A Culturally Proactive Approach to Literacy Instruction
ANTERO GARCIA & CINDY O'DONNELL-ALLEN

Newsworthy—Cultivating Critical Thinkers, Readers, and
Writers in Language Arts Classrooms
ED MADISON

Engaging Writers with Multigenre Research Projects:
A Teacher's Guide
NANCY MACK

Teaching Transnational Youth—
Literacy and Education in a Changing World
ALLISON SKERRETT

Uncommonly Good Ideas—
Teaching Writing in the Common Core Era
SANDRA MURPHY & MARY ANN SMITH

The One-on-One Reading and Writing Conference:
Working with Students on Complex Texts
JENNIFER BERNE & SOPHIE C. DEGENER

Critical Encounters in Secondary English:
Teaching Literary Theory to Adolescents, Third Edition
DEBORAH APPLEMAN

Transforming Talk into Text—Argument Writing, Inquiry,
and Discussion, Grades 6–12
THOMAS M. MCCANN

Reading and Representing Across the Content Areas:
A Classroom Guide
AMY ALEXANDRA WILSON & KATHRYN J. CHAVEZ

Writing and Teaching to Change the World:
Connecting with Our Most Vulnerable Students
STEPHANIE JONES, ED.

Educating Literacy Teachers Online:
Tools, Techniques, and Transformations
LANE W. CLARKE & SUSAN WATTS-TAFFEE

Other People's English: Code-Meshing,
Code-Switching, and African American Literacy
VERSHAWN ASHANTI YOUNG, RUSTY BARRETT,
Y'SHANDA YOUNG-RIVERA, & KIM BRIAN LOVEJOY

WHAM! Teaching with Graphic Novels Across
the Curriculum
WILLIAM G. BROZO, GARY MOORMAN, & CARLA K. MEYER

The Administration and Supervision of Reading Programs,
5th Edition
SHELLEY B. WEPNER, DOROTHY S. STRICKLAND,
& DIANA J. QUATROCHE, EDS.

Critical Literacy in the Early Childhood Classroom:
Unpacking Histories, Unlearning Privilege
CANDACE R. KUBY

Inspiring Dialogue:
Talking to Learn in the English Classroom
MARY M. JUZWIK, CARLIN BORSHEIM-BLACK,
SAMANTHA CAUGHLAN, & ANNE HEINTZ

Reading the Visual:
An Introduction to Teaching Multimodal Literacy
FRANK SERAFINI

Race, Community, and Urban Schools:
Partnering with African American Families
STUART GREENE

ReWRITING the Basics:
Literacy Learning in Children's Cultures
ANNE HAAS DYSON

Writing Instruction That Works:
Proven Methods for Middle and High School Classrooms
ARTHUR N. APPLEBEE & JUDITH A. LANGER, WITH KRISTEN CAMPBELL
WILCOX, MARC NACHOWITZ, MICHAEL P. MASTROIANNI, &
CHRISTINE DAWSON

Literacy Playshop: New Literacies, Popular Media, and
Play in the Early Childhood Classroom
KAREN E. WOHLWEND

Critical Media Pedagogy:
Teaching for Achievement in City Schools
ERNEST MORRELL, RUDY DUEÑAS, VERONICA GARCIA,
& JORGE LOPEZA

A Search Past Silence: The Literacy of Young Black Men
DAVID E. KIRKLAND

The ELL Writer:
Moving Beyond Basics in the Secondary Classroom
CHRISTINA ORTMEIER-HOOPER

Reading in a Participatory Culture:
Remixing *Moby-Dick* in the English Classroom
HENRY JENKINS & WYN KELLEY, WITH KATIE CLINTON, JENNA
MCWILLIAMS, RICARDO PITTS-WILEY, & ERIN REILLY, EDS.

Summer Reading:
Closing the Rich/Poor Achievement Gap
RICHARD L. ALLINGTON & ANNE MCGILL-FRANZEN, EDS.

Real World Writing for Secondary Students:
Teaching the College Admission Essay and
Other Gate-Openers for Higher Education
JESSICA SINGER EARLY & MEREDITH DECOSTA

Teaching Vocabulary to English Language Learners
MICHAEL F. GRAVES, DIANE AUGUST, &
JEANETTE MANCILLA-MARTINEZ

continued

For volumes in the NCRLL Collection (edited by JoBeth Allen and Donna E. Alvermann) and the Practitioners Bookshelf Series
(edited by Celia Genishi and Donna E. Alvermann), as well as other titles in this series, please visit www.tcpress.com.

Language and Literacy Series, *continued*

Literacy for a Better World:
LAURA SCHNEIDER VANDERPLOEG

Socially Responsible Literacy
PAULA M. SELVESTER & DEBORAH G. SUMMERS

Learning from Culturally and Linguistically Diverse
Classrooms: Using Inquiry to Inform Practice
JOAN C. FINGON & SHARON H. ULANOFF, EDS.

Bridging Literacy and Equity
ALTHIER M. LAZAR ET AL.

"Trust Me! I Can Read"
SALLY LAMPING & DEAN WOODRING BLASE

Reading Girls
HADAR DUBROWSKY MA'AYAN

Reading Time
CATHERINE COMPTON-LILLY

A Call to Creativity
LUKE REYNOLDS

Literacy and Justice Through Photography
WENDY EWALD, KATHARINE HYDE, & LISA LORD

The Successful High School Writing Center
DAWN FELS & JENNIFER WELLS, EDS.

Interrupting Hate
MOLLIE V. BLACKBURN

Playing Their Way into Literacies
KAREN E. WOHLWEND

Teaching Literacy for Love and Wisdom
JEFFREY D. WILHELM & BRUCE NOVAK

Overtested
JESSICA ZACHER PANDYA

Restructuring Schools for Linguistic Diversity,
Second Edition
OFELIA B. MIRAMONTES, ADEL NADEAU, & NANCY L. COMMINS

Words Were All We Had
MARÍA DE LA LUZ REYES, ED.

Urban Literacies
VALERIE KINLOCH, ED.

Bedtime Stories and Book Reports
CATHERINE COMPTON-LILLY & STUART GREENE, EDS.

Envisioning Knowledge
JUDITH A. LANGER

Envisioning Literature, Second Edition
JUDITH A. LANGER

Writing Assessment and the Revolution in Digital Texts
and Technologies
MICHAEL R. NEAL

Artifactual Literacies
KATE PAHL & JENNIFER ROWSELL

Educating Emergent Bilinguals
OFELIA GARCÍA & JO ANNE KLEIFGEN

(Re)Imagining Content-Area Literacy Instruction
RONI JO DRAPER, ED.

Change Is Gonna Come
PATRICIA A. EDWARDS ET AL.

When Commas Meet Kryptonite
MICHAEL BITZ

Literacy Tools in the Classroom
RICHARD BEACH ET AL.

Harlem on Our Minds
VALERIE KINLOCH

Teaching the New Writing
ANNE HERRINGTON, KEVIN HODGSON, & CHARLES MORAN, EDS.

Children, Language, and Literacy
CELIA GENISHI & ANNE HAAS DYSON

Children's Language
JUDITH WELLS LINDFORS

"You Gotta BE the Book," Second Edition
JEFFREY D. WILHELM

Children's Literature and Learning
BARBARA A. LEHMAN

Storytime
LAWRENCE R. SIPE

Effective Instruction for Struggling Readers, K–6
BARBARA M. TAYLOR & JAMES E. YSSELDYKE, EDS.

The Effective Literacy Coach
ADRIAN RODGERS & EMILY M. RODGERS

Writing in Rhythm
MAISHA T. FISHER

Reading the Media
RENEE HOBBS

teaching*media*literacy.com
RICHARD BEACH

What Was It Like?
LINDA J. RICE

Research on Composition
PETER SMAGORINSKY, ED.

The Vocabulary Book
MICHAEL F. GRAVES

New Literacies in Action
WILLIAM KIST

Teaching English Today
BARRIE R.C. BARRELL ET AL., EDS.

Bridging the Literacy Achievement Gap, 4–12
DOROTHY S. STRICKLAND & DONNA E. ALVERMANN, EDS.

Out of This World
HOLLY VIRGINIA BLACKFORD

Critical Passages
KRISTIN DOMBEK & SCOTT HERNDON

Making Race Visible
STUART GREENE & DAWN ABT-PERKINS, EDS.

The Child as Critic, Fourth Edition
GLENNA SLOAN

Room for Talk
REBEKAH FASSLER

The Brothers and Sisters Learn to Write
ANNE HAAS DYSON

The Testing Trap
GEORGE HILLOCKS, JR.

"Why Don't They Learn English?"
LUCY TSE

Conversational Borderlands
BETSY RYMES

Inquiry-Based English Instruction
RICHARD BEACH & JAMIE MYERS

PARTNERING *with* IMMIGRANT COMMUNITIES

action through literacy

GERALD CAMPANO
MARÍA PAULA GHISO
BETHANY J. WELCH

Foreword by María E. Fránquiz

TEACHERS COLLEGE PRESS

TEACHERS COLLEGE | COLUMBIA UNIVERSITY

NEW YORK AND LONDON

Published by Teachers College Press, 1234 Amsterdam Avenue, New York, NY 10027

Cover design by David Strauss. Cover art inspired by Circle of Culture and used by permission of © 2013 City of Philadelphia Mural Arts Program/Delia King.

Figure 1.2 created by David Low. Photography in Chapters 6 and 7 provided by María Paula Ghiso and David Low. Figure 3.1 created by Mary Yee.

Material in Chapter 9 was adapted with permission from Gerald Campano, María Paula Ghiso, and Bethany J. Welch, "Ethical and professional norms in community-based research," *Harvard Educational Review*, 85(1), 29–49. © 2015 by President and Fellows of Harvard College. All rights reserved. For more information, please visit: *http://hepg.org/ her-home/issues/harvard-educational-review-volume-85-number-1/herarticle/ethical-and-professional-norms-in-community-based*

Library of Congress Cataloging-in-Publication Data

Names: Campano, Gerald, author.
Title: Partnering with immigrant communities : action through literacy / Gerald Campano, Maria Paula Ghiso, Bethany J. Welch.
Description: New York, NY : Teachers College Press, [2016]
Identifiers: LCCN 2015051148| ISBN 9780807757215 (pbk. : alk. paper) | ISBN 9780807757222 (hardcover : alk. paper)
Subjects: LCSH: Immigrants—Education—United States. | Community Literacies Project. | Literacy—Social aspects—United States. | Church and education—United States.
Classification: LCC LC3731 .C32 2016 | DDC 371.826/9120973—dc23
LC record available at http://lccn.loc.gov/2015051148

ISBN 978-0-8077-5721-5 (paper)
ISBN 978-0-8077-5722-2 (hardcover)
ISBN 978-0-8077-7423-6 (ebook)

Printed on acid-free paper
Manufactured in the United States of America

23 22 21 20 19 18 17 16   8 7 6 5 4 3 2 1

Contents

Acknowledgments   ix

Foreword   *María E. Fránquiz*   xi

1. **The Community Literacies Project:**
   Social Justice Education in a Diverse Parish   1

   Contesting Views on Immigration   3

   Literacies of Immigrant Youth and Families: An Emphasis on Agency   8

   Precarity and Its Relevance to Education   10

   A Way of Being in Community: Fostering Interdependence in Research   12

   The Aquinas Center   16

   Discourse Communities at St. Thomas Aquinas:
       A Pluriversal Conceptual Model   18

   Overview of the Book   22

2. **Aquinas Center: Designing a Space of Radical Hospitality**   27

   A History of the Space   28

   Reusing, Repurposing, and Reclaiming   30

   Aesthetics of Identity and Change   31

   Responsiveness and Mutuality in Center Initiatives   33

   Conclusion   37

3. **Participatory Research with Parents: Mobilizing Social Capital**
   to Support Children's Education   39
   (Mary Yee, Karim Mostafa, & Gerald Campano)

   Building the Community Collaboration Process   40

   Indonesian Parents at the Parish   41

   Parental Involvement from the Ground Up   42

Accessing and Coconstructing Knowledge 43

Developing Community Capacity 48

Reflections: Lessons Learned 52

4. Collective Advocacy in a Latina/o Family ESOL Class **54**
(María Paula Ghiso, Alicia Rusoja, & Emily Schwab)

Publics and Counterpublics 55

Discursive (Counter)Publics Around Latina/os and Immigration 56

Codesigning Our Intergenerational Learning Space 57

Sharing "Class News" 58

Curricular Inquiries Based on the Class News 61

Conclusion 63

5. Cultivating Civic Engagement Through Literacy:
Francisco's Community Service Project **66**
(Robert LeBlanc & Bethany J. Welch)

Religious Engagement, Civic Engagement 67

Community Leader, Organizer, Public Speaker 69

Conclusion 75

6. Bidirectional Learning in a School–University Partnership **78**
(Lan Ngo, Katrina Bartow Jacobs, Gerald Campano, María Paula
Ghiso, & David E. Low)

Case 1: Linking a Graduate-Level Course with Mrs. Cruz's Classroom 79

Case 2: Young Children's "Inquiry into College" and Visit to Campus 84

Conclusion 90

7. Multiliteracies, the Arts, and Postcolonial Agency **92**
(David E. Low & Gerald Campano)

The Comics Inquiry Community 95

(Co)Creating Graphica: Randy's Lines of Flight 97

Conclusion 101

8. The Community Researchers Project:
    The Role of Care in Critical Work   103
    (Grace Player, Lan Ngo, Gerald Campano, & María Paula Ghiso)

    Background and Orientation of the Project   104

    Our Stance on Critical Literacy: Beginning with Care   105

    Researching from the Realities of Their Lives   106

    "A wound on our education system": Martin's Documentary Inquiry   107

    Intergenerational Care   111

    Moving Forward Together   113

9. Ethical and Professional Norms in Community-Based Research   115

    Developing Norms: Working the Dialectic of Theory and Practice   116

    Current Ethical and Professional Research Norms   118

    Conclusion   126

10. Collaboration and Advocacy in a Cosmopolitan Counterpublic   127

    Educational Advocacy   127

    Educational Precarity   128

    Returning to Our Conceptual Model: Nourishing Hope Through
        Collaborative Research and Practice   129

    Congregation: A Precondition for Solidarity   130

    First Circle of Solidarity: Communities of Inquiry with Educators   132

    Second Circle of Solidarity: Community Networks and Groups   134

    Third Circle of Solidarity: Our Youth   136

    Toward a Vision of Social and Educational Justice   138

References   141

Index   155

About the Authors   163

Acknowledgments

This book represents labor and thinking that was done in the company of others over many years. We would like to acknowledge several of the communities that have been invaluable in our personal and professional journeys.

We are grateful to the networks that have provided insights, encouragement, and care, including family, friends, colleagues, students, and mentors. Gerald is indebted to the support of the Literacy, Culture, and Language Education Department at Indiana University, Bloomington and the Reading/Writing/Literacy Division at the University of Pennsylvania. Scholars from The Future of Minority Studies Interdisciplinary Research Project made an indelible impact on his thinking early in his career. He is also appreciative of the Metro New York Chapter of the Filipino American National Historical Society, which is helping to honor histories and experiences that were excluded from the educational curricula of his youth. María Paula is thankful for the mentorship and inspiration from the Literacy Specialist team, colleagues in the Department of Curriculum and Teaching at Teachers College, and interdisciplinary collaborators from across TC and beyond. Bethany is grateful to all those who accompany and encourage her, including friends and colleagues from the Contemplative Leaders in Action and the Urban Affairs Association.

We've learned a great deal from the efforts and courage of grassroots immigrant rights advocacy groups in Philadelphia. We also continue to be inspired by all educators, such as those involved in the Philadelphia Writing Project, who unequivocally center issues of equity in their work in schools and neighborhoods.

Versions of chapters in this book have been presented at a number of professional conferences, including those sponsored by the Literacy Research Association, Practitioner Inquiry Day at the University of Pennsylvania Ethnography in Education Research Forum, the American Educational Research Association (AERA), and the Working Conference on Discourse Analysis in Education at The Ohio State University. We are blessed to have many brilliant, generous, and committed colleagues in the field of literacy who have both affirmed and productively challenged our work. This project has been supported by resources received from an AERA Education Research Service Project grant, the Netter Center at the University of Pennsylvania as part of its Academically Based Community-Service program, and a micro-giving initiative from the UPenn Graduate School of Education. UPenn GSE has a strong commitment to funding graduate students, who played an instrumental role in supporting and sustaining our research partnership over the years. The parish and center rely on generous gifts of time and talent from community members, donors, foundations, and collaborative partners from public, private, and nonprofit sectors. The incredible editorial team at Teachers College Press supplied incisive feedback throughout the whole process of writing this book.

We are deeply humbled by and indebted to the "beloved community" of St. Thomas Aquinas. Thank you for helping us find belonging at the intersections of scholarship and practice as well as faith and action.

Our parents were always there with love and guidance. This book is dedicated to their grandchildren, Gabriela Inés Campano and Connor Michael Canino Welch.

Foreword

In Spanish the closure for a message is sometimes, *en paz y solidaridad*, meaning, in peace and solidarity. It was a common closure during the Civil Rights era, specifically in relation to the United Farmworkers Movement. Non-violence was key in civil disobedience and arms locked together were emblematic of solidarity. I attended Mary Star of the Sea High School where the Catholic social teachings included partnering with the downtrodden, the poor, and the marginalized. Thus, I locked arms with members of the Sisters of the Immaculate Heart of Mary to protest for the civil rights of the oppressed. Years later, I was a teaching assistant for César Chávez at the University of California, Santa Barbara. He was teaching a course on the labor history of California. The lectures were centered on an unjust history of Mexican and Filipino workers who picked and packed the agricultural yield from the rich valleys of California. To protest the inhumane living conditions of farmworkers, César Chávez taught the importance of solidarity and coalition building. Sometimes closure for class was, *la lucha sigue*, or, the struggle continues. Sometimes it was, *contigo en la lucha,* or, with you in the fight.

In the 21st century, the uprooting of farmworker families continues. But, there are other uprootings increasingly occurring in the lives of families globally. The circumstances for men, women, and children to leave familiar spaces and cultural traditions for foreign ones is too often a response to war, failed economies, religious intolerance, and abductions, to name a few. The challenges families on the move face are precarious in terms of place, the labor market, and access to institutional supports such as those provided by schools and churches. The health, safety, and education of immigrant families through interactions in a faith-based community, St. Thomas Aquinas, is at the heart of the humanizing projects presented in this book.

As a reader I was struck by Gerald, María Paula, and Bethany's collaborative book organization and found the stories of their 5-year engagement in the Community Literacies Project absolutely captivating. Together the research team participates in "literacies of interdependence" in solidarity with a community-based center that aims to improve the educational outcomes of immigrant and refugee families within and outside a multi-ethnic Catholic parish. Rather than investing in reactionary distortions of hope this partnership dares to hope audaciously (Duncan-Andrade, 2009) in re-framing the negative impact of heated immigration debates. César Chávez would be fascinated with and approve of their coalitional practices that include, but are not limited to, sharing testimonials, resisting dichotomies, taking a stance of radical hospitality, practicing nonviolence, expressing concern for the dignity of all human beings and advocating sanctuary for immigrants.

The text is woven with nested inquiries and self-reflexive insights. An ethos of radical hospitality and cooperation is explored through a broad range of literacy projects such as repurposing a space for activism, fostering critical consciousness through community murals, examining the potential of multimodal literacies, teaching and learning about justice and health in the community garden, reading texts together with social justice themes, conducting and presenting research on issues that matter to youth, and grappling with the ethical dimensions of a partnership.

The diversity of immigrants and refugees at St. Thomas Aquinas includes families from Indonesia, Southeast Asia, Mexico, and the Philippines. Some are mixed-status families with children born in the United States. Since the parish serves as a site of civically engaged literacy practices it is a safe space to explore identities, provide social critique, and develop an activist stance. The authors learn that coalitional work among youth across their differences requires time. This means the bonds within a group such as Indonesian students at times is stronger than across groups such as Indonesian and Latina/o students. It is through sustained coalitional work that trust grows and the partnership is realized.

The first 5 years of a proposed 10-year study affirm and sustain a shared vision of a partnership for social justice. The overlapping histories and braided legacies are critical to the potentially agentive powers of literacies under construction across intersecting discourse communities such as cultural, religious, activist, legal, mainstream educational, and educational research discourse communities. The implications of the authors' work thus far is that an ethos of radical hospitality and interdependence yields circles of solidarity—solidarity with other educators, with community organizations, and with youth. These solidarity circles lock arms in audacious hope for a better future for immigrant communities. *Contigo en la lucha!*

—María E. Fránquiz, dean,
The University of Utah, College of Education

Chapter 1

The Community Literacies Project
Social Justice Education in a Diverse Parish

Probably you know my story. I just ran out from our country, that's it. I'm just coming here. First coming to Georgia, go to Florida, coming to Philly, and finally St. Thomas community. I'm just blessed to have this community.

—A leader in the Indonesian community

The stone that the builder refused has become the cornerstone.

—Psalm 118:22

This book documents the Community Literacies Project, our university partnership with a multilingual, multiethnic Catholic parish, St. Thomas Aquinas,[1] and its school and community center. Through examples of community-based research that occurred over a 5-year period, we investigate the following questions:

- What language and literacy practices are employed when individuals negotiate social, cultural, linguistic, and institutional boundaries to enact a shared vision of educational justice and immigrant rights?
- How do community members organize to provide resources for their families, with particular attention to education? What role might faith-based centers play in such efforts?
- How can the knowledge and interests of the communities we partner with inform literacy teaching and learning, both in school and out of school?
- How can universities foster sustained and ethical collaborations with community-based organizations?

St. Thomas Aquinas is a microcosm of a world increasingly characterized by migration and cross-cultural interaction. The parish serves a culturally and linguistically diverse congregation and is situated in a similarly

1

pluralistic neighborhood: There are longstanding African American and Italian American communities, Vietnamese and Cambodian refugees that arrived in the 1980s and 1990s, Filipina/o[2] parishioners, an Indonesian immigrant population beginning in the late 1990s, and newcomers from Latin America within the past 10 years, and most recently from Sudan and the Democratic Republic of the Congo. Fr. Shields, the monsignor[3] at St. Thomas Aquinas and himself of Irish descent, noted, "Our parish has been called 'Intercultural,' 'Multicultural,' 'Culturally Diverse,' but what we are, and have been calling ourselves, is a *shared Parish*. Shared by so many people [and] nationalities" (Fieldnotes, October 7, 2011). The parish offers services in English, Spanish, Vietnamese, Indonesian, and occasionally Tagalog and provides opportunities for the different communities to participate in culturally sustaining activities, such as native language youth groups and celebrations for Día de los Muertos and the Vietnamese Moon Festival. St. Thomas Aquinas also views itself as a teaching parish, where visitors are welcomed to become involved in the neighborhood through service learning projects. This vision includes advocating for immigrant rights to counteract the struggles many congregants face. St. Thomas Aquinas promotes an ethos of hospitality and universal human dignity, which may provide sanctuary for individuals who are stigmatized within other contexts of their lives. In 2013, the social justice–oriented Aquinas Center, of which Bethany J. Welch is the founding director, was established on the grounds of the church to provide educational, legal, and social supports for students and families.

In addition to us, the university research team consists of nine doctoral students who have been with the project long term (Mary Yee, Karim Mostafa, David E. Low, Robert LeBlanc, Alicia Rusoja, Lan Ngo, Katrina Bartow Jacobs, Grace Player, and Emily Schwab) and who have coauthored chapters in the middle part of this book, as well as several master's students who join each year. Many members of the research team are from minoritized communities themselves (e.g., Asian American, Hapa, Latina, Black) and have diverse backgrounds with respect to social class, gender/sexuality, and religious affiliation (Protestant, Catholic, Jewish, Muslim, and agnostic). They also bring a host of experiences as community activists, school leaders, and teachers from early childhood to adulthood, and share indebtedness to Freirian legacies of critical dialogue and pedagogy.

Our collaborative research combines traditional ethnographic methods (Erickson, 1986) with practitioner research (Cochran-Smith & Lytle, 2009) and participatory action research (Cahill, 2007). A primary concern for us has been the sustainability of research on broader scales of time and involvement. The research team has been immersed at St. Thomas Aquinas several times per week across the years, participating in parish events, attending leadership meetings, and designing a series of nested participatory studies with input from the St. Thomas Aquinas community regarding its goals for the partnership. We have striven toward a collaborative and transparent research methodology where community members are involved throughout the research process.

Our ongoing research collaboration with St. Thomas Aquinas affords an occasion to examine how the education of immigrant youth and families is impacted by social and political dynamics, as well as the ways that community members advocate for greater opportunities. A key contribution of this book is its focus on the knowledge that is already present in communities as people come together to take action on matters that directly impact their lives (Cushman, 1999). These critical insights are seeded in the soil of local contexts through culturally situated language and literacy practices and group legacies of resilience and resistance (Campano, Ghiso, & Sánchez, 2013). The diversity of the research context, and the opportunity to work together across cultural, linguistic, religious, institutional, and experiential backgrounds, allows for an exploration of languages and literacies in ways that are not bounded by a specific group affiliation. While there are rich portraits of particular groups in the educational literature, there is less attention to multilingual, multiethnic communities, whose experiences are braided by overlapping histories of colonization and shared present struggles. And while there are many stories of conflict between groups, we need more accounts of how diverse people work together for social change.

Partnering with Immigrant Communities also provides descriptions and guidelines for reimagining the practice of partnering in community-based research. Through our collaboration, we have sought to disrupt the secular missionary paradigm that positions universities as imparting knowledge in a unidirectional manner to under-resourced or minoritized communities. Instead, we have tried to enact more horizontal processes of partnering (Campano, Honeyford, Sánchez, & Vander Zanden, 2010) that value joint inquiry and view human relationships as ends in themselves rather than an instrumental means to an end. The book amplifies the voices of community leaders who desire to collaborate with universities to advance community goals but who are concerned about issues of equity, reciprocity, and mutuality.

CONTESTING VIEWS ON IMMIGRATION

In this section we share two vignettes—the self-representation of immigrant communities through a parish workshop that was our initial introduction to St. Thomas Aquinas and the representation of immigrant children in the public media. The examples call attention to the starkly divergent ways of framing the lives and learning of immigrant youth and families and contesting visions of what constitutes one's community. Their juxtaposition also suggests that, in addition to a dominant public sphere that positions individuals from immigrant and refugee backgrounds as racialized "others" who are at once excluded from and help define the national imaginary, there also exist counterpublics that resist these characterizations and enact alternative communities encompassing a fuller range of humanity. We believe the language and literacy practices at St. Thomas Aquinas contribute to such a counterpublic, one that is enriched by "the mutual exchange and change that occurs when cultural variety is actually valued" (Ortega & Alcoff, 2009, p. 8). This book documents our research partnership to support educational endeavors at St. Thomas Aquinas. Our particular lens into this work is through critical sociocultural perspectives on literacy (e.g., Lewis, Enciso, & Moje, 2007), which are attentive to power, and practitioner research and community-based methodologies (e.g., Cochran-Smith & Lytle, 2009) committed to democratizing research processes. Throughout our partnership, we have sought to understand the literacies of the St. Thomas Aquinas community, which help cultivate a counterpublic around issues of equity and access, and to work in collaboration with leaders to cocreate educational spaces that tap into these profound cultural, linguistic, and experiential resources.

An Immigrant Rights Workshop: Collective Agency in the Counterpublic

In the fall of 2010, Gerald Campano and María Paula Ghiso attended an immigrant rights workshop held at St. Thomas Aquinas. The workshop, hosted by the interfaith organization New Sanctuary Movement of Philadelphia, focused on how individuals might prepare themselves if confronted with questions about their citizenship status, especially given the collaboration occurring at that time between local police and U.S. Immigration and Customs Enforcement (ICE). During the discussion period, a number of the community members began to testify about the devastating effects that current immigration sentiments and policies were having on families, loved ones, and neighbors. People were afraid to report crimes, bullying, and labor exploitation for fear of having information forwarded to ICE; families were being torn apart because of recent raids and racial profiling; and parents were reluctant to develop strong relationships with their children's teachers given recent rumors that schools were to play a role in monitoring citizenship status. One of the local leaders, a priest, shared how he spends almost every weekend traveling to detention centers in order to provide guidance and counseling to detainees and their families. The sharing of testimonials—a community literacy event (Heath, 1982)—provided a nuanced portrayal of what many immigrants face daily in our city and nation.

The gathering was also an example of collective agency, where participants organized to interpret and respond to their circumstances and brainstorm ways in which to advocate for social justice. We were edified when a youth leader made links between challenges faced by immigrants and other communities of color. In response to frustrations voiced by attendees, she proclaimed that "we have to learn and take heart in the African American struggle" for civil and human rights and reminded the audience that "change doesn't happen overnight"; it is an ongoing endeavor, and the community needs to remain patient yet unwaveringly committed in their efforts to be treated justly (Fieldnotes, October 13, 2010). The comment was an example of intergroup solidarity that defied stereotypes, prevalent in the media, of a neighborhood solely fraught with conflict. This coalitional spirit we first witnessed would become a prevailing pattern in our involvement at the site and an organizing principle for our collaborative research partnership.

After the workshop, several of the community leaders discovered that we were education professors and former teachers with immigrant backgrounds ourselves and initiated a conversation about imagining possible work together. Although immigration issues were traumatic and demoralizing, the leaders nevertheless remained determined to advocate for education. The priest of the Indonesian community reiterated several times that education is what gives his community hope. His words resonated with us because in our own familial immigrant histories, education was a primary vehicle through which future generations could forge greater life opportunities. We soon met with the then head priest of St. Thomas Aquinas, who put us in direct dialogue with the parish leadership council, including representatives from the various cultural and linguistic communities, through a series of meetings to imagine our future work together. What initially attracted us to St. Thomas Aquinas was our desire for a sustained partnership with families. We wanted to communicate to contemporary youth from historically disenfranchised communities that universities, such as those we are affiliated with, would be lucky to have them as part of their intellectual communities, and that we would be there to support them in their aspirations.

The conversation that happened that evening is representative of exchanges taking place in churches, schools, or neighborhood centers throughout Philadelphia. Widening the lens, we trust it may also resonate with countless examples of solidarity building in cities and towns across the country, wherever families, neighbors, and strangers congregate to address the daily indignities faced by many immigrants, people of color, and those struggling economically. The discourse of social justice and interconnection emerging from the workshop was at once profound and unremarkable, making its contrast to how immigration is too often represented all the more revealing.

Immigrant Children at the Border: Scapegoating in the Public Sphere

Within the period described in this book, another story of immigration captured the national imagination for several weeks. Between October 2013 and July 2014, tens of thousands of children and teenagers migrated to the United States from Central America and Mexico. They fled their homes to escape violence and poverty. Many also sought to reunite with family members in the United States. The majority were detained and eventually deported back to their countries of origin, including El Salvador, Honduras, and Guatemala. What was referred to in the media as the "border crisis" of the unaccompanied minors elicited polarizing responses. Pundits opined that the children's presence signaled a threat to our national integrity and called for a further militarization of the border. There were crowds with signs reading "Stop Illegals" and chanting slogans such as "No one wants you" and "America, stand your ground" to children in buses en route to a Border Patrol processing facility, racializing immigration by referring to a law recently used to sanction the killing of Black youth. On the other side of the debate, immigrant advocates invoked the nation's image as a land of opportunity and refuge to argue for more effective legal remedies to address the children's predicament, including the possibility of asylum for them on humanitarian grounds.

Despite their differences, the various viewpoints on immigration presented in the public sphere often rested on some shared assumptions. In his discussion of the (im)possibility of hospitality toward others, using the example of immigrants, the philosopher Derrida (1999) suggests that conceptions of hospitality imply a sense of proprietorship. Genuine hospitality would require the host, including a host country, to relinquish control of the very spaces that enable its privileged position to be compassionate toward and welcoming of others. Actual hospitality, therefore, in some sense reinforces binary oppositions, like the ones between a host and a newcomer or an American and a foreigner. Too often these oppositions leave unexamined the power asymmetries between the two poles of the binary and their mutual dependence on one another. In the prevalent frame governing public opinion, the immigrant children were portrayed as either an unlawful threat to the integrity of the nation or the more or less deserving recipients of America's largess.

Postcolonial theorists have long deconstructed this type of dichotomous thinking and, perhaps more importantly, have begun to imagine more radical alternatives, uprooting dominant epistemologies that are employed to dehumanize others and clearing the ground for more intellectually egalitarian relationships. St. Thomas Aquinas is populated by communities that have endured histories of colonialism and oppression. This oppression is the product not just of overt force but also of Western intellectual and research traditions that have "othered" (e.g., Said, 1985) people of color, viewing them as objects rather than as intellectual agents themselves, and as behind in a single master narrative of human development and progress. Our project is inspired by postcolonial frameworks that seek to honor the multiple forms of knowledge, creativity, and solidarity that arise from marginalized experiences. St. Thomas Aquinas is best understood through what Mignolo (2011, p. 71) might label a "pluriversal" epistemological framework. Pluriversality exposes the tendency to universalize one particular, yet dominant, worldview. Yet it is not a form of relativism or separatism. Instead it seeks to learn from multiple, yet entangled, intellectual legacies, especially those that have been subordinated through histories of colonization, in order to more deeply understand our shared yet persistently unequal world.

A postcolonial perspective thus entails thinking critically about "borders"—the constructed nature of borders as based on colonial relationships that persist today, how borders shape our images of the "other," and the ways that people's migrations and their cultural and linguistic practices resist bounded demarcations. Anzaldúa (1999) uses concepts such as *mestiza consciousness* to center perspectives of marginalized communities who dwell in and draw insights from borderland spaces. Building on Anzaldúa, Mignolo's (2000) notion of "border thinking" emphasizes that decolonization is not just a matter of replacing a Eurocentric with a pure or essentialized non-Western worldview. That substitution would merely reproduce the binaries of coloniality, for example, 21st-century versus traditional literacy practices or individual versus community well-being. The value of border thinking certainly privileges subordinated perspectives, but it is also a form of critical inquiry that destabilizes either–or thinking as well as any knowledge regime that is used to exclude or devalue others, such as those that label vulnerable immigrant communities "illegal." Rather than casting immigration in us–them binaries, where communities from "developing" or "Third World" countries migrate to the "First World," a postcolonial orientation helps us ask questions such as the following: How is the predicament of immigrant children and families inextricably related to the lives of U.S. citizens? What entangled histories have been ignored in the debates around their fates? A broader account might include, for example, the United States' military interventions in Central America; the demand for and war on drugs that has fueled violent trafficking cartels; and the role that policies such as the North American Free Trade Agreement have had on local economies in Latin America through promoting the movement of goods and services, but not people. Both Anzaldúa and Mignolo remind us not to circumscribe any one group's experiences and to be attentive to the complex interpretive agency of community members who dwell within multiple borders and navigate languages, cultural practices, ideological perspectives, and power dynamics.

Contemporary activists and educators have also moved beyond the paradoxes of hospitality, which are grounded in assumptions of proprietorship around who owns land, who owns knowledge, and who owns a life that is more or less expendable, in order to flesh out a concrete decolonial social justice vision that foregrounds an ethics of care and interdependence. For example, Walia (2013) coarticulates indigenous and immigrant rights—two movements often kept separate—by delinking proprietorship, national or otherwise, from community and intellectual authority. She argues that recognizing our interconnections as part of a shared planet can foster new relationships based on kinship, mutuality, and humility, calling into question the very ideologies that separate people. Such transnational feminist activists and theorists remind us of the importance of constantly returning to a set of core ethical questions in our research at St. Thomas Aquinas. How are we implicated in one another's lives, and what are our obligations to each other? What are the possibilities for imagining, in the words of St. Thomas Aquinas's leaders, a more "radical hospitality" that does not merely reproduce insider–outsider dichotomies but instead conceives of community more expansively, beyond political borders and social boundaries? Who has the "right to have rights" (Arendt, 1976), including the right to an education, as stated by Article 26 of the Universal Declaration of Human Rights? Testimonials from the immigrant children from Central America conveyed their desires to attend schools in North America since back home they had become recruiting grounds for the drug cartels. This desire to flourish academically links the aspirations of youth in Latin America to youth who are undocumented in the United States, to the Indonesian youth congregating at St. Thomas Aquinas on that fall 2010 evening, to Syrian refugee families in Europe, and to anyone who still may find, following the words of the Indonesian priest, hope in education. If our research partnership does not support and nourish these educational aspirations, it is not worth pursuing.

LITERACIES OF IMMIGRANT YOUTH AND FAMILIES: AN EMPHASIS ON AGENCY

One of the most salient issues in education over the past decades has been the unprecedented linguistic and cultural diversity of student populations, with many policies directly geared toward the schooling of (im)migrant youth and families (Gándara & Hopkins, 2010). Scholars have documented the rich language and literacy practices and community-based funds of knowledge of children from immigrant backgrounds and the ways these may inform—and transform—the school curriculum (Fránquiz & Brochin-Ceballos, 2006; González, Moll, & Amanti, 2005; Gutiérrez, 2008). In line with strengths-based approaches (e.g., Yazzie-Mintz, 2007), our orientation has been to consider youth from (im)migrant and refugee backgrounds as "cosmopolitan intellectuals" (Campano & Ghiso, 2011) whose transnational lives, multiple languages, and comparative frames of reference resulting from global mobility are experiential resources that can be leveraged to collaboratively investigate social issues, in particular with regard to issues of power, access, and equity. We advocate for a "cosmopolitanism from below" (Appadurai, 2011, p. 32) that centers, in the educational curriculum, the unique knowledge of historically minoritized identities—what has been referred to as their epistemic privilege (Campano, 2007; Moya, 2002). The rich diversity of many 21st-century neighborhoods and classrooms, following Satya Mohanty (1997), offers an opportunity for collaborative ethical and intellectual inquiry into our shared world. And our deepest intellectual resources, we have come to learn, are the youth themselves.

Unfortunately, the climate of high-stakes testing in education and the remedial standardized curricula used to prepare children for such assessments (Genishi & Dyson, 2009) homogenize diverse experiences. Gutiérrez and Orellana (2006) discuss how dominant framings of students who speak languages other than English or are from immigrant backgrounds construct them as a "problem" through deficit ideologies that have persisted in notions of the cultural mismatch between home and school. Part of what "mismatch" suggests is that people occupy essentialized and bounded cultural contexts in particular spaces, and the goal becomes either to assimilate minoritized communities within the dominant discourse or to value the literacies and histories of each context while retaining them as separate. The prevalence of cultural mismatch theories, Gutiérrez and Orellana suggest, "obscure[s] differences within groups and within contexts, as well as similarities across groups and contexts" (p. 506). One important contribution of literacy research and pedagogy has been to challenge ideas of a universal literacy that is autonomous of ideology (Street, 1995) and to recognize the multiple literacies of diverse communities and how these are embedded in relationships of power.

While there has been a valuable emphasis on difference in literacy scholarship, there has been less attention to the literate practices of members of different cultural and linguistic groups working together in a shared space. A reorientation toward this coalitional dimension can be helpful in resisting the tendency to reify dichotomies (e.g., school vs. out-of-school literacies, standard vs. vernacular varieties) or to map a bounded literacy practice to a specific cultural group. It may also help us identify the procreative ways in which postcolonial communities mobilize literacies to make claims about and enact change in the world. For example, testimonials such as the ones we heard on our first visit at St. Thomas Aquinas are literacy practices shared across the Indonesian, Latina/o, and African American communities, not the purview of any one group, but they are innovatively employed in a specific context to foster a sense of solidarity. How, we wondered, might youth, families, and community members utilize literacies, whose multifariousness and hybridity reflect the diversity of their neighborhood, for coalitional work? How might they advocate for educational opportunities, even in an out-of-school context?

What role do literacies play in helping to cultivate more expansive notions of citizenship that challenge dominant discourses of immigration? How might language and literacy curricula—whether in school or out of school—become a vehicle for investigating and taking action on issues that impact the lives and learning of immigrant youth? How might educators and researchers learn from the knowledge and literate legacies already present in communities?

PRECARITY AND ITS RELEVANCE TO EDUCATION

We believe that to advocate for students within school contexts, it is necessary to attend to the complex intersecting forces that impact families, such as legacies of colonization (Ghiso & Campano, 2013), which necessitates looking beyond the school itself. In urban and, increasingly, suburban areas, newcomers no longer live in "ethnic enclaves" with neighborhood schools but rather in multicultural and multilingual communities. In these transcultural spaces, youth and families must navigate more complicated educational pathways because of developments such as the proliferation of charter schools, the defunding and consolidation of English language learning and bilingual programs, and the prevalence of high-stakes testing paradigms (e.g., Dutro & Selland, 2012; Menken, 2008). Immigrant communities have also found themselves vulnerable to police scrutiny, deportations, and xenophobic sentiments (Buff, 2008; Ngai, 2004).

Many families at St. Thomas Aquinas are surviving in conditions of precarity—social, political, economic, and educational insecurity resulting from neoliberal policies (Banki, 2013; Harker, 2012; Standing, 2013; Vagle & Jones, 2012). Particularly pertinent to our research partnership is understanding how these conditions are related to community members' "precarity of place": "the extent to which an individual is vulnerable to removal or deportation because of his or her legal status and/or possession of documentation, or lack thereof, in the host country" (Banki, 2013, p. 4). Immigrant rights issues were integral to the St. Thomas Aquinas community, whether because parishioners themselves had undocumented legal status, because they were ascribed by the state as "illegal" due to racialized policies, or because they joined the parish's mission to advocate for immigration reform, a cause from which, in the words of Fr. Shields, "we cannot exempt ourselves if we have passports" (Fieldnotes, December 5, 2011). Because of framings of citizenship and belonging as exclusive to the nation-state, individuals from (im)migrant backgrounds may find themselves at greater risk of labor exploitation, home displacement because of gentrification, health care instability, and detention by authorities. In circumstances of precarity, faith-based organizations, in addition to schools, often play an anchoring role for many (im)migrant and refugee populations (e.g., Hirschman, 2004).

The term *precarity* refers to the overwhelming potential for abuse or exploitation and not to the absolute certainty of such abuse (Banki, 2013). In the case of immigrant and refugee communities, social precarity speaks to the possible dismantling of their supportive networks and not to the absence of these networks in their lives (Banki, 2013, p. 2). Consider the following testimonials from St. Thomas parishioners that we documented through our research: Children in the school district discover that their school is slated for closure due to city budget cuts; an otherwise healthy individual finds a sudden illness exacerbated by the lack of health care; a young child's asthma becomes life threatening when schools can no longer afford nurses to help monitor and control such ailments; a dedicated immigrant student becomes criminalized as a truant because he is reluctant to travel to school on public transportation, where he had previously been physically assaulted (Campano, Ghiso, Yee, & Pantoja, 2013). Reporting bullying or crimes—or even a broken car headlight—may put a family under greater scrutiny by authorities, who may target them for deportation. The concept of precarity, on the one hand, describes a shared condition of many individuals at our research site, who have to contend with social, economic, and educational insecurity. On the other hand, the parishioners may experience different degrees and types of precarity in their day-to-day lives. For example, they may have similar economic hardships, but one individual may be more vulnerable to racial profiling from the police while another is more vulnerable to labor exploitation in a sweatshop.

Butler (2009, 2011) also talks about ontological precarity. She argues that, from a global perspective, all people are vulnerable by virtue of their shared humanity and thus mutually dependent on one another. At the same time, precarity is regulated politically by positioning groups hierarchically through "normative frameworks [that] establish what kind of life will be worth living" (Butler, 2009, p. 53). Often, the categories of nationhood, race, social class, gender, ability, and language are used to differentiate between groups and to determine whose interests and security are most important. Shifting the perspective to one of global politics, Butler contends, spotlights precarity as an essential condition of all life, "expos[ing] our sociality, the fragile and necessary dimensions of our interdependence" (Butler, 2011, p. 20). Once the illusion of independence is dispelled and there is a recognition of human sociality and vulnerability, the productive dimension of precarity is that it provides an opening to develop new ways to organize and to cooperate across social boundaries. Coalitions may in part develop from these overlapping and intersecting precarious conditions. As people gain critical consciousness (Freire, 1970) about their own experiences of oppression, they may foster empathy for and be moved to take action on other people's conditions. Commenting on Butler, Walia (2013) asserts that "enacting a politics of decolonization also necessitates an undoing of the borders between one another" (p. 11). Even those whose lives are relatively secure may come to understand their privilege as historically contingent and subject to change, perhaps questioning the individualistic or meritocratic ideologies that rationalize inequality. Our research partnership with St. Thomas Aquinas seeks not only to deconstruct how power operates in the vein of critical ethnography but also to work collaboratively to prefigure and help reconstruct an alternative form of sociality premised on a sense of social justice and shared responsibility toward one another, what Ghiso (2016) has characterized as "literacies of interdependence" (para. 4). We are interested in understanding collective agency across boundaries and borders, as well as the role that literacies play in coalitional projects for social justice.

A WAY OF BEING IN COMMUNITY:
FOSTERING INTERDEPENDENCE IN RESEARCH

What originally inspired the partnership described in this book was our desire to understand how some immigrant communities support their children's education; a Catholic parish was a potentially rich site to build relationships with families. The three of us self-identify as Catholics, but this research was not designed to be about theology or religion per se. Nevertheless, the context of a faith-based site could never easily be suppressed. As we have developed our collaboration over the years, involved more students on the university research team, and presented our work to various audiences, we have grappled with questions about what it means to engage in progressive literacy research and pedagogy within the context of a Catholic parish. One research team member, Karim, put it well from the beginning: "How do I see myself, as a Muslim man, fitting in or not fitting in to this work?" In a transnational Catholic context, where some of the parishioners had been a Christian minority in a Muslim-majority country, Karim was concerned that various historical experiences and conceptions of religious difference abroad would make his presence a source of discomfort within the community. Those who self-identify as Queer questioned if a religious institution would be a safe space for them, but were also aware that official church doctrine may differ from its instantiation in local parishes. Mary and Alicia wondered to what extent the research at St. Thomas Aquinas could lead to the types of direct action that characterize grassroots organizations, such as Juntos and Asian Americans United, local affinity groups that have forged coherent political platforms and strategies. As educators and researchers committed to critical intellectual traditions, we also considered the tensions involved in doing community-based research in a Catholic parish, such as whether the faith context might limit political possibilities or even reproduce social inequities. How, then, do we make sense of the politics of our collaboration?

To our surprise, at no point in our partnership has anyone on the research team been the recipient of didactic Church rules that could come across as judgmental or indoctrinating. In fact, in all our work alongside parish members, there has been very little explicit discourse around church dogma. Everyday parish activities do not seem to be shaped by adherence to a set of top-down decrees but instead are organized around one agreed-upon idea: a stance of radical hospitality and cooperation. While this orientation is certainly reinforced by St. Thomas Aquinas's leaders, such as the priests, from the very beginning of our partnership the ethos of hospitality has been conveyed in practice and collectively embodied in social interaction.

The Italian philosopher Giorgio Agamben (1998, 2013) provides a way to begin conceptualizing the exclusion and vulnerability of immigrant and minoritized groups, as well as the political possibilities of places such as St. Thomas Aquinas to offer more radically inclusive models of community. Agamben is perhaps best known for his examination of *homo sacer* (Agamben, 1998), a figure in Roman law signifying a person who is banned and may be killed on a whim, who exists in a "state of exception" from the law—for example, during a political season when fears of terrorism or a faltering economy are channeled into the scapegoating of immigrants, as was the case during the writing of this book. The example of *homo sacer* unmasks how state sovereignty is predicated on the ability to break social contracts during perceived crises. To deem that someone is outside the protections of the law—that they can be detained or killed without due process, forcefully interned or deported, denied health care or education—is also paradoxically an act of law, deciding what rules apply when and to whom. While we may conventionally consider laws to be an outside force superimposed on a preexisting life, Agamben's interest has been in the ways in which law and life become indissoluble. His political work involves displaying how *homo sacer* is relevant to contemporary populations, such as prisoners in black sites or stateless migrants, a group served by St. Thomas Aquinas. When someone is from a predominantly Muslim country, or is accused of being a communist, or is profiled as being an "illegal," there could be a sudden suspension of juridical protection, making minoritized social identities more vulnerable to sovereign power. This state control over life and death of populations, what has been termed "biopower" (Foucault, 1990), exposes how the "human" has been a historically variable category, with shifting conventions regarding who is deemed fully human and thus deserving of rights.

Agamben's recent work has been interested in more positive illustrations of how forging a life according to rules may lead to less exploitive human relationships. His book *The Highest Poverty* (Agamben, 2013) in part examines the Franciscan social movement as a paradigm that might help us imagine alternatives to dominant social orders. Here, Agamben makes a distinction between the Church as an institution, and its laws, and the Kingdom of Heaven, which is about living a life in the spirit of the gospels. He suggests that there are higher rules that might govern how people live, often in the shadows of hierarchical institutional authority. In this case, the inseparability of rules and life potentially enables more inclusive ways of being in community that exist alongside of or in resistance to sovereign power. The early Franciscans challenged the top-down dogma of the Church; they also voluntarily adopted a monastic rule in order to emulate a highest poverty through "forms of life" (p. 121) that disavowed property ownership. Everyone could use objects and resources, such as food and clothing, in order to survive and live collectively together, but no one was entitled to own them, what Agamben characterizes as use without appropriation (p. 137).

The contemporary parishioners at St. Thomas Aquinas, of course, do not live a monastic existence. Many are of the working poor who participate in both formal and informal economies in their daily lives in order to survive and provide for their families. There may nonetheless be useful resonances of Agamben's paradigm for understanding the dynamics at St. Thomas Aquinas. We have documented how parish leaders invoke a higher sovereignty that contests state power in order to advocate and provide sanctuary for immigrants, reflected in phrases such as "God did not create anyone illegal" and "We are all citizens of Heaven." In bulletins and homilies, parish priests place the words "documented" and "undocumented" in quotations, destabilizing their ontological authority. No one group owns what it means to be a citizen, and everyone, irrespective of the contingencies of history, is deserving of basic human resources, care, and opportunities. In Agamben's terms, the parish aspires to provide sanctuary for those exiled in a constant state of exception. It contributes to a counterpublic that resists the force of laws that ban some human beings to the margins of civil society. The St. Thomas Aquinas community was energized by the election of Pope Francis, named after St. Francis of Assisi, who perhaps more than any other Catholic figure in current history has brought together Church law with forms of life that embody its social teachings, including a commitment to fostering nonexploitive relationships to the poor and to the environment, a message he reiterated during his visit to our city.

The ethos of radical hospitality at St. Thomas Aquinas is not simply one espoused by parish leaders and transmitted to those they serve. Rather, we believe the leaders themselves have been influenced by the various cultural and linguistic communities who enact their own "forms of life"—ways of living and being with one another that value an ethos of interdependence, mutual care, and reciprocity (Ghiso, 2016). Over the years, The Concerned Black Catholics (CBC), a group formed by African American parishioners to advocate for youth in the parish and the broader neighborhood, has organized an annual community health fair, taken schoolchildren to theater productions, raised funds to help build a playground, and opened its doors and made dinner for college students who are assigned to learn about the history of the neighborhood. Members of the Indonesian community pool resources to provide native language programming for youth and network with one another to learn about local schools. The Vietnamese community, which has been in the parish for many years, has created opportunities for intergenerational learning where youth gain knowledge from elders about language, cultural traditions, and educational access and can in turn mentor younger generations. Parents in the Latina/o community have built important bridges between St. Thomas Aquinas and grassroots immigrant activist groups such as New Sanctuary Movement in order to more directly address educational issues affecting youth who are undocumented.

In a very practical sense, St. Thomas Aquinas is also a "shared parish." There is a collective expectation that its resources will be of use to everyone but owned by no one, from the actual space of the Aquinas Center to basic office supplies and books for children. Individuals and communities also share their talents for the betterment of the whole. They join together to lead youth groups that contribute to the parish, beautify the church for celebrations, repair building infrastructure, and organize community events. While Christianity has historically been an instrument of imperialism, St. Thomas Aquinas is composed of postcolonial communities, with legacies of war and genocide, who now occupy formerly sacred and exclusive church space—such as a convent converted into a community center—in order to organize for their survival and for their rights—an example, alluding to Audre Lorde (1984), of using the Master's tools to reimagine and repurpose the Master's house. They also use the space and its resources to sustain cultural traditions, celebrate community, and engage each other in often compassionate and joyful ways.

This is not to deny, however, the existence of tensions. Ultimately, the diocese owns the parish; an outside nonprofit organization now runs the parish school; and even among those involved in the research collaboration, frictions may arise when people feel a sense of ownership over aspects of the partnership. Nonetheless, on a day-to-day level, we have seen continued evidence of St. Thomas Aquinas's attempts to de-link use from ownership and to emphasize cobelonging, reciprocity, and support for those who are most in need. Our research methodology has aspired to honor this ethos.

Given the shared nature of the parish, it was important for us to align research with cultivating membership in a community, especially since the former often brings power asymmetries and its own histories of exclusion and appropriation. Gaining research access to St. Thomas Aquinas was not simply about procuring approval from parish leaders or providing some degree of benefit to members to outweigh research risks. Rather, it involved nurturing relationships by participating in happenings that were already a regular part of the parish and thoughtfully co-organizing additional events with leaders based on their visions for the partnership. One decision Gerald made early on in the collaboration was that the doctoral students working with him would dedicate a good portion of their funded hours to immersion in the community; other students have joined the research team and volunteered their time and labor. Every contributor to this book has spent significant months, sometimes years, building relationships with parishioners before the decision was made to proceed with research. The host/visitor and researcher/participant distinctions have not been rigid, and efforts to sustain the partnership have been bidirectional. Just as a number of initiatives brought university faculty and students to St. Thomas Aquinas, youth and community leaders came to the university campus, including in an Inquiry into College with young children from the aftercare program (Campano, Ngo, Low, & Jacobs, 2015) and a research presentation by Indonesian and Latina/o youth at the Ethnography in Education conference. We have tried to build a research relationship predicated on being in community and mutually sharing resources. Over time, these principles have evolved into collaborative research norms—not "laws" or top-down decrees but parameters through which we strive to embody egalitarian relationship (Campano, Ghiso, & Welch, 2015). We describe these norms and how they have informed our partnership in Chapter 9.

THE AQUINAS CENTER

Fast-forward several years after the Know Your Rights workshop to a ceremony in that same basement on January 27, 2013 that officially inaugurated the Aquinas Center, a social justice–oriented community center directed by Bethany. Her opening presentation at the event described its coalitional spirit and philosophical orientation as a hospitable environment to all, and this vision was reflected throughout the inauguration. The priests of St. Thomas Aquinas—Indonesian, Latino, Vietnamese, and Irish—offered remarks and led the congregation in a multilingual prayer. Bethany called up to the front of the room leaders from the respective cultural and linguistic groups, as well as community partners such as the University of Pennsylvania, and presented them with scissors, the purpose for which would soon become clear. The crowd then moved across the parking lot to the repurposed convent that had become the grounds of the center.

The procession made its way through the main entrance and down the hallway toward the back of the building, passing doors adorned with the Aquinas Center logo created by Bethany that denoted the uses of each of the spaces: a room hosting the Indonesian Sunday School for young children with whom a university literacy course partnered on the multiyear "PennPal" project; a gathering place where members of the Filipina/o community spearheaded a fundraiser for Typhoon Haiyan; and a room where the Education and Research (EaR) Group, composed of university- and St. Thomas Aquinas–affiliated members, would meet regularly to share updates on the research and coplan future inquiries. The dining area, festooned with Mexican flags and bursting with Filipino lumpia, Vietnamese spring rolls, Mexican tamales, and Indonesian curries prepared by

St. Thomas Aquinas families for the celebration, would become a central touchstone to our collaboration: It is where we would facilitate literacy engagements around *Charlotte's Web* in partnership with the CBC, who took youth from the neighborhood to see a theater production of the classic tale; where we would host a retreat for our research team to deepen our orientation to partnering; and where an inquiry group with Indonesian and Latina/o youth focused on reading and writing nonfiction texts would share their research findings with elders in the community. The procession moved to the back of the building, where a large red ribbon flanked the doorway. Photographs from the event portray leaders from the multiple cultural and linguistic groups at St. Thomas Aquinas linking arms and using their scissors to cut the ribbon and officially open the center. The group then made its way to the basement, where the research team would facilitate a language and literacy class with Latina families and young children, and later with Vietnamese youth and elders, for cake to honor the occasion.

One of the paradoxes of the Aquinas Center is that the very conditions of precarity that it was envisioned to address are also its raison d'être. In the absence of a robust public sphere to provide childcare, mental health services, educational enrichment activities, legal counsel for immigrants, and contexts for sociality and solidarity, the center labors to fill in these gaps. For example, individuals may have the opportunity to take on leadership positions not available to them at their jobs; gain access to an arts curriculum that has been virtually eliminated from public schools because of the emphasis on high-stakes testing and the under-resourcing of the district; or discuss ways to take action on labor rights or new immigration legislation, topics that would put them at risk in other public contexts. At a time when community members' well-being is precarious and many find themselves vulnerable, the Aquinas Center provides a space where people can nurture their humanity more fully. The inherent contradiction, however, is that through these actions, the center runs the risk of perpetuating the very neoliberal logic that leaves so many of its members vulnerable, whereby the social safety net becomes the responsibility of individuals and faith-based entities rather than a public and human right.

Community-based research is precarious as well. Because it may not conform to dominant epistemological paradigms, it is often considered mere service and not always easy to fund. Its collaborative and relational nature in some ways contradicts the academy's privileging of individual stardom. This book is written by multiple authors to capture the collaborative nature of knowledge production. We also hope to call attention to the situated nature of inquiry—that is, that there is no neutral position or "zero-point" (Castro-Gómez, 2005, as cited in Mignolo, 2011, p. 80) from which to analyze the world and how diverse perspectives may lead to more comprehensive interpretations of social phenomena.

DISCOURSE COMMUNITIES AT ST. THOMAS AQUINAS:
A PLURIVERSAL CONCEPTUAL MODEL

We find the concept of "discourse community" a useful way of unpacking the complexity of St. Thomas Aquinas as well as understanding how its diversity might be mobilized in order to advocate for the rights of immigrants and vulnerable populations. The term *discourse community* refers to "a grouping of people who share common language norms, characteristics, patterns, or practices as a consequence of their ongoing communications and identification with each other" (Bazerman, 2009, para. 1). Guided by our research questions and the goals of the partnership, we focus specifically on those discourse communities that have an orientation toward advocacy. As community-based researchers, we are less interested in adopting a distant ethnographic perspective that seeks to classify literacies from above. This blinkered academic gaze risks casting community members as social dupes who need the tools of an outside researcher to gain critical consciousness (Guerra, 2004). We are more concerned with community agency, how participants at St. Thomas Aquinas employ and in fact create their own power codes by drawing on multiple literate resources to both navigate the social world as well as make normative claims about it and how it might be better.

Through our research partnership, we have identified six major advocacy discourse communities at St. Thomas Aquinas (see Figure 1.1):

1. A *religious discourse community* that urges empathy for those most vulnerable and attempts to transcend unjust human laws by appealing to a higher morality and a more universal ethos of human dignity.

2. An *educational research discourse community* that emphasizes sustained deliberation to support collaborative inquiry and, borrowing from critical pedagogy and practitioner research traditions, is concerned with democratizing research processes and highlighting issues of power in education.

3. An *activist discourse community* organized around cogent political visions with the goal of taking direct action to speak truth to power.

4. A *legal discourse community* that utilizes a professional register to address the juridical power codes that criminalize people's identities as, for example, "illegals."

5. A *service discourse community* oriented toward discerning and addressing the pressing needs of community members through programming.

6. *Cultural discourse communities*, specifically, community members' epistemic privilege—knowledge derived from their historically minoritized identities that is especially relevant to social justice advocacy efforts (Moya, 2002).

Figure 1.1. Advocacy Discourse Communities at St. Thomas Aquinas

ADVOCACY DISCOURSE COMMUNITIES

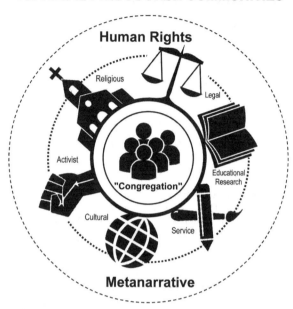

Our thesis is that the respective discourse communities reflect multiple, entangled forms of knowledge and exist in a constant state of synergistic promise: They potentially complement each other and, taken together, constitute a *cosmopolitan counterpublic* that provides opportunities for fostering nondominant social arrangements and advocacy on behalf of immigrant rights and educational justice.

The Synergistic Relationship of Discourse Communities

The six advocacy discourse communities we have documented at St. Thomas Aquinas have respective language, literacy, and social practices (Barton & Hamilton, 1998). Each has its own strengths with respect to knowledge production and advocacy, but they also have their limitations. Together, they provide complementary resources and perspectives that can be mobilized toward collective action. We offer a window into their synergy below.

Educational research provides opportunities for sustained inquiry but at times uses language that can be needlessly obscurantist and alienating, a limitation that would be well complemented by more plain-speaking registers from the community itself. Academic research can also become mired in deconstruction and critique (e.g., in endlessly analyzing the intractability of an oppressive system) without envisioning projects of reconstruction and transformation. It might therefore benefit from the political urgency and call to action that activist organizations and community-based programming forefront in their missions. For their own part, the tone of *activist* groups writ large can feel polarizing or self-righteous, which may potentially stifle dialogue or prevent others from joining the cause. The inclusivity of the religious discourse may mitigate exclusive language. The premium placed on the urgency to enact change may be tempered by a more deliberate research orientation or by community programming that can underscore how action and resistance may take multiple forms, including in more subtle, less politically legible ones.

In advocacy efforts, *religious* discourse appeals to universalism as a means of identifying common vulnerabilities and fostering compassion for others. This emphasis may elide the particular experiences of various groups or may imply a facile overcoming of difference, and it can be complemented by the different cultural and linguistic groups at St. Thomas Aquinas, who share with others what is unique about their lived experiences. In our research site, the *legal* discourse community has been contending with undocumented immigration status from a technical perspective, such as by helping individuals file for Deferred Action for Childhood Arrivals, which would grant them a permit to work in the United States. This code of power can provide people with concrete advice about how to move forward. The legal language, however, is bureaucratic and at times dehumanizing, and it may be augmented by the more relational discourses of community programming and of the various cultural groups. Another potential critique of the legal discourse is that it supports individuals in navigating the system but is not necessarily orientated toward changing it. An activist discourse that sees current laws as fundamentally flawed may contribute to agitating for systemic reforms or even more revolutionary transformation. For organizations like the Aquinas Center, the notion of *service* becomes more egalitarian and bidirectional when community programming takes seriously the experiences and knowledge of different cultural groups, which can prevent presupposing their needs or positioning community members as mere victims through a type of missionary ideology. A university–community partnership can provide time for deliberation and analysis to inform the services offered.

Many community members at St. Thomas Aquinas have navigated shifting social and political contexts by virtue of migration and may be uniquely situated to interpret social issues through a comparative transnational lens. Groups such as the CBC have had to contend firsthand with racial oppression and can offer perspectives of how Black youth are often scapegoated and criminalized. They are also heirs to rich activist legacies regarding educational access and civil and human rights. These multiple knowledges are made public through literacy practices such as testimonials or in dialogue at culturally defined spaces such as the Indonesian Sunday School or the Vietnamese youth group. One consideration for *cultural discourse communities* may be the interrelationship of specific group experiences, and how dialogue might proceed across boundaries.

The religious discourse provides a sense of common humanity that can balance particular group interests, and activist and academic discourses can highlight common logics of domination, such as White supremacy and patriarchy (Rodríguez, 2010), that impact all communities. The service discourse community can provide opportunities for people to come together in a shared space, both honoring groups' epistemic privilege as well as cultivating relationships and mutual commitments. We have found that the robust diversity of St. Thomas Aquinas profoundly enhances all the respective discourse communities and is the cornerstone of all our work together.

As these examples suggest, literacies and languages do not merely reference the world. They also act on it, what Susan L. Lytle (2013) characterizes as "work in the world": "thoughtfully and intentionally engaging the wider socio-cultural and political struggles that drive current educational controversies" and highlighting issues of "access and equity in the local discourse and practices of our schools and universities and communities" (p. xix). The various advocacy communities at St. Thomas Aquinas do "work in the world" by mobilizing literacy for interpretation, making social justice claims, and attempting to transform inequitable conditions.

Human Rights Metanarrative and Congregation

The heterogeneous discourse communities of advocacy flowering at St. Thomas Aquinas overlap yet retain their distinctive identities. What enables them to cross-pollinate and flourish are circulating tropes that constitute a type of human rights metanarrative. These tropes include the aforementioned principles of radical hospitality, especially to those who are dispossessed, nonviolence, and a concern for the dignity of all human beings. Although these tropes have Catholic roots (Moyn, 2014), they have diverse secular and religious dimensions as well. For example, discourse communities may arrive at the ideal of nonviolence in multiple ways: The CBC is inspired by the Civil Rights legacy of peaceful dissent and King's vision of a beloved community, and refugees have expressed a revulsion to violence after witnessing war and genocide firsthand in their home countries. The Human Rights metanarrative does not reflect a fully coherent or uniform political philosophy, but its flexibility is in many ways its strength. It offers a language through which community members name inequities and appeal to a social justice vision that links their disparate and overlapping struggles. Individuals at St. Thomas Aquinas can find common ground by invoking this metanarrative, and the premium placed on inclusivity may mitigate the impulse to resolve conflict by scapegoating any particular individuals and groups (Girard, 1986). As the chapters in this book document, there is also one final superordinate ideal central to the human rights metanarrative in the context of our own collaborative efforts: the right for everyone to have access to a high-quality education. Throughout our partnership a leitmotif has been the belief that education may be transformative and a vehicle for self-creation, a way of superseding past hardships and the contingencies of history.

The core of the model is congregation. There can only be a genuine exchange of ideas when individuals come together to learn from one another's experiences, expertise, and epistemic privilege. The chapters in this book showcase opportunities for congregation within the various projects of our partnership. As educators who align ourselves with critical perspectives, our role has been to work alongside community members to cocreate spaces for learning and advocacy. We are one of many groups at St. Thomas Aquinas committed to doing work in the world and have sought to learn from others and better understand how diverse perspectives, including our own, may function synergistically as part of collective knowledge projects.

OVERVIEW OF THE BOOK

The various chapters in the book feature insights from some of the nested inquiries that form part of the Community Literacies Project (see Figure 1.2).[4] Chapter 2 is about the realization of the Aquinas Center, which became the heart of the partnership after our 2nd year. This chapter provides an account of how the community center was first conceived and then came to fruition in a former, repurposed convent: a new world literally taking root in the shell of the old one. This new world, echoing a vision put forth by the Zapatistas, is a pluriversal one striving to encompass the many social and cultural worlds of the larger parish, neighborhood, and Church, as symbolized by the center's murals. The chapter describes the challenges involved in attempting to create a material place that reflects an ethos of radical hospitality and cooperation. The details of the chapter are meant to demonstrate the intentional yet tenuous daily labor involved in making a "counterplace" to dominant ideologies of how neighborhood space might be appropriated: one that endeavors to nurture cultural, educational, physical, and spiritual flourishing in a context of deepening economic and social inequality. From the outside, St. Thomas Aquinas and its community center may look like any number of the city's countless churches. But behind its facade, there is a rich underground of creative, intellectual, and political work, of which the remaining chapters of the book try to give a sense.

Chapters 3 and 4 focus on the advocacy efforts of adults at St. Thomas Aquinas. While there is robust literature in the field of literacy studies on youth participatory action research (e.g., Mirra, Garcia, & Morrell, 2015; Tuck & Yang, 2014), what perhaps has been given less attention is the complex cultural work of parents and families who organize to support their children's educational and life opportunities. Many of the youth at

Figure 1.2. Overview of the Community Literacies Project

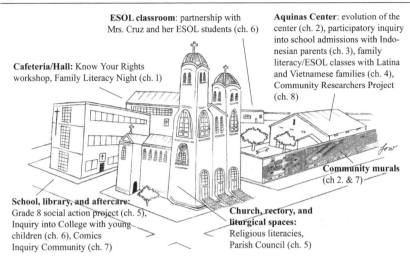

St. Thomas Aquinas have deep respect for their elders and the sacrifices previous generations have made on their behalf. Chapter 3 describes a participatory inquiry with parents directed at navigating the stressful and bureaucratically convoluted high school admissions process. The chapter introduces in more detail the Indonesian community at St. Thomas Aquinas, who originally invited our partnership, and reviews what we have done over the years to develop the trust necessary to engage in a collaborative research together. The chapter also analyzes how parents mobilize their social capital (Bourdieu, 1986) and transnational perspectives to navigate a distressingly under-resourced school system.

Chapter 4 describes a language and literacy class with Latina/o families and children, which evolved to include Vietnamese youth and elders, spotlighting how community members drew on their multilingual literacies to cultivate alternative forms of civic engagement that may not be visible in the dominant public sphere. Chapter 4 pairs two concepts, precarity and counterpublics, that are germane to all of our research at St. Thomas Aquinas. When taken together, chapters 3 and 4 contribute to research that challenges stereotypes of immigrant parents as passive or merely victims. The chapters also provide a sense of the heterogeneity within broad social categories. The unique history of Indonesian Christian immigrants, for example, is not easily subsumed under generalizations regarding Asian Americans, and it would be hardly accurate to portray the activist Latina mothers in Chapter 4 as fearfully "living in the shadows." At the same time we can begin to look across immigrant groups to tease out important differences in their racialized experiences as well as the shared struggles that might become the basis for coalition building (such as in the Fight for Drivers Licenses described in Chapter 10).

In Chapter 5, we turn our attention to youth who are at once part of their families but also forging identities and affiliations in "transnational local" contexts (Ghiso, 2016; Saldívar, 2012), such as St. Thomas Aquinas. The chapter showcases a Mexican American student, Francisco, who drew on religious literacies to shape a class project as social action, galvanizing others to aid victims of a devastating typhoon in the Philippines. Through concepts from scalar theory, we can see that Francisco's learning and social commitments do not easily conform to in- and out-of-school binaries, and that his literacies cross boundaries of space, audience, and genre. Being a good citizen of the parish, which is part of a larger constellation of Catholic networks, is ineluctably entwined with his school identity. Francisco's experience is an important reminder of how educators need to understand students within the broader social ecologies of their lives and reconceptualize teaching practices and university–community partnerships accordingly.

Our research has been conducted during a time when universities in general and education schools in particular are trying to reimagine their commitments to surrounding neighborhoods. Our partnership with St. Thomas Aquinas, a parish with a school and aftercare program that served neighborhood children, afforded a unique opportunity to begin investigating how "universities, schools, and communities work together" (Zeichner, 2015, p. 49) to learn from one another's respective expertise. Chapter 6 captures the potentially bidirectional nature of knowledge production. We describe the role of our community partnership in Gerald's course on Literacy and Assessment, a requirement for a master's program in Reading/Writing/Literacy. In the chapter, we foreground some of the ways in which the master's students learned from Mrs. Cruz, an English for speakers of other languages (ESOL) teacher at St. Thomas Aquinas with expertise in culturally responsive pedagogy.

Chapter 6 also explores what happened when we invited young children in the aftercare program at St. Thomas Aquinas, a number of whom had Mrs. Cruz as a teacher, to engage in a sustained Inquiry into College, which involved their own ethnographic experience in the form of a field trip to Penn's campus. Many of the children lived within several miles of the campus but had never visited it, and the field trip reminded us why this might have been the case. Our university, not unlike many elite institutions, is near impenetrable to young children without specific social capital, such as parents or siblings who are alumni. Nevertheless, the young children displayed agency through their own organic forms of sensemaking, or what we characterize as critical play (Campano, Ngo, et al., 2015). They took up our invitation to represent their inquiries by using humor and imagination to demystify the university and make it part of their own social worlds.

One of the ongoing tensions of the partnership has been the challenge of forging shared projects that work across difference to value a multiplicity of diverse identities and perspectives. In diverse neighborhoods, how do educators acknowledge shared and overlapping histories without compromising attention to the specificities of experience? What new identities and communities may emerge in the process of creative collaboration? Chapters 7 and 8 highlight rich forms of youth intellectual and creative production in contexts that are out of school but not necessarily in opposition to young people's academic aspirations. Chapter 7 examines how youth in a comics inquiry community that was part of the parish afterschool program used multimodal literacies to develop a shared literary character that could morph into different identities and traverse social worlds. Chapter 8 presents insights from the Community Researchers Project, a participatory inquiry with Indonesian and Latina/o youth in which they read high-quality nonfiction texts with social justice themes and then, inspired by the books, conducted research on issues that mattered to them, sharing their insights with others at the parish and beyond. Both chapters demonstate how inquiry may become a vehicle through which to nurture the creative and intellectual desires of students. In the process, members of a learning community develop new collaborative relations that defy the ideology of the normal curve and of individual aptitude. They also actualize curricular possibilities that neither homogenize experience through standardization nor essentialize identities as insular but instead remind us of how a multiplicity of perspectives is necessary for envisioning and enacting a better collective future.

Chapters 9 and 10 weave insights across the various inquiries, describe the collaborative methodologies in which we engaged, and elaborate on implications for education, community-based research, and the practice of partnering. Chapter 9 explores the role of ethical and professional norms in community-based research, especially in fostering trust within contexts of cultural diversity, systemic inequity, and power asymmetries. We describe a set of guidelines for community-based research that developed through collaborative inquiry into our partnership. The norms emerged from investigating the reciprocal and recursive relationship between our roles as both scholars and practitioners. We hope making our norms transparent will inspire others engaged in community-based research to explicitly attend to the ethical dimensions of their own partnerships. In Chapter 10, we return to the conceptual model that explains how the various advocacy discourses circulating through St. Thomas Aquinas exist in a productive synergistic relationship with one another. Doing good "work in the world," we argue, requires cooperation across diverse communities and perspectives. The model may provide a heuristic for others to help identify and cultivate the rich, pluriversal intellectual and activist resources already present in communities as people negotiate boundaries in projects of change and transformation. Chapter 10 also describes further inquiries and implications for the scholarship, practice, and teaching of community-based research with an educational focus. These include the importance of scholars directly naming educational precarity as a strand of social precarity while simultaneously supporting the agency of families, educators, youth, and community leaders who, on a daily basis, advocate for education through sophisticated and culturally inflected literacies. We have learned from our collaborative research at St. Thomas Aquinas that hope is a project that entails nurturing ever widening and overlapping circles of solidarity that have as their foundation congregation in the service of social justice and human rights.

NOTES

1. While this is the real name of the parish, we have used pseudonyms for research participants and changed identifying details to protect their confidentiality.

2. We have chosen to use the terms "Filipina/o" and "Latina/o" rather than "Filipino"and "Latino." We realize these are still imperfect referents that may exclude individuals who identify as being outside the gender binary. For an article that uses "Latinx" and addresses the intersections of race, immigration status, and gender, please see: Mejía, C. E. (2015). Mixed status Latinx families: Love and chosen family as a means of resistance to the American Dream. *Tapestries: Interwoven Voices of Local and Global Identities*, 4(1).

3. Monsignor is an honorific term given to recognize length of service or particular administrative roles in large Catholic parishes.

4. There was an inadvertent lapse in Institutional Review Board approval between December 14, 2012, and June 22, 2015, which was discovered and addressed in June 2015.

Chapter 2

Aquinas Center
Designing a Space of Radical Hospitality

Bethany J. Welch and María Paula Ghiso

The parish has, I don't want to say an aura, but it certainly has a reputation for being a welcoming community to many of our brothers and sisters who might land on these shores or come into this city and might now know exactly where to go, where they won't be conspicuous, where they will be welcomed, where they will be fortified in the Word of God, and supported by a community of people who are on a journey with them.

—Fr. Shields

The globalization of neighborhoods has created layered communities where people from different backgrounds and cultures come together in the same densely populated location. In these transnational contexts, residents begin to unintentionally and intentionally rework how space is used, experienced, owned, navigated, and understood. This chapter explores how members of St. Thomas Aquinas repurposed a former convent on the grounds of the parish into a community center that strives to embody the ideal of radical hospitality. Churches and houses of worship are often the first point of contact or attachment for immigrants and refugees arriving in a new place (Hirschman, 2004). Not only are families welcomed into the faith community for worship (possibly in their own language), but the place-based nature of faith-based organizations in these neighborhoods also plays a critical role in mediating the resettlement or relocation experience for new arrivals and catalyzing their civic engagement (Silverman, 2013; Welch, 2012). Research on social service provision in the post–welfare reform era of neoliberalism identifies the urban church as an essential hub of support for under-resourced neighborhoods (Owens & Smith, 2005). English classes, social gatherings, devotional or feast celebrations (e.g., *Feast of Our Lady of Guadalupe, Simbang Gabi, Tet*), food, shared languages and advocacy opportunities complement the worship experience and, in some cases, become the primary, rather than secondary, attachment to these spaces.

This chapter describes Aquinas Center as both a physical place with a distinctive material presence in the built environment and a cocreated community of communities that lives and breathes within the walls of a former convent. The brick and mortar aspects of Aquinas Center cannot be separated from the worldviews and practices of people who (re)make the space through continued activity. As scholars in disability studies have noted, built environments are never neutral but rather always ideologically saturated: They privilege certain identities and exclude or delimit others (Siebers, 2010). The chapter thus begins to explore questions such as the following: What is the relationship between the built environment of Aquinas Center and the diverse identities of the parishioners? How is a "shared" and "teaching" parish actually materialized and structured? How do decisions about space and resources balance the need to honor particular cultural practices while simultaneously creating opportunities for collaboration across social boundaries? What can be done to ensure that visitors to the center, such as service learning students, disrupt instead of reproduce deficit ideologies of the neighborhood? How does a grassroots community center keep its lights on in a neighborhood feeling the squeeze of gentrification?

We explore three ways in which the St. Thomas Aquinas community has worked to create an inclusive place that values a multiplicity of diverse identities: how the Aquinas Center was collectively conceived, planned, and repurposed; the role of aesthetics, as exemplified in the center's designed murals, in helping to forge a shared identity across difference; and how the center has facilitated programming responsive to community members' unique contributions and needs. We believe our efforts at fostering equitable university–community partnerships have helped develop educational opportunities based on mutual learning and on valuing the knowledge of St. Thomas Aquinas's diverse communities. Despite our progress, we continue to be concerned about St. Thomas Aquinas's sustainability in a neighborhood that is experiencing significant real estate and redevelopment pressure as well as anti-immigrant policies that threaten families and youth.

A HISTORY OF THE SPACE

What is now Aquinas Center has seen three distinctive iterations. The 8,500-square-foot brick structure was built in 1965 to house Servant Sisters of the Immaculate Heart of Mary. These women, commonly referred to as nuns or sisters, would have worked for many decades in the adjacent parochial school as teachers and administrators. The convent, as it was known during that time, is situated in the northeast corner of the parish campus, which occupies an entire city block or approximately five acres of land.

Improved economic and social standing for women increased educational opportunities outside religious life, reducing the number of sisters who entered the vocation and became teachers. In the early 2000s departure of the religious order left the building vacant, at which time the parish opened a day care center, a move popular for ensuring a steady flow of students into the parochial school and that for many years provided a consistent source of income. When the state changed policies for how child care was subsidized, the rate of reimbursement for families was no longer sufficient to cover costs, and the day care began to lose money. Sociocultural shifts and neoliberal policies all factored into the emergence of the Aquinas Center.

At the beginning of the university partnership with St. Thomas Aquinas in 2010, when space in a former convent in the parish became available, members of the research team attended a meeting to discuss and workshop a mission statement for the center, then tentatively called the "Cabrini House":

> We will network and collaborate with other parishes, community and cultural organizations, government and other agencies toward the goal of creating within our own neighborhood and the larger community of South Philadelphia *a place of welcome* for the immigrant and the stranger. We will do this by advocating for the rights of immigrants, attending to the needs and concerns of new immigrants and by striving to build understanding among different cultures. (Artifact excerpt, February 4, 2010)

In 2011, a new priest was assigned as senior pastor of St. Thomas Aquinas. Fr. Hugh J. Shields brought extensive experience in the global South as well as multilingual settings across the Archdiocese of Philadelphia. He revived conversations with the parish community about how the building might be reused. In these discussions, he emphasized that everyone's ideas be heard and stressed the need to "put social justice into the mix" (Fieldnotes, June 2012).

Bethany was invited by Fr. Shields to visit the former convent space in the summer of 2012 with the hope that she would assist the parish communities to reenvision it, and soon after she was asked to take the lead on efforts to create a new space that addressed community goals. A year later, in her capacity as founding director, Bethany invited María Paula to join the Board of Directors as the center began its transition to a nonprofit organization. With a separate Board of Directors, the Aquinas Center functions in a collegial relationship with parish leadership. Day-to-day program activities are managed by Bethany, and the board provides fiduciary and policy oversight. Income to operate programs is generated by the Aquinas Center as an organization and is paid to the parish, which owns and maintains the facility. Fr. Shields provides insights into the community but is not a member of the Aquinas Center Board of Directors.

REUSING, REPURPOSING, AND RECLAIMING

During the 9 months leading up to the formation of the center, Fr. Shields made four important changes: (1) relocating the parish chapel from the parochial school to the building, (2) inviting parish leaders and outside experts to continue discussions about how the building might be best used, (3) asking parish leaders to review the spaces available in relationship to their envisioned needs, and (4) holding a community-wide renovation day to paint over the distinctly child-oriented visual themes and wallpaper from the day care years.

Moving the chapel was a symbolic action and a placemaking move. It signified to guests and parishioners that the purpose of the new building would not be solely social or educational but would be spiritual as well. It created a central gathering space for the weekday life of the building by holding daily Mass there Monday through Saturday. Placemaking, an urban planning concept (Jacobs, 1961) that has been employed across a number of disciplines, refers to how color, shape, and structural form are used to create distinctive feelings about a physical space or suggest certain uses. In a city park, a fountain and benches might invite passersby to linger. In another, decorative metal arches ringing a large stretch of green grass imply that pedestrians can admire the well-groomed lawn but should not venture onto it. A school as a "place" may house contesting visions of education, teaching, and parent engagement derived from the different perspectives of policymakers, testing companies, and local families (Sánchez, 2011). Placemaking frameworks underscore the notion that places are not preexisting realities with which we interact but are social as well as material constructions that both reflect and reproduce ideologies. As such, placemaking necessarily calls attention to power—whose vision is being enacted and how, who is included or excluded from that vision—and the tensions that arise from competing interpretations (McCann, 2002, as cited in Sánchez, 2011).

Scholars have argued that democratic placemaking engages existing or potential users in the planning and implementation of a space (Lefebvre, 1970). At St. Thomas Aquinas, the reimagining of the convent space into the Aquinas Center was a collective one. Rather than dictating the course of action in a top-down manner, group discussions infused community perspectives into decisionmaking. Parish leaders identified a desire for multicultural cooperation across languages, levels of education, religious affiliation, and social class and also emphasized inviting others to join the positive work already occurring in the neighborhood. Given these visions, the group sought complementary insights from beyond the St. Thomas Aquinas community on trends in repurposing church property and concrete strategies for facilitating their vision. Bethany suggested that hosting service experiences might be one way to pursue their goals. These experiences typically involve inviting high school or college students, often from suburban or rural areas, to stay in the city for 3 days to 1 week and participate in hands-on volunteer or "service" projects during their stay. Tenets from Catholic Social Teaching inform dialogue around visitors' experiences and help challenge assumptions about the neighborhood. St. Thomas Aquinas community leaders agreed to this model, which would generate a revenue stream to help offset the cost of keeping the building open and provide an occasion to teach others about the neighborhood and work alongside them on service justice-oriented projects. As we describe later in the chapter, through initiatives such as Youth Voices, members of the different cultural groups at St. Thomas Aquinas play an integral role in sharing their knowledge and representing the parish and its mission during service learning experiences.

AESTHETICS OF IDENTITY AND CHANGE

Part of placemaking at the Aquinas Center has involved balancing shared space with areas for particular groups. The various cultural communities at St. Thomas Aquinas and other partners, including a legal clinic and the University of Pennsylvania, have dedicated space of some kind. For example, based on priorities shared by each community during initial planning sessions, the Filipina/o community was allocated a small room on the first floor near the center's chapel where they could meet together and also store meeting items (coffee, tea, hymnals, prayer books, etc.). At the same time, there are vibrant areas of the building that serve multiple purposes and invite congregation across groups. A dining room and kitchen may be occupied by a high school service group one day and host an intercultural women's group meeting the next; a shaded outdoor space has large picnic tables for shared meals and a culturally relevant community garden planted by children from the neighborhood; and a large basement might host, on alternating days, ESOL classes, workshops on immigration or health support, and youth participatory research. Spaces shift with priorities and needs: For instance, the university office was seldom occupied because we were usually in larger rooms that could accommodate educational activities; thus, in later years our materials were moved to a designated closet and the work we created with families and youth was displayed throughout the building.

Aesthetics were a primary consideration during the first few months in the new space. Bethany spent many hours considering, with community input, how the physical environment might reflect the range of new activities taking place in the former convent as well as how to express a unified identity across the many partners, cultural groups, and organizations that had begun to utilize the space. On a pragmatic level, this involved a type of "branding": A new logo adapted from the parish emblem hangs over

individual rooms, denoting all particular spaces as part of a collective enti-
ty, and was replicated on the facade of the building, letterhead, and T-shirts
worn by staff, community members, and visitors alike. In the spirit of local
artistic tradition, murals became one of the mediums of choice to aestheti-
cally represent the emerging vision of the center. Philadelphia, a postindus-
trial city with historical contributions to democracy and civic participation,
has become an epicenter of community murals. At present, there are over
3,500 murals across the city, many the result of the Mural Arts Program.
Cocreating these beautiful walls, ranging from expansive canvases of brick
and stucco to small panels installed on existing structures, can be the im-
petus for fostering critical consciousness about contested urban spaces.
Murals offer a counter-representation to pervasive discourses and images
of deprivation perpetuated in the media and dominant public sphere. The
process of developing a mural often engages diverse individuals in a unified goal, develops a sense of a shared use for city locations, and illuminates
rich local legacies and subaltern group histories (see Chapter 7). When
conceived and executed collaboratively, murals can become one means by
which community members gain control of the images and metaphors used
to represent their neighborhoods.

Aquinas Center is now home to six community-constructed murals.
They all reflect local knowledge and, taken together, an ethos of radical
hospitality. They range from major yearlong projects to more modest expressions of identity. Each one is unique and has a different purpose or
message, yet they draw on the rich cultural and linguistic diversity of the
parish. For example, a partnership with the Mural Arts Program and the
nonprofit organization PhillyRising, coupled with funding secured from
Bloomberg Philanthropies, resulted in the collective design of an exterior
mural to capture the diversity and ethos of hospitality of the St. Thomas
Aquinas community. It features textile designs from Vietnam, Indonesia,
and Mexico threading together in a common composition. The mural was
designed by artist Delia King based on collective discussions to generate
its vision, and it was executed by more than 160 participants ranging from
parishioners to neighbors to medical students from a local university to
returned Peace Corps volunteers. A sixth mural was developed during the
summer of 2015 with the theme of Flowers and Feasting to capture the rich
connections between flora and fauna as expressed in the feasting traditions
of the many St. Thomas Aquinas communities. The Vietnamese New Year
celebration (Lunar New Year) incorporates a soft yellow apricot *mai* flower
into many of the visual elements of the event. The celebration of Our Lady
of Guadalupe focuses on the roses in Juan Diego's cloak during the appari-
tion of the Virgin Mary in the hills above Mexico City. In the mural, these
varied flowers and traditions blend and cross-pollinate, at once reflecting
the particularities of spiritual traditions and the new possibilities spurred
by cross-cultural encounters.

Companions on the Journey was the first, and perhaps most modest, mural, yet perhaps more than the others, it captures the philosophies that led to the creation of the center and that it strives to embody. Designed and painted over 1 month in January 2013 by youth catechists from the Latina/o community, the mural concept was intentionally allegorical, operating on both theological and historical levels. The image of the Holy Family fleeing (or returning) to Egypt is symbolic of the forced movement experienced by many contemporary immigrants and refugees, such as those at St. Thomas Aquinas. In the sacred text, the governing leader of an occupied Israel, King Herod, was threatened by the birth of what many were calling their future king. To quell a potential overthrow, the king decreed that all male Jewish children under the age of three be killed. Scripture describes Mary and Joseph relocating to Egypt, a nonoccupied neighboring country, in order to save their son. As they drew inspiration from the Biblical story for designing the mural, the St. Thomas Aquinas youth shared their own experiences in navigating national borders to flee difficult circumstances and to work for better life opportunities.

Aquinas Center volunteers used a colorful, visually accessible image of this flight as the jumping off point for the design of *Companions on the Journey*. This framed reprint of a painting by local artist Brother Mickey McGrath, donated by a Catholic immigrant advocacy organization that was closing, was hung at one end of a long hallway. Its colors, extended into the mural, brought vibrancy to the narrow corridor and imbued the area with meaning. The mural design stretched about 10 feet from end to end and depicted a landscape of abstract trees, water, and hills in the same style as the painting. It gives viewers the illusion of walking in the same landscape as the Holy Family and is complemented by a prayer—a show of solidarity—for all who experience displacement and the people that accompany them. As part of the built environment, the mural communicates not just hospitality but a preferential option for people who have been dislocated or live in exile, values that stand in stark contrast to ones that criminalize immigrants.

RESPONSIVENESS AND MUTUALITY IN CENTER INITIATIVES

In the context of social and economic precarity due to neoliberal policies that have eroded affordable housing, access to education, and employment opportunities, parishioners and neighborhood residents increasingly rely on community organizations for these services. Aquinas Center strives to be responsive to community members' unique contributions and needs as determined by community members themselves. One challenge is to try to be mindful of not assuming what others require. In this section, we describe two initiatives developed with ongoing community input: the center's multicultural garden and the Youth Voices program. These examples illustrate the ways the Aquinas Center has been code-signed as a teaching and activist space that takes the lead from parishioners' interests and goals.

Learning from Others and Enlisting Collective Support

While visions for how to repurpose the parish building had been collectively generated over time, these discussions did not stop when the Aquinas Center became a reality. Over a period of 5 months, Bethany sought input in a range of ways: attending community activities, where she could learn about others through informal conversations; visiting worship and devotional settings to get a sense of the religious dimension of the work being done at St. Thomas Aquinas; and consulting one-on-one with community leaders to hear what was important to them. These listening sessions revealed common goals for the space:

- Cultivating solidarity across boundaries
- Providing space for both church and cultural activities (food, art, language, music)
- Creating a safe(r) space for dialogue
- Fostering educational opportunities
- Supporting community leaders with social action/advocacy
- Inviting guests to help achieve community goals

Once established, the Board of Directors worked together to construct a mission statement reflective of community members' visions, highlighting the values of hospitality, responsiveness, solidarity, and transformation that threaded the various articulated goals. The resulting statement—*Aquinas Center builds unity in diversity, supports learning, and inspires thoughtful action*—resonates with the long history of parish discussions about the place they wished to make together.

With no start-up capital to begin the center, it was essential to build coalitions to support this vision. Some of the partnerships with the parish, like the University of Pennsylvania, were already in place, whereas new ones were intentionally pursued to address additional goals articulated by the community. For example, to further leadership development for social action and advocacy, Bethany and a member of the Latina/o community at St. Thomas Aquinas reached out to the Catholic Campaign for Human Development (CCHD), which funds social change efforts, to present a proposal for supporting Spanish-speaking leaders who were anxious about police stops, interaction with immigration officials, and conflicts with landlords. Aquinas Center received funds from the CCHD for advocacy and organizing around immigration reform. The Youth

Voices program, which we describe below, was one concrete instantiation of the community's desire for strengthening the leadership capacity of younger generations.

Youth Voices Program

Several years ago, students in the 8th-grade class featured in Chapter 5 "adopted" the Aquinas Center for their social action project, aiming to contribute to its redevelopment through their ideas and the labor needed to actualize them. The youth came from a range of cultural and religious backgrounds but all of them attended the parish school. The youth's interest and initiative harmonized with goals expressed by the St. Thomas Aquinas community of cultivating existing local leadership. The students' involvement in the center became the cornerstone of the Youth Voices program, which meets after school once a week and a few Saturdays a month. The youth have valuable knowledge about their community and ideas for change. However, because of what Fricker (2007) characterizes as testimonial injustice, a deflation of one's credibility as a knowledge generator due to systematic identity prejudice, their perspectives are often devalued within the broader public sphere because of their age, race, language, and class. The goal of the Youth Voices initiative is to support the teens in making their voices and perspectives more audible: They may practice public speaking to gain fluency in articulating their ideas, design presentations for their proposals, or anticipate how to address contesting perspectives on issues they are investigating. Youth Voices participants have taken on greater leadership roles in the Aquinas Center, becoming the spokespersons who introduce the area to visitors undertaking service learning experiences and helping facilitate discussions on a range of social justice issues and advocacy efforts.

Ana, one of the young women involved, described what she saw as the benefit of the program:

> I have learned to believe in what I say, I don't back down anymore. There is a mixture of being encouraged to speak and getting to practice in front of people that care about you. It is a big thing to know people believe in you.

Ana, 14 at the time she was interviewed, highlights the *care* she felt—encouragement, belief in her abilities—as well as the opportunities to concretely develop her voice and share her talents with wider audiences. Ana attended St. Thomas Aquinas for all of grade school and graduated as class valedictorian in the spring of 2015. Her artistic gifts are evident in some of the center's murals and most recently in a T-shirt she designed to celebrate the pope's visit to Philadelphia in the fall of 2015.

In discussing with Bethany what they valued about Youth Voices and what they would change, the teens all mentioned the importance of care. While no space is ever fully "safe" and there are always silences (Leonardo & Porter, 2010), trusting relationships, built consistently over time, helped foster an environment where students felt safer to express their experiences and opinions and could work through dissensus and conflict, which are necessary for growth. These conversations, part of ongoing evaluation, are designed to ensure that programming remains sensitive to community interests. In bringing to fruition their ideas for improving the center, and practicing how to convey those visions most effectively, the youth frequently engaged in informal exchanges about issues affecting their lives. For example, Youth Voices became a space where conversations about documentation status and immigrant rights took hold organically. Since the students had forged relationships with one another, differences that in other contexts might have been politically divisive were received in a generous spirit. The youth claimed their knowledge while simultaneously cultivating what Fricker (2007) would characterize as a stance of virtuous listening, being self-reflexive regarding one's own identity prejudices vis-à-vis others. This type of relational labor lays the necessary groundwork for coalitions across lines of race, gender, language, and immigration status.

Multicultural Garden

One example of a coalition that involved multiple communities was the multicultural community garden. The community garden germinated as a collaboration between Bethany and Mrs. Cruz, the parish school's ESOL teacher whose partnership with a university class we feature in Chapter 6. Many of the parish's immigrant communities had extensive knowledge of gardening from their home countries, and food was also central to families' cultural and literate practices. Volunteer labor and creative funding sources helped to make the project a reality. The garden has expanded from its original small patch of soil to become a primary feature of the center's 1,500-square-foot courtyard—a central gathering place for the St. Thomas Aquinas community and an educational hub for a range of initiatives. Youth from the Community Researchers Project (featured in Chapter 8) used the garden as a context for learning about qualitative methods, and the space has progressively become more integrated into youth programs such as a Summer Green and Growing Camp, where young children honed literacy skills within the context of science explorations, and teens mapped the space to guide the spring planning, blending math and horticulture through hands-on experiences.

At the insistence of the youth, who were proud of their work and wanted to show off the garden to their families, the center established open hours so that parents and elders from different communities in the parish could mingle and share with one another stories of the culturally relevant food items being grown there; this will be formally expanded through food and folklore programming linking the bounty of the garden with transnational storytelling practices. The garden and courtyard are also spaces frequented by visitors to the center, many of them students at local universities who stay overnight for service learning projects, and offer both neighbors and guests a space in which to serve side by side and commune with one another as equals.

The possibilities for the garden continue to expand with passing years and in response to feedback from community members. This year, the Aquinas Center received a grant for $15,000 to provide fresh, culturally relevant food to immigrant and refugee communities in South Philadelphia. The garden will be a centerpiece of this initiative, serving as a demonstration space for families who will learn how to transfer the gardening knowledge they bring from their home countries to a city context and who will also receive gardening kits for their homes. Other ideas are in the works, including a multicultural cooking club. Foucault (1990) famously used the garden as an example of heterotopic spaces, a single real space that juxtaposes plants from all over the world. The place of the Aquinas Center, too, might be thought of as a heterotopia. On the surface it looks like just one of many church buildings throughout the city. However, behind its walls thrive a heterogeneity of transcultural influences and alternative forms of sociality that resist exclusionary ideologies. The creation of the garden afforded an opportunity for community members across the diverse constituencies of St. Thomas Aquinas to work alongside one another and share cultural knowledge. All this was done under a shared vision to address issues of food justice and health disparities that impact the broader neighborhood.

CONCLUSION

One of the biggest challenges to the Aquinas Center is gentrification. Where simple two-story row homes once dominated the streetscape, now five-story single-family dwellings are being constructed with considerable amenities and are selling for four to five times the price of houses on either side. Nonprofit organizations, schools, and churches are impacted by this real estate pressure. Even the decision to repurpose the empty convent instead of selling it was made against the backdrop of this reality. Since the early 2000s, parishes similar to St. Thomas Aquinas, in comparable financial straits, had begun to sell off individual properties when they could no longer maintain the structures or manage the utility bills. At the same time, parochial education began to decline in the face of increasing numbers of publicly funded, tuition-free charter schools.

The result has been a large inventory of vacant properties that were eligible for sale or reuse, a trend common across cities in the Northeast (Welch, 2009). For example, a parochial school in the area was sold for $3.1 million (Whelan, 2012) to a private developer who turned the space into 48 apartment units. A few years prior, a local Catholic high school for boys was combined with a nearby girls' school, then repurposed by the Archdiocese's Office for Community Development, a community development corporation (Archdiocese of Philadelphia, 2007). The property became a low-income housing facility for seniors. Both of these adaptive reuse projects were undertaken by major institutions with significant capital that had the internal capacity to navigate rezoning, access to tax incentives (abatements and credits), and the ability to front the multimillion-dollar expenditures to redevelop the properties.

In contrast, Aquinas Center was forged out of a community-based grassroots effort to respond to the immediate needs of the neighborhood. However, everyday people's goodwill and innovation are tenuous factors within a larger economic and political context. As the Aquinas Center looks to the future, there are several lingering questions: Will existing households be able to stay in the neighborhood as rent and property taxes rise? Will new arrivals to the gentrifying area be invested in the same kind of bridge building and advocacy work that characterizes the center now?

In a recent address on the Feast of the Holy Trinity, Pope Francis remarked, "We are not called to live without the other, above or against the other, but with the other, for the other and in the other" (Vatican Radio, 2015, para. 4). If the center is to persist in the face of redevelopment pressure, it is this spirit that must prevail. For the immigrant youth facing an uncertain future due to the lack of Congressional action on immigration reform, and for other St. Thomas Aquinas community members living under conditions of precarity, Aquinas Center could continue to serve as a "Companion on the Journey," a place for dialogue, empathy, and hospitality.

Chapter 3

Participatory Research with Parents
Mobilizing Social Capital to Support Children's Education

Mary Yee, Karim Mostafa, and Gerald Campano

Relationships are the strength for us.

—A leader in the Indonesian community

The Philadelphia neighborhood where St. Thomas Aquinas is located has, for the last 40 years, been the first landing for immigrants and refugees, especially from Southeast Asia. The Indonesian community started to form around 2000, as individuals fleeing religious and ethnic persecution in their home country arrived. Like the Vietnamese, Cambodians, Lao, Burmese, and Bhutanese, many immigrants from Indonesia are navigating a new school system while encouraging their children to get a good education as a path to a more secure existence.

Our personal histories as educators from immigrant/transnational families familiarized us with the kinds of challenges the Indonesian parents face in adapting to a dominant culture and language, dealing with issues of maintaining home language and heritage, making choices in an unfamiliar and confusing educational landscape, and struggling daily to provide a decent livelihood for their families. With this project we sought to demystify the bureaucracy of American schooling and work together with families to support their children's education. Our research questions— "How do immigrant parents advocate for their children's education?" and "What further supports can we build together?"—reflected our ongoing interest in understanding the strategies families employ to help their children and how university–community collaborations might assist them in their efforts. The families' desire to advance their children's opportunities was evident in their enthusiastic participation in all the literacy projects at St. Thomas Aquinas, several of which are detailed in this book.

Our inquiry evolved into participatory action research focused on the local school district's high school application process and culminated in a community workshop that explained and advised parents about this confusing bureaucracy that had significant gatekeeping implications for college admissions. Moreover, parent voice and agency in guiding the project challenges deficit characterizations of immigrant families' school involvement. At St. Thomas Aquinas, parental involvement and leadership emerged from grassroots concerns—it was not dictated by district policy or mandated by federal law. Parent agency was also evident in the resourcefulness and tenacity of families seeking opportunities for their children to thrive academically.

BUILDING THE COMMUNITY COLLABORATION PROCESS

Our collaboration with the Indonesian parents germinated from our earlier activities with the parish leadership team that included organizing a Family Literacy Night. Gerald had been partnering with the families for several years to facilitate a letter exchange (the "PennPal" project) between children in the Indonesian Sunday School and Penn master's students. It was clear that the Indonesian families were concerned about their children's education, were eager to involve their children in literacy enrichment activities, and wanted more resources and information about American schooling. Given her administrative work in the local school district and community work with immigrant families and students, Mary felt a natural connection to the group, which led her to approach Dina, a mother with school-age children on the leadership council, about working together. Karim was drawn to the inquiry because of his own transnational educational experiences. As one project in a larger research initiative, we grounded ourselves in the foundational principles of the university research team: the Ethical and Professional Norms for Partnering detailed in Chapter 9.

Our approximately year-and-a-half-long project consisted of four general meetings and three planning ones that culminated in a High School Workshop for the Indonesian community at the parish, as well as review of workshop evaluations and interviews with parent leaders. Proceeding from our belief that parents should be equal partners and that their community knowledge and lived experience would be paramount resources, we began by asking parents about their interactions with the American educational system. During our first meeting parents raised questions and concerns about school practices, available services, and educational rights. The discussion converged around several themes, which became clear to all of us at the end of the meeting. The parents chose three topics for the group to focus on: language access, the negotiation of school choice, and support for undocumented students. The following meeting, parents came to a consensus that the first initiative would be a workshop on the public high school admissions process, an immediate issue since a significant number of families had children in middle school. As we set out to learn together about the process, participatory action research was developing organically. The goal of subsequent meetings was to gather and share questions and information and finally to plan the agenda and logistics of the workshop. The parents relied on Karim and Mary to jointly facilitate the meetings and to be resources for the project, while they provided input for the agendas and made decisions on how to proceed.

INDONESIAN PARENTS AT THE PARISH

In the early 2000s, the Indonesian community in South Philadelphia formed after virulent riots against ethnic Chinese and non-Muslims in Indonesia in the spring of 1998 propelled many ethnic Chinese Christians who had settled in Indonesia to seek refuge in the United States. Most of these families arrived on tourist visas and applied for political asylum upon arrival. Many left behind a livelihood and valuable property in search of security and a future for their children. A majority had high school diplomas; a significant proportion had college degrees.

As with many refugees, they arrived with few resources and generally little English proficiency or knowledge of American culture. Most adults were underemployed, working as day laborers or at other low-wage jobs. Although there are mixed-status families with American-born children, some community members have been unsuccessful in obtaining legal status and remain constantly anxious about being apprehended (Bernsterin-Baker, personal communication, March 11, 2015). At its height, the Indonesian community in Philadelphia was estimated to number about 10,000; however, in 2010, it was thought to have diminished to about 4,000 (Kase, June 15, 2010), still ranking it as the ninth largest in the United States (Spolan, June 14, 2011, *Philadelphia Weekly*). After 10 to 15 years here, the community's presence is felt not only in the Catholic parish but also in local schools, which have hired Indonesian-speaking professionals to serve the critical mass of families requiring language access services. In addition, Indonesian family restaurants, cafés, and grocery stores—many with citywide reputations—have sprung up in South Philadelphia, and a number of first generation students have entered professional fields such as nursing. Community members have continued to be a presence at local immigrant-serving social service agencies that provide legal assistance and English as a Second Language (ESL) classes.

The circumstances surrounding immigration have greatly influenced the day-to-day experiences of families at St. Thomas Aquinas. Despite having intermarried and being a few generations removed from China, they identify and are identified as ethnic Chinese—even though they are Indonesian citizens. Enmity against ethnic Chinese in Southeast Asia has persisted because of their perceived domination in the business and corporate sectors (Rohr, February 5, 2001, *Inquirer*). As Catholics fleeing from religious persecution and as ethnic Chinese escaping ethnic violence, since 9/11 the Indonesian community in Philadelphia has experienced the cruel irony of increased scrutiny and anti-immigrant sentiment because they are from a predominantly Muslim country.

Our project involved the ethnic Chinese Indonesian community that has congregated at St. Thomas Aquinas. Over 30 families belong to the parish, which has served as a place for worship and succor and also for building community among its Indonesian members. Indonesian leaders participate in the Parish Council, organize their own Sunday School and Catholic youth activities, and share the division of labor for special events at the church, such as preparations for Christmas and Easter celebrations. As participatory action researchers, we worked to leverage the leadership, sense of community cohesion, and organizational know-how already in place.

In the following sections we contrast our practice of parental involvement with how it is implemented in schools and show how the Indonesian families mobilized social capital in support of their children's education.

PARENTAL INVOLVEMENT FROM THE GROUND UP

We are accustomed to hearing about the need for and lack of parental involvement as if this were the missing ingredient in advancing student achievement (Nakagawa, 2000). Parental involvement has a typology ranging from preparing children for school to decisionmaking at school (Epstein & Dauber, 1991) and is mandated in Title I of the No Child Left Behind Act for schools and districts that qualify as poor, often through top-down policies with only token representation of parent voices (Doucet, 2011; Fine, 1993).

Our approach to parental involvement resists two strands of the dominant discourse about minoritized parents, including immigrant parents, and their children's education: (1) that parents do not care and really cannot help their children, and (2) that districts and schools should determine and set the form and content of parental involvement. Only more recently has ethnographic research distinguished between ethnic groups within pan-ethnic categories such as Latina/o or Asian and broadened our knowledge of families' engagement in education: the values they transmit, their strategies for gathering pertinent information, and the actions that they take to support their children's academic achievement (Suárez-Orozco, Suárez-Orozco, & Todorova, 2008). Moreover, those who have worked for a long time in grassroots communities know that the first stereotype is far from true (Delgado-Gaitán, 1991). A nexus of institutional constraints and power differentials prevents many schools from engaging with parents in a meaningful and respectful way and parents from having an effective voice in decisionmaking about their children's education or how the school will function (Fine, 1993; Nakagawa, 2000).

Our collaboration with parents arose directly from their priorities. Their involvement with us was motivated by both personal interest and their perception of the needs of their community as a whole. Rather than proceeding from a mandate, such as Title I, which dictates a structure, representation, and funding, our project grew organically as a loose configuration of interested community parents facilitated by the university researchers. Instead of focusing on a single school, our group involved families from several schools. Since we believed in nurturing local parent leadership, the group made decisions through consensus on what kind of project to implement, who the audience would be, and what format we would use. Within the parent group, two mothers, Dina and Mega, rose to the challenge of acting as a liaison with the rest of the families.

Parental involvement policies have inferred an "ideal parent," who is modeled on a stay-at-home English-speaking middle-class mom who participates in the Parent–Teacher Association and bake sales, chaperones class trips, attends report conferences, helps with homework, and monitors attendance and progress (Nakagawa, 2000). Most working-class and poor immigrant parents cannot be at school during the day, and schools do not frequently provide language access services. Despite this, the Indonesian parents were heavily invested in their children's progress: They assiduously attended report card conferences, signed off and oversaw homework completion, were strict about attendance, and helped with homework in the lower grades. Monitoring occurred even when signing off was not required because the parents, who had grown up in Indonesia, were accustomed to the watchful eyes of their own parents. Many of the parents in our group were computer literate, and those with public school students went online to check test scores, grades, and assignments on the district website.

ACCESSING AND COCONSTRUCTING KNOWLEDGE

While the Indonesian parents looked to us for expertise about the American schooling system, we came to recognize their resourcefulness in finding the best placements for their children. The families had many questions and critiques about discipline, cooperative learning, competition, and test scores. One parent did not understand why the school did not address the bullying of her son; another wondered why her high-achieving child had to help a student who was struggling; others felt that there should be a more competitive environment where grades and test scores are posted. We realized that the parents' schooling in Indonesia influenced their attitudes, expectations, and concerns about the U.S. system.

In the following sections we look at how the Indonesian parents enacted their *habitus* and mobilized their *social capital* in particular in the *field* of education to find ways to support the academic success of their students. We employ these concepts from Pierre Bourdieu to understand the dynamics among the parents within the larger social context. *Habitus* can be understood as the complex expression of an individual's personality, dispositions, accent, even bodily mannerisms, formed at a young age, which is in constant dialectical relationship to social context (Bourdieu, 1990). In general terms, *cultural capital* includes such things as upbringing, education, special knowledge, and strategies for success (and even strategies for developing new strategies); *social capital* is the advantage bestowed on a social agent as a result of networks of relationships and membership in various groups (Bourdieu, 1986). *Field* is the social arena, such as domains in the arts, education, sports, or finance, in which actors demonstrate their *habitus* and exercise their various forms of *capital* (Thomson, 2008).

In our early meetings, parents told us of the various ways in which they learned about and investigated schools. We had assumed (incorrectly), given the families' strong involvement in church activities, that many children attended the local parish school. On the contrary, we found out that children typically attended parochial school only for a short time and then transferred to district or charter schools. In order to explain their decisionmaking, the parents described the educational hierarchy in Indonesia: Catholic institutions are considered the most elite while government schools occupy the lower tier. Families make economic sacrifices to send their children to parochial schools, even to the point of taking out loans. As Bernard, a parent, explained, "Parents are willing to make the sacrifice because they know that the education will be high quality," and consequently, the future of their children would be secure. As all the parents in our group had attended Catholic school through high school, and some even through university, they had high expectations of Catholic education, derived from their experiences in their home country. To their surprise, the parish schools here did not meet their standards of educational quality. Another disincentive was the parochial school tuition, which was a hardship for these families where adults were often working in multiple low-wage jobs simultaneously.

In short, the parents were accustomed to Indonesian schooling where, like in many Asian countries, a transmission model of pedagogy prevailed. Discipline was strict—corporal punishment, the norm; great effort demanded; respect for teachers, absolute. Other characteristics included a standardized curriculum, high-stakes testing, stand-and-deliver methodology, and rote learning. Several parents remarked that they admired their children's confidence in asking questions in American schools and also questioning the adults at home—actions that would have been frowned upon in Indonesia. The educational experiences, expectations, and beliefs of the Indonesian parents in the home country, factors contributing to their *habitus*, shaped their expectations of their children and schooling as well as their changing attitudes about the American educational system.

Mobilizing Social Capital

As researchers have found, immigrant families have used their *social capital*, that is, they have often taken advantage of resources, social connections, and networks both in and outside of their communities, to support their children's education (Bankston & Zhou, 2002; Suarez-Orozco et al., 2008). This also proved true for the Indonesian parents with whom we collaborated. Parents who were dissatisfied with the children's current schools sought other alternatives through their social connections. They employed various strategies, always alert to potentially useful information.

Although the parish did not typically help the families with educational options, they did host an informational session for a start-up charter school established near Chinatown. This event led one particular family—Althea's—to enroll children at that school, an act that led to a stream of Indonesian children attending it over the years. Althea's children were among the older K–12 students in the community at the time; thus, her children were seen as pioneers (or guinea pigs, according to one parent) in the public school system. Althea shared that she and her children liked the school. Sometime later, Dina was asked by a friend, who was the lunchroom assistant at the school, to help translate for a parent meeting. Dina, impressed by what she saw, made a mental note about the school, which has a rigorous math curriculum; a thriving arts program; and multiethnic, multilingual parent engagement. Consequently, she applied for her daughters, who were accepted the following year. Many more Indonesian parents have followed suit. For information on high schools, Dina's cohort of parents again turned to Althea, whose children arrived in their middle school or high school years. Althea credited the school counselor with guiding her children to special admissions schools, much better alternatives than the neighborhood comprehensive high school, a "persistently dangerous" school by federal standards. Thus, parents were alerted to choices among high schools.

Parents were not shy about using their emergent language abilities to gather information. Nancy asked her former employer and customers at a café about the high school choices for their children. She learned about a magnet middle school when her son asked to apply because his classmate was applying. Having known Nancy since kindergarten, the classmate's parent guided her through the process. However, while they had some knowledge that there were different tiers of high schools, the Indonesian parents felt there were an overwhelming number of choices, and they were unclear about the relative advantages or requirements of one school compared to another—thus the need for a workshop on the HS admissions process.

The various kinds of *social capital* ranging from the connection with the parish and parents of older students to ones at the workplace and other community sites enabled most parents to garner sufficient information for elementary and middle school. What one family learned was shared through the Sunday School network of parents or social media such as Facebook. Our arrival on the scene added to the *social capital* with another connection, which provided "insider" information on the workings of the school district. Thus, parents demonstrated their agency in optimizing school choices by using their *social capital*, despite the fact that the local educational system constrained their access (e.g., by not having adequate interpretation or translation) to knowledge that would have helped in the decisionmaking.

Intergenerational Closure: A Facet of Social Capital

Research on other Asian immigrant communities, such as the Vietnamese, has revealed high academic achievement rates undergirded by cultural values transmitted via "bounded social networks" of parents and other adults surrounding children (Bankston, 2004, p. 177, citing Bankston & Zhou, 2002). The St. Thomas Aquinas Indonesian community reflects this characterization, being tightly knit, connected by face-to-face congregation at the parish as well as social media. The Indonesian families knew each other's children. Coleman (1988) terms these linkages as "intergenerational closure" and a facet of *social capital* (p. S106). The significance of these bonds is that they provide additional *social capital* to the parents and also reinforce group norms regarding sanctions and behavior. Within our parent group, parents usually had detailed knowledge about the grade level and school trajectory of other people's children. Parents continually stressed the importance of high academic achievement based on personal discipline and hard work. Not surprisingly, a high proportion of children in the community attended magnet or special admissions schools or well-regarded charter schools. This was patently clear during our High School Workshop, which included a half dozen high school students who had been invited by the parent leaders to relate their experience applying to their particular competitive high school. These high school students embodied the educational values and desired outcomes of the parents.

Literacy and the Interaction of *Habitus* and *Capital*

Using Bourdieu's definitions of *habitus* and *capital* (*cultural, social,* and *economic*) as well as sociological definitions of social capital, advanced by researchers such as Coleman (1988), Zhou (Bankston & Zhou, 2002), and Bankston (2004), we sought to understand the many ways that our Indonesian parent coparticipants as agentive social actors have engaged literacy practices to advance their children's education. By starting with the parents' sharing their own educational experiences in Indonesia, we were able to ascertain how the school literacies they brought were operationalized as a form of transnational *cultural capital*. Along with their values, expectations, and dispositions toward education, we could also observe how aspects of their *habitus*'s interacting with *social* and *cultural capital* pointed them toward taking advantage of certain opportunities, such as enrollment at the charter school near Chinatown and the collaboration with the university.

As Bourdieu theorized, *habitus* with *capital* in a *field* (i.e., an arena of social action) propels individuals, groups, or institutions toward certain actions.

We began to see the parents' dispositions toward education as a facet of their *habitus*. From schools, they expected rigorous instruction, strict discipline, and public student ranking; from their children, high academic achievement, maximum effort, and good behavior; from themselves, a commitment to obtain the best education for their children and to support them academically. In our meetings, parents recounted the kind of scrutiny of homework and grades to which they had been subjected by their own parents and shared how they continue that tradition. As he wondered whether parents were pressuring their children too much, Peter said, "We only know to do the same thing to our kids that our parents did to us." This included the literacy practices of daily homework monitoring and parental home tutoring and continual exhortations on the importance of academic success. While the *cultural capital* embedded in Indonesian language and culture are not valued to the same degree here, nonetheless certain parental behaviors are considered exemplary by the public educational system. This combination of *habitus* and the type of *cultural capital* that aligned with that valued by the public educational system worked in favor of the Indonesian parents. The Indonesian parents read the educational landscape around them and used that knowledge to act on behalf of their children.

Despite the fact that the Indonesian parents were nonnative speakers of English, they were able to marshal their many language and cultural resources or communicative repertoires, that is, "the collection of ways an individual uses language and literacy and other means of communication (gesture, dress, posture, or accessories) to function effectively in the multiple communities in which they participate" to support their children's education in very effective ways (Rymes, 2010, p. 528). At home they drew on their *linguistic habitus* and *capital* (Bourdieu & Thompson, 1991), including home language, acquired English, and cultural ways of expressing and being, to help their children with homework; also, using multilingual resources at their disposal, in various settings, they gathered information from coworkers, other parents, and texts about schools and schooling. They used multimodal digital literacies (e.g., Facebook postings and email) to communicate with other parish families. In the activist space that we shared, we learned about the literacies parents developed for the multiple settings of their lives—the home, parish, workplace, hospital, and children's schools.

Bourdieu and Thompson (1991) speak specifically of *linguistic habitus* and *linguistic capital*, signifying both the resources and power differentials that come into play in different *fields*, or arenas of social action, between individuals or groups who have command of the dominant language and those who do not. As Gutiérrez and Orellana (2006) note, "In a stratified society, differences are never just differences; they will always be interpreted and ranked according to dominant cultural values and norms" (p. 506).

In opposition to this kind of ranking, we acknowledged but did not emphasize or stigmatize language differences; we tried to ensure that everyone in the gathering could comprehend and participate in the conversation by encouraging the full range of communicative repertoires, especially multilingual dialogue and interpretation. Thus, we were able to co-construct knowledge about differences between American and Indonesian schooling and about ways to negotiate the school district's high school admissions process. This knowledge represented not only additional *cultural* and *linguistic capital* but also a specific educational literacy, which involved the content and register of the school district's high school admissions process. Gaining power through this new literacy, parents and their high school–ready children demonstrated their agency through the successful navigation of the process as evidenced by the students' acceptances at special admissions and magnet schools.

DEVELOPING COMMUNITY CAPACITY

The importance of the high school admissions process in Philadelphia lies in the gatekeeping function it performs. Which high school and which tier of high schools one's child attends can have a major influence on chances for college acceptance and on college choice. The process is largely bureaucratic and paper based, punctuated sometimes by interviews, portfolio presentations, and auditions. For more prestigious and academically rigorous schools, it is highly competitive and based overwhelmingly on standardized test scores and grades. For other schools, admission is based on a lottery, sometimes modified by preselection of student applications beforehand according to attendance and behavioral criteria. Because the applications for 9th grade are processed during the child's 8th-grade year, it is the 7th-grade test scores, grades, and attendance that are most weighted by admissions committees. This fact is often obscured so that parents and students do not fully realize the importance of school achievement and performance 2 years before high school admission.

Navigating the District High School Directory

The main district resource for parents was a 52-page guide, the *2013 High School Directory*. The district did not have the budget to print these for distribution, so it was only available as a pdf downloadable file, despite the additional barrier this might present to families without Internet connectivity or computer access in the home. Over 70% (37 pages) of the publication consists of descriptions of high schools and their offerings; other parts include a greeting from the superintendent; a sample application form; and a section on "additional information," which is actually the description of the application process. The expectation is that parents actively engage in advising their children on high school choices. As the superintendent's greeting states,

> You will also want to review your child's academic history, visit the school and talk to teachers, administrators, students and parents to determine the best fit. . . . I hope that you will take the time to consider your goals and how The School District of Philadelphia, with its vast array of programs and services, can help you to achieve them. (*2013 High School Directory*, p. 2)

While the Indonesian parents review their children's academic history through copies of report cards, they were unlikely to go to prospective schools and consult with anyone because of work obligations, transportation difficulties, or lack of confidence with respect to communicating in English. Moreover, the opportunity offered by the superintendent did not necessarily exist; many schools did not have open-door policies that allowed parents to come at any time and meet with school personnel.

Even though the technocratic language was tempered somewhat in this publication for parents and students, for immigrant parents with less than native proficiency in English, it was nonetheless a dense text with terms and references that are not obvious. The layout and font size of the text in the high school descriptions discouraged thorough reading of the *2013 High School Directory*. The official application form, called the "High School Voluntary Transfer Form," as well as the parent verification at the bottom of the page, is equally intimidating. The directions are difficult to follow: They indicate completion of the form whether you want to "transfer" from your "neighborhood/feeder high school" or not and direct parents to "check the box . . . that so indicates" without any signal as to where this section is on the large application form reproduced (in rather blurry print) below the instructions. Referring to the process as "apply[ing] for a voluntary transfer to high schools other than your neighborhood/feeder school," as opposed to the more direct "apply[ing] to high schools," can be confusing since students would be transferring without having ever attended a particular high school. The form is overwhelming, perplexing, and when you take the time to look closely, even nonsensical in places.

As the *Philadelphia Public School Notebook*, the local education newspaper, noted,

> In a system where studies have found that parents are already befuddled by the process, students and their families have a dizzying array of high school choices—small schools, large schools, themed schools, charter schools, themed charter schools, neighborhood schools that have become charter schools—the list goes on. (Mezzacappa, 2012, p. 3).

For immigrant parents, this process is all the more opaque and confusing—and the anxiety increased—because of language difference, lack of knowledge about the school hierarchy, and the implications of attending one school or another. Given this situation, immigrant communities and communities of color find their students are underrepresented in schools with better reputations for achievement and overrepresented in neighborhood comprehensive high schools, which is the default setting in the admissions process—that is, the placement that occurs if the student makes no application or none of the student's choices pan out.

Finding Sources and Scaffolding Information

From the onset of this project, we wanted to do more than just point the parents in the right direction for resources and information on high-school admissions. We also wanted to support them in gleaning information from these resources, taking into consideration language and culture as possible barriers to accessing, navigating, and, ultimately, comprehending informational materials. Hence, in the initial phase, Mary, Karim, Dina, and Mega collected as many resources as possible and held a meeting for the Indonesian parents to explore the materials. As we introduced a local educational newspaper's issue on admissions, we quickly realized the barrier to entry was quite high; hence, we supported the families by explaining the design and format, skimming headlines, and highlighting text. For the main workshop itself, in contrast to the district's written description, we prepared some simple visual schematics to illustrate the steps in the high school application process (see Figure 3.1).

This adapted text uses a more direct title ("Public School Students Applying to School District High Schools") and includes a visual of the High School Voluntary Transfer Form that is labeled succinctly as "Application Form." The illustrated steps trace the application cycle from its origins at the school or district website to the form's return to the school counselor. Rather than parents having to wade through information buried in a lengthy directory and rendered in needlessly complex language, these redesigned schematics attempted to communicate the information parents were asking for visually and directly.

Community Members: Building Confidence and Taking Leadership

From the project's onset, Mary and Karim agreed to be continuously attuned to how they positioned themselves and were being positioned by the parents as knowledge holders of the high-school admissions process in Philadelphia. For parents to gain this kind of "insider" knowledge is a significant step in learning how to navigate the school system (Doucet, 2011). Having agreed with the parents early on that this was a collaborative learning exercise, we wanted to present to the community what we had learned together. This was not to deny our privilege, stance, or access historically, but, rather, it was a way of acknowledging that we would

Figure 3.1. Revised Graphic of the High School Admissions Process for Parent Workshop

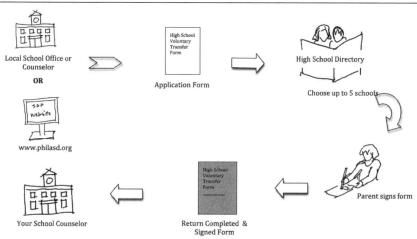

learn from the parents about their experiences with schools, what information might be most relevant, and the best way to convey it. Given our lack of proficiency in Indonesian and our hope that community members would "own" this information, we proposed that the parent leaders facilitate the meeting with our presence as resource people and not prominent speakers.

The night before our main workshop, we were asked by the parents to present *everything* the following day. We surmised later that this was a case of agita, brought on by lack of confidence in their knowledge of the topic and possibly last-minute stage fright. This concern led to a conversation about our own limitations, such as communicating in Indonesian. Despite the parents' resistance to presenting, we all agreed that together we had the skills and knowledge required for a complete workshop, including the high school students who would share their admissions experience. In this division of labor, the parent leaders agreed to introduce the workshop and translate the high school admissions timeline. However, the parents quickly assumed leadership roles in running the whole presentation; that is, there was a marked difference in how they carried themselves as followers in the planning meeting versus as leaders at the workshop itself. Mega remarked later, "I did not realize how much I know from translating the timeline." Dina responded immediately to the way the workshop participants positioned her as the knowledgeable spokesperson in their home language. Her footing (Goffman, 1979) changed from an ancillary speaker to the main speaker and facilitator. Among the community with whom they were familiar and with the necessity to speak in Indonesian, the parent leaders found the confidence to present the materials they had learned well through preparing for the workshop.

REFLECTIONS: LESSONS LEARNED

Our purpose with this project was to address educational issues experienced by the Indonesian families at St. Thomas Aquinas who were new to the U.S. educational system and to support the broader university–community partnership. Through our collaboration, the parent leaders gained more confidence in approaching materials in English and dealing with the bureaucracy of the high school admissions process. On our side, we developed social and organizational ties within the Indonesian community and came to understand how Indonesian parents mobilized their *capital* (*social* and *cultural*) to support their children's education and how intergenerational closure also reinforced the norms of high academic achievement and personal discipline within the community.

We and the parents had greater aspirations for the future work of our inquiry group, including investigating other topics they had raised such as financial aid, underemployment, and the impact of parental stress on students. However, despite a number of initial contacts and expressions of interest, nothing materialized in the year after our work. Reflecting on this collaboration, we identified various factors that would have enhanced our effort: having more frequent contact with the parent group as a whole and with individual members, not depending so much on a couple of parent leaders to reach out to the community, working to transfer facilitation of the group to parents, and having a clearer picture of the interrelationship between various university projects in the parish. Because there were other university–community literacy projects in which the Indonesian families wanted to be involved, as well as regular parish obligations such as Sunday School, there were many demands on the same leaders—thus making it difficult to schedule both planning and general meetings and to ask them to do work outside of meetings.

Given the stresses in the lives of most immigrant families in the Indonesian parish seeking a livelihood and keeping their families healthy psychologically and physically, and the range of other leadership roles they had taken on, the time may not have been ripe to deepen this particular inquiry. We did not reach the point of directly addressing the systemic inequities in the school district around high school admissions—for instance, improved counseling, language access services, and better dissemination of information to parents whose first language is not English. We also did not address the dilemma that an individual student's valued access to a high-performing school continues to reproduce a system of tracking often divided along lines of race and class. Nonetheless, the relational ties and experiences remain as resources for members of the university research team and for the Indonesian parents who were part of our project. We all learned in many ways from each other and were enriched by our connections, which became the foundation for the Community Researchers Project (described in Chapter

8) in which Indonesian youth researched issues of interest to them and their community, including systemic school inequities. Looking ahead, we are extending on our work with the parent inquiry group in a cross-cultural direction by inviting parents from different backgrounds to learn from each other about how they support their children's education and to investigate together how to address challenges they experience. The seeds of our work together continue to bear fruit in unexpected directions.

The Indonesian parents reflect the experiences of many migrant communities who express a profound gratitude for the opportunities afforded to them in the United States, but who also have come to learn that no nation, territory, or neighborhood is ever truly secure. There are only better and worse options for survival, and increasingly movement is becoming a necessary and defining feature for much of humanity. Because of their first-hand experiences with social precarity across national contexts, we believe the parents have developed a profound agility with "border thinking" (Mignolo, 2000), romanticizing neither a previous homeland nor the possibilities of assimilation into a new one. In the participatory action project, the parents demonstrated this border thinking in their advocacy for their children's education. Through a comparative transnational framework, they weighed their previous knowledge of schooling in Indonesia with what they were learning about education in the United States, in the process navigating a mystifying city bureaucratic system by mobilizing multiple forms of cultural and social capital. This innovative collaborative inquiry was in the service of finding classrooms where their individual children might intellectually and emotionally thrive. The flourishing of individuals, we have learned from many families at St. Thomas Aquinas, has been inseparable from the broader community's well-being. Although many of the children are growing up in neighborhoods and attending schools very different from those of their parents, what has perhaps traveled across nations and generations are social practices of interdependence and collective mutual care, reflecting values that continue to flower through congregation at St. Thomas Aquinas and in our university partnership.

Chapter 4

Collective Advocacy in a Latina/o Family ESOL Class

María Paula Ghiso, Alicia Rusoja, and Emily Schwab

We may be from there or here, but we are all from the same world...That is what I believe. We need to be united like a chain.

—A Latino parishioner (translated from Spanish)

One Saturday morning in the fall of 2012, Latina families, their young children, and members of our university-based research team (María Paula and Alicia) gathered for the first meeting of what would become an intergenerational ESOL class. The parents, immigrants from Mexico, had expressed a desire for classes where they could learn English and work together to support their children's education. During our first session, we asked families to reflect on what had worked well for them in previous language learning contexts, what brought them to the group, and what goals they envisioned for our time together. They mentioned a range of aspirations that emphasized both specific grammar skills in English as well as communicative purposes such as "talk with my boss or with my daughter's teacher," "go to medical appointments," or "search for jobs."[1] At the end of class, Ángela, one of the mothers, approached us to share several concerns. She worked on alternate Saturdays, she told us, and would thus not be able to come on a weekly basis. We also learned that she, like the other parents, walked a half hour with her young children to get to the parish, even in inclement weather and during the winter months. They made these sacrifices because they felt it was an important part of supporting their children's education.

This chapter explores how we co-constructed curricula with Latina/o immigrant parents (primarily mothers) and their young children in the family ESOL class. Specifically, it focuses on how participants mobilized their cultural resources for social critique through learning experiences that reflected community concerns, promoted civic engagement, and challenged definitions of citizenship that denied their human rights. In the context of these learning experiences, families discussed challenges they faced while navigating broader issues that were impacting their lives, including xenophobia, immigration policies, monolingual ideologies, labor exploitation, and the upheaval of the public school system in the city.

PUBLICS AND COUNTERPUBLICS

The concept of publics and counterpublics has helped us think about how individuals, including those with undocumented status, engage issues that impact their children's education and advocate for immigrant rights. Habermas's (1991) conceptualization of a public sphere where citizens participate in decisionmaking through reasoned and dispassionate argumentation laid the groundwork to further investigate the limits and possibilities of such deliberative democracy when there are systemic social inequities. Some scholars, like feminist philosopher Young (2000), have challenged Habermas to think more expansively about what constitutes reasoned dialogue to include rhetorical and disruptive acts, such as street protests, which may reflect forms of communication arising from marginalized social locations. Others have suggested the ideal of a unitary and inclusive public sphere to be premature and utopian (e.g., Benhabib, 1996). How can, for example, individuals with undocumented immigration status raise issues regarding their children's education and future aspirations if doing so may put them at risk of detention or deportation? The move to pluralize the public sphere to encompass multiple publics has been one way to account for the intersectional social issues that divide people and stymie dialogue across boundaries of class, language, gender, race, (dis)ability, and citizenship.

The degree to which various linguistic publics also map onto the experiences of racialized and minoritized identities raises the importance of affixing the term *counter* to publics. Fraser (1992) argues that counterpublics provide "parallel discursive arenas where members of subordinated social groups invent and circulate counterdiscourses, which in turn permit them to formulate oppositional interpretations of their identities, interests, and needs" (p. 81). Counterpublics are not merely political in a narrow sense but also reflect countercultures and alternative ways of being in the world not explicitly directed toward a concrete, shared political cause (Warner, 2002). Asen's helpful (2000) review of counterpublic theory argues that its focus should indeed be on "alternative discourse norms and practices" rather than being attached solely to specific persons, topics, or places (p. 424). This is an important reminder that people enact agency through their participation in counterpublics, not as a result of an individual person (such as an educator who brings about critical consciousness), a place (such as St. Thomas Aquinas), or a predetermined topic (like immigration reform). The mothers in our ESOL class nourished and were nourished by a counterpublic that existed beyond the parish, where alternative notions of citizenship were threaded through the multiple and intersecting topics of their lives. When seeking to understand the experiences of Latina/o immigrants in the United States, and of members of St. Thomas Aquinas, the notion of counterpublics can shed light on oppressions they face and also on collective practices of working toward changing these inequities.

DISCURSIVE (COUNTER)PUBLICS AROUND LATINA/OS AND IMMIGRATION

Latina/o immigrant youth and families have been subject to a deficit orientation in public discourse (Buff, 2008; De Genova, 2005; Perea, 1997), particularly post-9/11, through dehumanizing language that portrays them as criminals. These characterizations are prevalent in the public sphere—our local city paper, for example, often blasts headlines about "illegals." Scholars have argued that such positionings are tied to histories of racism and nativism (Pérez Huber, 2009), including the colonization of portions of Mexico by the United States (Castro-Salazar & Bagley, 2010). Framings of the immigration debate target Latina/o communities with undocumented status (Chávez, 2008), circumscribing participation and belonging along national boundaries that are contingent and racialized. For example, in times of economic growth, the United States has instituted programs to encourage border crossings in order to supply a cheap labor force, and many of the conditions that have resulted in current migration patterns were created through U.S. policies (Castro-Salazar & Bagley, 2010). The dominant public discourse of Latina/o immigration elides these histories.

Alternative discourses and practices around immigration are, however, taking place (e.g., Mangual Figueroa, 2012). Many of the participants in our study, whose perspectives are often excluded from conventional civic participation because of immigration status, engage in political activity and social change, or what scholars have referred to as Latino cultural citizenship (Flores & Benmayor, 1997; Honeyford, 2013; Rosaldo, 1987). Within these counterpublics, individuals can "claim space and social rights" (Flores, 2003), enacting definitions of belonging that contest the hegemony of civil society and the boundaries between citizen and noncitizen established by the state. Following Warner (2002), these alternative communities are not organized solely around a political cause (e.g., immigration rallies) but also entail cultural and linguistic practices. Delgado Bernal, Alemán, and Carmona (2008) examine how culturally situated literacies such as *testimonios* and *pláticas*, and the multilingual practices that are needed to navigate and claim rights to across spaces, help Latinas/os construct notions of belonging that can affirm cultural identities while understanding these as heterogeneous and intersectional. Such language and literacy practices, we suggest, work to create a counterpublic whereby citizenship can be defined apart from the nation-state.

CODESIGNING OUR INTERGENERATIONAL LEARNING SPACE

We premised our work with Latina/o families at St. Thomas Aquinas on trying to understand, value, and learn from the knowledge of community members. Many ESOL and family literacy programs ostensibly strive to provide access to the dominant language and literacies, but too often they are based on an assimilationist paradigm whereby immigrants have to downplay their language(s) and cultural practices in order to "belong" (Rivera & Lavan, 2012; Valdés, 1996). This type of family language and literacy program is often designed to address parents' presumed lack of involvement in their children's education or lack of skills in supporting them academically, which critics have denounced for aiming to change families to better align with White middle-class norms (Auerbach, 1995). Related research also has found that the perspectives of Latina/o parents tend to not be considered when designing and implementing school policies (Segura & Facio, 2007), meaning that the opportunity to learn from the parents' perspectives is missed. These realities exacerbate the cycle of exclusion and deter parents from effectively communicating with and participating in their children's schools, which in turn can be misread as families not being invested in their children's education.

Rather than "deliver a service" or try to change families' practices to align with a predetermined norm, we hoped to create a space for mutual learning/teaching that would be enriched by multiple perspectives and participatory approaches. An initial difficulty was that caretakers often had young children with them and child care would be needed to "free up" the parents' time. We chose to deal with this challenge by designing the class as intergenerational, so that we could build on the ways Latina/o children support their families (e.g., Ghiso, 2016). We provided time for pedagogical explorations among the children and adults, as well as opportunities for each age cohort to explore related topics independent of each other. Over the course of 2 years, an average of 15 parents and five children attended each session.

Having felt as immigrant students that our own cultural and linguistic resources were excluded or derided in school, we employed a number of strategies so that the knowledge of the Latina/o families was an integral part of the curriculum. During our initial meetings, we drafted "golden rules" that included a collective decision that our 2-hour weekly sessions be bilingual and that news and issues (from our lives and from the world) be part of the content of our lessons. We alternated between joint inquiries that involved both adults and young children working together and times when each of the age groups explored the same theme separately in age-appropriate ways. The participants transacted with real-world texts of their choosing, such as menus from pricey restaurants where they prepped food and notes from bosses at housecleaning services, to foreground their own questions and interrogate issues of power (Auerbach, 1997; Freire, 1970).

Such pedagogies aimed to cultivate a shared learning community that was not centered on the transmission of skills as determined by the university-based facilitators. In fact, during the first months of our time together, one of the mothers brought in a Spanish-language grammar book to give to a graduate student helping out on the project, thus underscoring that there were skills to be learned by all involved and overturning preconceptions of who is considered a "language learner." Through their multiple perspectives and funds of knowledge (González et al., 2005), the families taught us and each other about critical issues in their lives while gaining particular language and literacy tools to address day-to-day concerns.

SHARING "CLASS NEWS"

One generative routine for our ongoing inquiries was the "Class News." The mothers took turns going around the room and sharing any news they had that week, which was recorded on chart paper and used to spark discussion, teach specific language elements, or plan future inquiries. The Class News grounded our inquiry community in the issues facing families and also provided opportunities to attend to the technical aspects of language and literacy learning that parents had envisioned for the course (such as possessives and verb tenses).

A representative example of the Class News featured in Figure 4.1 illustrates the range of issues families contributed to our conversations and mutual learning as they participated in this discursive counterpublic. Emilia, a member of the inquiry group who was also involved in the local immigrant rights organization Juntos, began the Class News for this day by telling us about two activist events. The first was a vigil against the closing of city's public schools, at which 16 community leaders had been arrested. The protests were a response to the severe school district budget cuts that would result, later that year, in the shutdown of 24 schools and a significant reduction of services, including nurses, social workers, teachers, and other staff to some of the poorest areas of the city. School closings were a recurring topic in our inquiry group. Parents were concerned, for example, about their ability to take their children to school without cars or driver's licenses when public transportation was often unreliable, and about how the relocation away from their own neighborhoods would impact children's physical and emotional well-being. Julio, a kindergarten student, rejoiced in a Class News activity a few months later that "they saved my school" (Artifact, February 2013), a testament to children's awareness of these issues and to the potential power of a collective action. Unfortunately, many schools were ultimately closed despite these efforts.

The second event Emilia spread the word about during this particular Class News session was a march for immigrant rights. Scholars note that

Figure 4.1. Class News Example

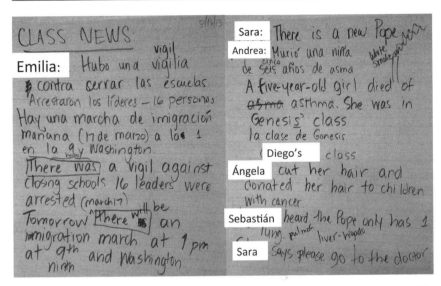

undocumented status exacerbates social duress through more intangible factors like fear of deportation or discrimination (Banki, 2013). While in this instance Emilia named political action for immigrant rights explicitly through a protest organized by a local activist group, documentation status was a cross-cutting theme that impacted many of the issues the participants identified. Immigration could not be teased out as a discrete topic in the counterpublic but was interwoven through the lives and learning of the families and children in our class, including their relationships to medical and educational institutions.

One salient topic the mothers raised was health, and through the Class News they worked together to expose its complexity (including how health is impacted by immigration status) as well as to try to address the problem. In our discussion, Andrea mentioned that a classmate of her daughter's had died a few days prior as a result of an asthma attack. Ángela was particularly alarmed because both she and her two children also suffered from asthma, and with budget cuts schools often lacked essential nursing staff. Health insurance was difficult to come by given the contingent nature of their jobs and the labor exploitation that often occurs when immigrant workers have little alternative but to participate in the informal economy (Lopez, 2006). Sara shared that a friend had passed away because, without health care, her cancer had not been detected and treated in its early stages. This tragedy was compounded by the militarization of the border: Sara recounted that her friend's body could not be returned to the family she left behind in Mexico, including the son she had not seen since he was a baby. The conversation also prompted Sara to tell the group about a mobile health van that was coming to the parish to conduct breast cancer screenings. One had to make an appointment in order to take advantage of this service, a task that may be intimidating for recent immigrants who have trouble communicating in English and are reluctant to write personal details on official forms. Sara thus provided everyone with the name and number of a Spanish-speaking nurse involved in the initiative who would be able to assist in scheduling the exam. She chose to represent her contribution to the Class News chart with the phrase, "Sara says please go to the doctor." The Class News activity both made visible the social and economic struggles faced by Latina/o families and helped members of our inquiry group pool collective resources.

Hope and joyful solidarity are also part of the dialogue of the counterpublic. Following the group's sobering conversation about death, family separation, and immigration, Ángela shifted the discussion, noting "I have a lot of struggles but I want to share something more positive." She went on to recount that she had cut her hair and "donated it to children with cancer," a concrete action she took to ease the suffering of others. Other joyful news included the birth of children or, on this occasion, the election of Pope Francis, the first Latin American pope. The families saw this new leadership as an important turning point in the church, signaling greater representation of Latina/os within an institution historically dominated by European leadership. Through dialogue around the Class News routine, the mothers, who were of Mexican descent, worked to construct a pan-Latina transnational identity whereby spiritual affiliations transcend nationhood and immigration status. Drawing on the discursive counterpublic by sharing their joy at the Pope's election or the family names they selected for their newborn babies provided opportunities for all involved to participate in positive dialogue, moments of mutual learning, humor, and affective connection.

On other occasions, the Class News focused specifically on how broader dynamics were influencing the school context and the ways in which the mothers advocated for their children's education. During our 2nd year, this exploration began when one mother contributed that because of recent violence, security at her child's school had become more stringent. She had been asked by the teacher to come in for a meeting regarding her son's progress, but because she was not proficient in English she was not able to decipher the intercom at the school's entrance and had missed the appointment. She wanted to learn English, she noted, so that she could know "how to enter the school." While this occurrence has the potential to be characterized as a lack of involvement (e.g., the teacher calls a meeting, and a parent fails to attend), the mother's sharing within the counterpublic of the inquiry group raises issues of access—literally—that may not otherwise be visible. Other parents concurred that English had been a barrier for them in becoming more involved in the schools, and that they wanted to focus on further developing these linguistic skills within the context of our class. This included learning "the parts of the school," "how to ask teachers about the progress and behavior of the children," and "to inform them [the school] if there are problems of bullying" (Artifact, November 2013). The language and literacy practices of the inquiry group afforded openings for such perspectives to be shared and for the topics raised during the Class News to become a curricular focus.

CURRICULAR INQUIRIES BASED ON THE CLASS NEWS

Through the Class News, the Latina mothers reframed debates about immigration and advocated for their community's rights. As practitioner researchers at St. Thomas Aquinas, we were able to co-construct learning opportunities that enabled participants to negotiate meaning and connect their experiences to larger social, political, and historical dynamics. In this section, we explore some of the pedagogical inquiries that resulted from the Class News, focusing on one example from our 1st year (addressing health concerns) and one from our 2nd year (using English to communicate with the school).

"Nosotras te ayudamos" (We will help you): Advocating for Health

After learning about families' health concerns from Class News discussions, we designed lessons around navigating these issues and invited nursing students to role-play healthcare visits in English. The collective nature of our learning community was evident when nursing student Jane asked one of the mothers, Valentina, if she had any additional questions as part of the role-playing, to which Valentina replied "No." Pamela, a fellow member of our class, asked Valentina "What do you mean no? Of course you must have questions. Ask her why you have to take those pills twice a day," which led Valentina to begin to articulate her concern in English but then stop again. Warmly, Pamela added: "Ask the questions in Spanish and we all will help you put them into English." Valentina then tried again, supported by her fellow classmates Pamela, Carmen, and Paula and by nursing student Jane, each making Valentina feel more at ease as they helped her identify, pronounce, and then spell the words to communicate with Jane. Carefully and jointly, the mothers worked to raise questions in English related to their health care. They also taught Jane, as a future medical professional, the importance of listening to patients from immigrant backgrounds (with the assistance of a translator if necessary) and taking the time to unearth underlying queries together rather than assume these are not there.

During another instance of role-playing, one of the mothers, Carmen, asked the visiting nursing student, "What happens when your cough doesn't go away?" Carmen looked noticeably unwell that morning; her eyes were red and watery, and she noted that she had been coughing a lot and been very congested since leaving her cleaning job the day before. When asked whether her boss provided protective gear for the harsh chemicals, which is mandated by law, Carmen replied by shaking her head and saying, "I am not protected." We then discussed how Carmen's boss had ignored the responsibility that cleaning companies have to supply (and ensure correct use of) protective gear when workers clean, and what she might do to change the situation. Pamela looked through the health-care packet that accompanied the role-playing activity and found one health center that might welcome uninsured individuals with undocumented immigration status. Carmen appeared physically and emotionally drained by the situation. How could she protest her work conditions given her vulnerable immigration status? Pamela encouraged Carmen to sit with the possibilities; she did not pressure Carmen to make decisions immediately. We later learned that Carmen did end up going to the health center because she called one of us for language support while she was there.

Mutual support and solidarity are crucial to survival when facing precarity of place (Banki, 2013). Within our inquiry community, self-efficacy was reframed from a characteristic that individuals have or do not have (or can acquire through explicit teaching such as in family literacy programs) to a group achievement. We sought to nurture language and literacy learning spaces that support their members in relying on each other—at times, quite literally by building on the words of peers to construct one's own—as a form of advocacy. Although not all the problems the mothers raised could be adequately addressed or solved, it was essential to foster a humanizing and supportive environment (Paris & Winn, 2013; Simon, 2011), one that contrasts with the dehumanizing discourse of immigration in the public sphere.

"Hay racismo" (There is racism): Concerns for Educational Access

The mothers' *testimonios* of their difficulties accessing monolingual school contexts led us to organize a series of bilingual explorations about communicating with schools. Conceptualizing community members' Spanish language proficiencies and their cultural and transnational experiences as resources necessitated that we devise pedagogical approaches that valued their insights. We began by asking families to compare and contrast schooling in Mexico and the United States using the language of their choosing. This activity led to a discussion of the questions families had about certain U.S. practices and of how anti-immigrant sentiments impacted their participation in their children's education and the children's success in school.

The mothers underscored the racism and linguistic stigma to which they and their children were subject. One participant commented, "They get upset that one doesn't speak English but they don't go beyond English." This contribution captures the paradox of how Latina/os were being positioned as deficient because of their emergent knowledge of English when in fact, by acquiring the language, they had surpassed the monolingual standard by which they were being judged. Being Mexican made their stigmatization cultural in addition to linguistic, and families connected their reception in schools with assumptions regarding their immigration status as fueled by the dominant public discourse on race. In subsequent class sessions, we went on to inquire together as to how families could communicate with the school and teachers, while recognizing the power dynamics that impacted home–school interactions. Throughout the class, the English learning taking place was not predetermined by us as facilitators but driven by the epistemic privilege (Campano, 2007; Moya, 2002) of Latina/o families.

Based on these conversations and families' transnational knowledge, we introduced relevant vocabulary in English, which inquiry group participants then used to create sample dialogues about the issues they had raised. The scenarios included children being bullied, the stress of high-stakes testing, difficulties they were having with the classroom reading curriculum, and the penalties of being late to school. In the last example, the mothers learned from each other that the district considered lateness equivalent to an unexcused absence, which could result in their children being labeled as truants and summoned to court. A mother in the group reported that the new school to which her daughter was transferred because of district closings was too far away from her home for her to arrive on time, given the need to travel on multiple forms of (quite unreliable) public transit. Ironically, according to administrative guidelines, she lived just close enough to the school that she did not qualify for a school bus. The mothers worked together to discuss these issues and practice how they might address them with teachers and administrators. A hovering threat was the families' precarity of place (Banki, 2013), and their very real fears of police scrutiny. One of the mothers, Bendición, nonetheless urged her peers to speak up, exclaiming that "we have rights," and that, moreover, "the children have rights." For the sake of their children, Bendición urged others to not walk with their heads lowered no matter what racism and discrimination they may experience. Through their discussions, including those fostered in our Class News, the Latina mothers connected their lived experiences and concerns to a larger supranational discourse of human rights.

CONCLUSION

The women and children in our study participated in a discourse community that reflected collective intellectual and activist engagement around systemic inequities, thus challenging the characterization of immigrant communities as either criminals or the passive benefactors of others' hospitality. A practitioner research stance, which situates teaching and learning within larger sociopolitical contexts, has taught us that trust, intellectual respect, and political solidarity are preconditions for participatory teaching, especially when working with minoritized communities. It has also helped us discern how community members are agents within counterpublic spheres and how our pedagogies might mobilize their knowledge, commitments, and inquiries in the classroom.

The families needed to feel relatively safe to voice their insights and questions. Viewing teaching as social and political rather than merely neutral (Cochran-Smith & Lytle, 2009) helped us shift these considerations to the forefront of the classroom. We were transparent about how our political stance was partially shaped by our own immigrant family backgrounds and by prior involvement with activist organizations. Because practitioner research entails asking critical questions, such as who decides what gets done and whose interests are served by a classroom interaction, it may help educators become sensitized to topics that matter to families but remain invisible in the dominant public sphere. It may also facilitate centering participants' own visions for the class, even when these are in tension with our own preconceptions. For example, our pedagogy at times involved direct instruction of specific language elements, traditional arrangements that we viewed with skepticism because they seemed illustrative of a banking model of education (Freire, 1970). We learned, however, that families had a great deal of investment in teacher-directed classrooms associated with school in Latin America. Many of the families told us that they felt as if their own educational trajectories had been prematurely curtailed, and they wanted the opportunity to take up successful academic identities in the ways that were conventionally valued. They negotiated and traversed multiple publics in their lives. An inquiry stance enabled us to be less dogmatic and more conscious of the situated nature of the families' desires for the class.

Beginning in fall 2014, the language and literacy class at the Aquinas Center has taken on new life. Along with Alicia, research team members Emily and Marina are helping to cofacilitate the class. After reflecting with community leaders about how to best continue to serve the evolving goals of immigrant families at the center, we decided to offer a beginner ESOL class for members of St. Thomas Aquinas's various cultural groups. Currently, about 25 students from the Latina/o and Vietnamese communities participate in an inquiry community that is grounded on the types of inquiries documented in this chapter. Five Aquinas Center volunteer cofacilitators have also joined the team, bringing new perspectives that have shaped the direction of the class. We now meet biweekly during evening hours, an expenditure of valuable time for participants who work all day.

One of our current inquiries is about cultivating community across cultures, languages, and immigration histories. We have sought to apply lessons from our work with the Latina/o families within an intercultural configuration that highlights the possibilities of coalitional work. While everyone is still in the beginning stages of building relationships, the Vietnamese and Latina/o participants have already found commonalities that serve as a foundation for shared learning. For example, one of our concerns during this phase of the project has been to cocreate a space where individuals with varying levels of comfort with English can learn together, without needing to be separated into "levels" or native language or cultural groups. Beatriz, a current class participant of Mexican descent, mentioned one evening that she was already familiar with most of the English we were teaching but had decided to keep coming to the sessions nonetheless. She told us, "I feel inspired by the Vietnamese elders, I feel solidarity with them. They remind me of how difficult it was when I had just arrived in the U.S. and didn't speak English and I didn't know anyone and they remind me of all that it takes to keep going." Beatriz added that she wanted to keep coming to class to learn alongside them: "I do learn a lot when I help other people in class and I'm learning a lot from their commitment." Like Beatriz, we continue to be inspired by these moments of mutuality and humanizing connection in our partnership.

NOTE

1. All participant comments in Chapter 4 were originally in Spanish and have been translated by the authors.

Chapter 5

Cultivating Civic Engagement Through Literacy

Francisco's Community Service Project

Robert LeBlanc and Bethany J. Welch

There's a vibrancy and a hope that is very, very powerful and it's good to be part of it and good to be walking with people who believe things can be better and they want to try. It's great to be part of that movement.

—Fr. Shields

On a Thursday afternoon in late April, a small group of activists, parishioners, academic specialists, working parents, immigrants, and community leaders gathered in the basement of the Aquinas Center to hear more about the Catholic Church's work for global solidarity through local action. Clustered in fours and fives at small, round tables to discuss, debate, and listen, the group spent the day in dialogue around shared themes such as "Global Issues Affecting the Poor and Vulnerable," "The Church's Response to Globalization in the United States," and "Taking Action Locally Through Accompaniment and Advocacy." The final presentation included a legal expert, an academic dean, and the head of an immigrant rights advocacy group; however, it was an 8th-grade student and Mexican immigrant to the country who made the most moving contribution. When his turn came, a normally shy and reserved Francisco stood in front of the large group and discussed his advocacy for global food justice and disaster relief. As a youth who was an integral part of the parish, Francisco represented a unique viewpoint on the panel. He spoke about being the principal organizer of a fundraiser for those in the Philippines affected by Typhoon Haiyan, and he noted confidently, "People felt they were helping the Philippines because maybe someone else helped them in the past, so they want to help." Francisco's rationale for working on civic projects invoked the Gospel's moral imperative, "Do unto others as you would have them do unto you," that frequently circulated at the parish and the school.

This chapter examines how the religious life of St. Thomas Aquinas parish promotes civically engaged literacy practices for students often denied those opportunities by systemic exclusion from systems of power (Patel, 2012; Vieira, 2011). We specifically look at how religious spaces at St. Thomas Aquinas facilitate opportunities for students to use literacy to write and think across temporal and spatial scales (Blommaert, 2007): to tack back and forth between the "local" and the "global." Blommaert (2007) writes that "social events and processes move and develop on a continuum of layered scales, with the strictly local (micro) and the global (macro) as extremes, and with several intermediary scales . . . in between" (p. 1). The parish is in the unique position of being a neighborhood anchor, a local intermediary organization, and also part of the international network of the global Catholic Church. Networks are one of the mechanisms by which people, texts, and ideas are distributed across scales. Employing scalar theory helps illuminate Francisco's agency—the way he is able to access the social networks of St. Thomas Aquinas and move across various discourse communities (including religious, activist, educational, and cultural) to engage civically in ways that resonate beyond his immediate context.

The entwinement of St. Thomas Aquinas parish and school creates its own unique meaning-making opportunities, a nexus for the patterned movement of ideas, texts, and practices. The Catholic Church is an example of the "transnational local" (e.g., Ghiso, 2016; Saldívar, 2012): It has historically been a gathering place for immigrants (Mora, 2013) who carry on cultural practices from home while simultaneously forging new identities, and a site where texts and practices can be projected beyond the local and into national and even international conversations. This provides an opportunity for civic engagement on various scalar levels: from the local to the global and back again. For Francisco, St. Thomas Aquinas provides a place to "scale" his literacy practices, to speak on behalf of himself and his community and distribute his words and ideas widely. By offering both a network and an ethos of advocacy, St. Thomas Aquinas is a pathway for Francisco to reach leaders, policymakers, and community members and to speak with authority.

RELIGIOUS ENGAGEMENT, CIVIC ENGAGEMENT

St. Thomas Aquinas is a hub of civic activity, from health fairs to voter registration drives to marches for immigrant rights. While research has illustrated the relative decline of civic engagement in contemporary American life (e.g., Garcia & Sanchez, 2008), religious institutions continue to support inclusion and democratic participation (e.g., Mora, 2013). By providing opportunities to organize, speak publicly on a range of topics, take on leadership roles, and volunteer, religious organizations support groups that are disenfranchised from local, state, and federal politics. The tension of religion's role in civic society is not new to America (cf. Tocqueville, 1835/2000), but it has taken on new meaning in light of the decline of intermediary associations—community organizations such as the Lions and the Elks, the Boy Scouts and the Girl Scouts, labor unions, bowling leagues—in the face of changing economic and social circumstances (Putnam, 2000). The retraction of government services, particularly in under-resourced contexts, raises questions regarding spaces for democratic participation and what role religious organizations can play in offering supports in relation to the State (Stepick, Rey, & Mahler, 2009; Wuthnow, 2004). Of specific relevance to the St. Thomas Aquinas community is the way the modern Catholic parish is a place where both documented and undocumented members take on leadership and decisionmaking roles.

The Parish Council, which is responsible for guiding St. Thomas Aquinas's mission, allocating resources, and determining stewardship of space, represents the diversity of the faith community and the ways the institution has sought to be attentive to and learn from their cultural practices. In 2012, St. Thomas Aquinas operationalized a policy of ensuring several representatives from each language community were included, thereby diminishing a type of "tokenism" where one person is expected to speak for the whole. Additional time for decisionmaking was added to honor the emphasis many of the parish's cultural communities place on dialogue. This allowed the leaders to go back and discuss specific action items within their language groups and return at a later meeting with input from others. In terms of scale, this local instantiation of church leadership is informed by the national and global perspectives of its members. While this council does not have a specifically civic function, nor can several of its members vote in local, state, or national elections, the church space amplifies their voices as part of a larger collective that is recognized within the municipal area.

Literacy scholars have described churches as crucial "sponsors" (Brandt, 2001, p. 27) that support immigrants' literacy practices. Immigration is a process regulated by the authority of texts, including the production of state-authorized documents, the negotiation of "high-risk literacy events" at borders (Beach, Campano, Edmiston, & Borgmann, 2010, p. 12), or the possession of multiple passports and green cards in a highly fluid global economy. Beyond the more visible English classes run by religious groups (Ebaugh & Chafetz, 2000), literacy researchers have shown how churches can sponsor identity documents for individuals who are denied them by the government, as well as offer public platforms for community advocacy and the use of texts such as the Bible to critique unjust immigration policies (Levitt, 2003; Mora, 2013; Vieira, 2011). Religious organizations have the capacity to be crucial centers in the civically engaged literate lives of immigrants in the United States.

COMMUNITY LEADER, ORGANIZER, PUBLIC SPEAKER

In this chapter, we explore how St. Thomas Aquinas provided opportunities for immigrant youth such as Francisco to develop civic engagement and distribute that engagement widely. We examine Francisco's completion of a fundraising project for Philippines disaster relief, which culminated in his presentation to the Global Solidarity workshop over the course of several months. We utilize the work of Cathy Kell (2009) to conceptualize literacy meaning-making across time and space.

Kell offers the idea of the *meaning-making trajectory*: that activity and meaning are not isolated in time and space but are often spread out over multiple events using many modes and tools. Texts and literacy practices remain key to following how meaning is transposed through and across various artifacts and spaces. Kell's (2009, 2011) work helps illuminate how a local religious practice like the composition of a prayer for Mass may be the product of multiple social actions (a person's personal prayers at home, conversations about prayer with a friend, the physical action of writing it on paper) and equally projected across many spaces through a network, as that prayer is perhaps memorized by another reader, read at Mass, and then recited by someone else in their home.

The value of this approach is multifaceted. First, it highlights the agency of the actor, who continues to encode his or her meaning-making through various entextualizations/recontextualizations. Recontextualization refers to the way the "elements of one social practice are appropriated by, relocated in the context of, another" (Fairclough, 2003, p. 222). As we describe in this chapter, Francisco is able to use the network of the church to expand his social advocacy for disaster relief across spatial and temporal scales, locally, nationally, and even internationally. When something is placed into a form (entextualized), it can be moved or recontextualized to other places, sometimes verbatim and sometimes in new forms. Second, the notion of a meaning-making trajectory draws attention to the movement of texts and practices beyond a single object or instance. To understand Francisco's work, we must look past a singular instance to the many events (fundraisers, speeches, mundane moments of writing) that work together to help him create meaning. Third, Kell highlights the multimodal means of communication, as a single meaning-making trajectory may include reading texts, writing, reading out loud in a meeting, and employing visuals. By following the trajectory of Francisco's meaning-making through literacy practices and texts, we can see its circulation through social networks, ones that rely on many modes (documents, speeches, audio, etc.). In the process, we gain a deeper understanding of the broad audiences he reaches as well as his agency to reconstitute his identity as a civically engaged student within the local context of his parish and school.

Setting a Trajectory

For Francisco, the meaning-making trajectory of the Philippines disaster relief began as a school project initiated in the fall of the academic year by his
8th-grade teacher as part of Religion class. While a number of the classes at
the parish school include community involvement, Francisco's Religion class
had a 50-hour service component where students participated in charitable
projects in relation to classroom work. The core of this obligation came in the
form of their Community Service Project, which Francisco's teacher, herself
an active member of the parish, had conceptualized and made part of the
curriculum. Students were to research a charity; draft a written proposal for
a fundraiser (including a full budget and projected revenue); present their
proposal to their classmates, to the principal, and to Fr. Shields at the parish
for critical feedback and approval; and then carry out the fundraiser.

Francisco and his group were immediately drawn to the work of
Catholic Charities USA, an organization dedicated to providing "leadership and support for the work of local agencies in their efforts to reduce
poverty, support families, and empower communities" (Catholic Charities
USA, http://108.166.114.95/about-us/). The parish had recently highlighted through its bulletin the overwhelming humanitarian need in the Philippines following Typhoon Haiyan. A number of the parishioners at St.
Thomas Aquinas are first- and second-generation Filipina/o immigrants,
including some of Francisco's schoolmates and basketball teammates. During the same week that the class began researching possible Community
Service Projects, Catholic Charities USA put out a pressing call for aid on
their website. The call included a set of pictures and text to which Francisco energetically pointed when the page loaded. Francisco's initial idea
to the group, which they wholeheartedly took up, was to charge a small
admission at the door of the upcoming Catholic Youth Organization (CYO)
basketball game (of which he was a key member) in tandem with a parish
bake sale. When asked why this issue seemed so important to him, Francisco responded, "It's our duty as Catholics to help other people." This
theme of moral obligation continues throughout his narrative, echoing the
voices of his teacher, parish priest, and other leaders who proclaim, in the
words of Fr. Shields, "Christ's example is saying that we're all brothers and
sisters; it doesn't matter the language, culture, color. . . . We're all called to
love God and serve God, serve our people" (Interview, May 29, 2014).

Already embedded in the framing of this community service project
was a time–space scale that differs from much classroom reading and writing. Bloome, Beierle, Grigorenko, and Goldman (2009) note that prototypical classroom literacy practices fix temporal and spatial scales to that
moment and that space: The literacy event or text is something to be under-
taken right then (filling out a worksheet, reading a short story) with consequences for that location (for a grade, for completion of something called
"English class"). This is especially the case in an era of standardization

and high-stakes testing when too often students do not have the opportunity to read and write for a purpose and for authentic audiences. Through the Community Service Project, however, students could engage in literacy practices that had implications beyond the immediate goals of the classroom. Bloome and Katz (1997) highlight that some classrooms relate activities and projects to those of the community. A global event like Typhoon Haiyan reframes the spatial logic of these literary practices since it was both local and global for those who live in South Philadelphia. Families immediately engaged with digital and social media in the aftermath of the typhoon and connected with their relatives on the ground. Students brought their own feelings, experiences, and family narratives into the classroom. By invoking a seemingly timeless principle like "Catholic moral duty" to complete a classroom project and connecting it to multiple timescales (including the time of their event and the present moment of need for disaster relief), Francisco and his teacher reframed the temporal logic of the classroom literacy practices. This reframing allowed Francisco to construct his identity as a community leader, a Catholic, and a global citizen whose reading and writing have temporal–spatial implications beyond this particular classroom in this particular moment.

This movement of a classroom practice across spatiotemporal scales demonstrates the network capacity of the St. Thomas Aquinas parish and its power as a linguistic resource for students. Warriner (2013) notes that language has resources for flexibly manipulating time–space relations: By using reference, categories, and personal pronouns, people can situate their literacy practices within different time and space scales and in doing so change the relationships between things, events, and participants (Wortham, 2006). For example, in a reflection on that Sunday's Gospel passage (Luke 16:19–31), Fr. Shields threads international, national, and local action and authorities together in his weekly homily: "[Pope Francis] is clearly indicating that it is our responsibility as Catholics to live our Faith in its entirety which definitely includes tending to the needs of the Lazaruses among us . . . the ill, dispossessed, undocumented, troubled, persecuted, victimized, stigmatized, marginalized, despised" (Artifact, November 29, 2013). This is complex scalar work, and we can see how in one instance the Father uses language to frame something as operating at many different scalar levels: The priest invokes papal authority (an international scale), national issues like legal documentation, and local personal and communal obligation ("our responsibility" and "among us") through a specific Biblical passage (Christ's parable about the need to attend to the poor). "Up-" and "downscaling" of this nature is a linguistic resource (Baynham, 2009) of and for the parish that Francisco and his classmates can draw on in formulating the meaning of a classroom practice. The national and local Church's international presence fosters what Wuthnow and Offutt (2008) call "transnational religious connections" (p. 209) and works in tandem with the multiscalar language of Catholic tradition (often upscaling beyond traditional borders of race, ethnicity, and nationality) to offer a range of resources for individuals to transform the time–space relations of an event. It is this set of resources for scaling interaction and meaning-making that makes the Catholic Church and its adjacent school at St. Thomas Aquinas such a unique site of inquiry.

Tracing the Trajectory

Simply having access to a resource (like a proposal for a fundraiser) is not enough to generate meaning: The resource has to be recognized and circulate to meaningful audiences (Kell, 2011). Often the circulation of practices and resources is dependent on access to what Latour calls "centers of calculation," places where documents and texts are moved back and forth and "weighed" for quality (Latour, 2005, as cited in Kell, 2009). One example of the scaling and networking possibility of the parish is the movement of Francisco's meaning-making trajectory between the classroom and the larger community. Where Francisco's desire to help Filipina/os affected by Typhoon Haiyan began as a series of small entextualizations on the school computer in the form of flyers and planning documents, they were quickly "upscaled" to the parish level by an excerpt in the parish bulletin, a document that is transmitted physically and electronically to over a thousand people each week. Student writing recontextualized in the parish bulletin immediately upscales the distribution beyond the single classroom and presents it as relevant to the "entire parish." Francisco's own text, shown in Figure 5.1 (it begins with the bold, underlined heading), was included in this document on Sunday.

Within the parish bulletin, Francisco's language is framed within a larger religious discourse of compassion, empathy, and interconnection. Notable here is the use of familial language to describe those affected by the typhoon in the Philippines. While some members of the parish are Filipina/o, most are not. However, positioning people in the Philippines as "brothers and sisters" to the reader both helps cultivate a moral obligation of care and blurs national and ethnic boundaries to produce a superordinate identity of a cosmopolitan human family (Juzwik & McKenzie, 2015). As well, Francisco's effort ("Our CYO basketball team") is understood within the context of this document to be part of a larger collaborative effort to provide aid and relief to an international crisis.

Following the December fundraiser, Francisco's effort was once again recontextualized, this time in a small blog post written by Bethany for the Catholic Relief Services website. Testifying to the networking capacity of the Catholic Church, this blog post was subsequently excerpted and recontextualized by Catholic Relief Services for their national newsletter (see Figure 5.2), which goes out to thousands of people across the country and the world. It was picked up by the local neighborhood paper, the *South Philly Review*, as well.

Figure 5.1. Excerpt from the December 8th Parish Bulletin

A "Thank you" to all who so generously contributed to their brothers and sisters in the Philippines. The amount from the parish totaled $8,210, which included $827 raised by our Vietnamese youth group (Our CYO basketball team is working on a fundraiser for the Philippines—a $2 admission to their next game [see accompanying announcement]) . . .

Fund Raiser for the Philippines by the Basketball Team

On December 16 at the game a $2.00 donation at the door will take place. Raffle tickets will be sold also for $2.00 to one of the two Sixers games, court side seats. . . . This should be a great night. All monies collected will go to Catholic Relief Services Typhoon for the Philippines.

Once again, Francisco's civically engaged meaning-making has moved from the very local (his classroom) to the national level, this time as a distillation of his project. This movement happened through an "intertextual chain" (Fairclough, 2003), a report of an event written up as "news" and then transmitted by media outlets (in this case, Catholic Relief Services) to a wider audience. However, following Latour (2005), we can see "traces" of Francisco's influence along each step across the spatial and temporal scales of these entextualizations.

Beyond the distribution of Francisco's project through social networks and forms of entextualization to a national (and potentially international) audience, and its framing within the CRS newsletter as an example of a global Catholic effort for disaster relief, this excerpt demonstrates the capacity of language to gain broader meanings as it travels (Baynham, 2009; Bloome et al., 2009). St. Thomas Aquinas's fundraiser is rhetorically pitched as an example of a larger Catholic principle, in this case the "golden rule," articulated by one of the youths in the newsletter excerpt, "You should treat others how you would want to be treated" (which itself is a reframing of the Biblical imperative from Matthew's Gospels to "do to others what you would have them do to you"). This situates the fundraiser simultaneously as a unique act with particular spatial–temporal boundaries (this parish, at this time) but equally as representative of a longer tradition of Catholic moral principles.

It is notable that Francisco's voice/presence is absent from both the original blog posting and the CRS newsletter. His literal words may be absent from the prose, but his initial meaning-making trajectory continues. In this case, Francisco's participation in civically engaged literacy practices entailed a certain sacrifice of control over future iterations of his writing and meaning-making, a sacrifice common when writing or meaning are scaled up beyond the local. It reflects how much public writing is rarely solely authored, and in this case they are products of multiple people and are influenced by the diverse discourse communities circulating through St. Thomas Aquinas.

Figure 5.2. Excerpt from Catholic Relief Services January/February 2014 *Partnership Newsletter*

St. Thomas Aquinas School Basketball Squads Puts Golden Rule in Action

The boys' and girls' basketball teams of St. Thomas Aquinas School in Philadelphia held a fundraiser at their games and raised over $300 to support CRS' typhoon relief efforts in the Philippines. When asked why this fundraiser was important, a seventh-grade player remarked, "It is about the Golden Rule: You should treat others how you would want to be treated." Msgr. Hugh J. Shields, pastor of St. Thomas Aquinas Parish, felt similarly: "Our community will often say, 'today someone else; tomorrow me.'"

The predominantly immigrant inner-city parish of over 4,000 households, including a large Filipino population, raised $8,545 in total for typhoon relief from two second collections during weekend Masses, as well as food sales by the Vietnamese youth group and the income from the basketball games. A typical second collection would be about $1,000. Msgr. Shields suggested that the donation from St. Thomas Aquinas is about the Incarnation: "The presence of our Filipino community here helped us identify with the people in the Philippines. Just as Christ helps us identify with people throughout the world and to be in relationship with them." (Excerpt adapted from CRS Faithworks blog post written by Bethany J. Welch, PhD. Read the post in its entirety here: faithworks.crs.org/today-someone-else-tomorrow-me/)

Completing the Trajectory

The Global Solidarity workshop mentioned at the start of this chapter represents the culminating iteration of Francisco's meaning-making trajectory. The successful fundraiser prompted members of the workshop to invite Francisco and a classmate to speak to others about how they responded to a global issue with local action. The invitation solidified his identity as a young voice for change. While Francisco's speech to the assembled teachers, academics, community members, and clergy was short, we quote it here as a representation of his continual adoption of various literacy resources available through the parish's network of social ties, and equally as an example of the potential for parishes to serve as sites of civically engaged literacy practices.

Francisco's speech included a PowerPoint presentation, which he created for the workshop with the help of several of his classmates and Bethany. While he spoke, the PowerPoint presentation was displayed on a projector screen immediately behind him, and he used a nearby laptop computer to control the movement through the slides:

> *Francisco:* Well hello, I'm Francisco. I'm a student from St. Thomas Aquinas and I'm talking to you about Catholic Relief Services. And how we helped the Philippines. (*Changes slide—reads from PowerPoint*) "How did you choose this charity or issue?" My friends and I decided to choose this charity because we think it's

our responsibility as Catholics to help others who are in need. Like the Philippines who got hit by the typhoon and we wanted to help them as much as we can. (*Changes slide—reading*) "How did your class do?" Our class had a bake sale and basketball. The game, it was a game, it was girls versus boys. It was fun.

Audience: Who won? (*laughter from audience*)

Francisco: Well . . . the girls (*huge laughter and applause from audience*) . . . People helped us by bringing goods like cookies, brownies, and marshmallow chews. A lot of stuff. We raised about three hundred and ten dollars. The event took place in February. (*Slide change—reads*) "What went well?" We had a fun. We had a fun time. Everyone who came enjoyed it. And we sold a lot of baked goods. They were good. I bought myself some too (*laughter from audience*). People felt that they were helping the Philippines. Because like maybe someone else helped them in the past. So they want to help.

Francisco's presentation draws on a number of resources. The first example is his previously noted recontextualization of the Biblical "Golden Rule" and Fr. Shield's prompt "today someone else; tomorrow me" in the Partnership Newsletter. Francisco phrases this imaginatively, intuiting the motivation of his fellow parishioners whereby past aid initiates present action: "Because like maybe someone else helped them in the past. So they want to help." Further, he imparts his group's actions within the language of moral obligation rooted in their Catholic faith, noting, "It's our responsibility as Catholics to help others who are in need. Like the Philippines who got hit by the typhoon." The actual specifics of their action and of the devastation they are working to aid are presented as "cases of," specific illustrations of an abstraction deemed "Catholic responsibility." While helping those in the Philippines affected by Typhoon Haiyan is important, it is just one example of a larger directive toward helping those in need. This points toward Francisco's potential future action along similar lines, as well as his emerging identity as an activist.

CONCLUSION

The ability to "upscale"—to frame an action, artifact, or practice as more than simply influencing the here and now—"depends on access to discursive resources that index and iconize particular scale-levels, and as such access is an object of inequality" (Blommaert, 2007, p. 7). For Francisco, access to the rich discursive tapestry and complex social network of St. Thomas Aquinas helps move his own community action across multiple scales: from the local (classroom), neighborhood (through the parish bulletin), national (through Catholic Relief Services), international (as affecting disaster relief efforts in the Philippines and by crossing traditional ethnic borders through inclusive and familiar discourse). It equally provides him with an opportunity to speak to a range of stakeholders, many of whom play crucial roles in the policies that frame his young life. The tightly knit parish and school offer a unique network for meaning-making and for developing new roles and identities, ones that might have ramifications beyond the borders of St. Thomas Aquinas.

Just as the local Parish Council is transnationally transformed by the diversity of parishioners, Francisco's literacy practices situated his voice as part of a larger collective. It elevated him to a recognizable leadership position that has had additional implications and benefits within his own cultural community, in the neighborhood at large, and in the municipal context through a unique documentary short, "Communities of Grace," that has been shared widely. During his 8th-grade year, Francisco expressed a desire to attend a unique private Catholic school that blends studies with work experience. The competitive college prep education is funded by corporations and nonprofit or public agencies that pay the school the equivalent of a salary for four or five students who share one entry level job, such as data entry, receptionist, or program assistant. In order to participate, all students must be authorized to work in the United States, something that was not possible for Francisco as a childhood arrival. Francisco applied for the Deferred Action for Childhood Arrivals, a recent administrative relief option for youth who meet certain criteria established by the federal government. The legal clinic, housed at Aquinas Center, helped Francisco and his family prepare the detailed application, and an Aquinas Center donor sponsored the $465 filing fee for the United States Citizenship and Immigration Services. His compelling story—one of hope and aspiration—was well received by the intended audience of donors, attorneys, and the public.

We should not, however, overly idealize Francisco's networks. In many ways, Francisco's experience mirrors those of his peers in the neighborhood. He deftly juggles academics; a robust social life; and, like other children of immigrants, work responsibilities that help pay his family's household bills. And yet, in a mixed status home, Francisco is continually aware of the vastly different opportunities awaiting him after high school. His two younger siblings, born in the United States and therefore citizens, have access to driver's licenses, federally subsidized student loans, and other rights and privileges. Despite his emerging identity as a leader in the community and his evolution as someone who is called upon to speak civically, Francisco faces an uncertain future. Because of his immigration status, Francisco still has limited options for higher education and employment under current state and national policies. Perhaps it is for this very reason that Francisco has flourished in the parish space. The parish—from the academic classroom to the basketball court to the altar—has been a safer place for him to cultivate civic engagement. Francisco's voice has also traveled through literacy practices that circulate through his parish and beyond. His role as a leader has offered him the platform to speak to civic authorities and educational leaders who can influence policies that shape the life opportunities of immigrant youth.

Chapter 6

Bidirectional Learning in a School–University Partnership

Lan Ngo, Katrina Bartow Jacobs, Gerald Campano,
María Paula Ghiso, and David E. Low

My grandmother, my mother, their siblings always helped people. Always. Always
took anyone in, any friends that come, like today: my kids bring their friends home, I
host students from St. Thomas Aquinas, from different colleges. You just make people
feel welcome. And they open up to you . . . You have to love people and want
to help them and support them. Your heart has to be big enough for all the different
communities.

—The Head of the Concerned Black Catholics

Every year, Mrs. Cruz and the children in her ESOL classes at St. Thomas
Aquinas host a celebration to honor the cultures and languages of the community. The day before the 2012 event, preparations were in full swing with
the help of upper-grade youth, St. Thomas Aquinas family members, and
several master's students from the University of Pennsylvania. Younger siblings joyfully laughed and played in the open space as the older children,
parents, and grandparents chatted in English, Spanish, and Vietnamese while
taping up artwork that displayed information about their home countries.
Master's students busied themselves setting up tri-fold display boards on a
row of tables. They had spent the past weeks helping Mrs. Cruz's class put
together the boards, which were covered with the children's writings, immigration stories, and family photos. Mrs. Cruz spread individual portfolios on
the tables to accompany the tri-fold boards. On the day of the celebration,
students, teachers, community members, and neighborhood guests streamed
into the gym, which had been transformed into a colorful auditorium, and
began taking their seats under sparkling, student-made signs, such as, "Ms.
Smith, 5th Grade" and "Parents and Family." A paper reading "Fr. Shields"
was affixed to a chair in the front row, next to another seat reserved for the
school principal. A sign for "Penn" was propped up by the other guests of
honor, a gesture of hospitality signaling the university's sustained collaboration with St. Thomas Aquinas parish and school (Fieldnotes, April 2012).

This chapter highlights two projects that together represent the bidirectional nature of the partnership: how master's students from a course on literacy assessment entered the space of St. Thomas Aquinas and learned alongside Mrs. Cruz and her students and how children from the aftercare program at the school conducted an "Inquiry into College" and visited the university campus. In the first case, the research team taught a graduate course that foregrounded issues of equity and access in the education of children from (im)migrant and refugee backgrounds, many of whom are labeled English language learners. Since there are intersecting social and political factors that influence students' educational opportunities, it may not be enough for pre- and inservice teachers to think about access narrowly in terms of the acquisition of discrete skills. They also need to become familiar with the greater ecology of students' lives, to gain a deeper understanding of the obstacles families navigate as well as the funds of knowledge (González et al., 2005) present in communities.

The partnership with St. Thomas Aquinas afforded a context to explore university–school–community collaborations in teacher education. As the master's students began to get to know the children and families more holistically, it became clear that many at St. Thomas Aquinas had questions about the university and a desire to learn about higher education. This realization led to the research team's planning an Inquiry into College, where young children learned photography as a method of inquiry and, primarily through an "ethnographic" visit to the university, researched college. Contrary to partnerships that locate expertise solely within the academy, the two projects unsettled binaries between knowledge and practice (Cochran-Smith & Lytle, 1999) in order to enact "more democratic ways of working with schools and communities" (Zeichner, 2010, p. 89).

CASE 1: LINKING A GRADUATE-LEVEL COURSE WITH MRS. CRUZ'S CLASSROOM

During the spring of 2012, Mrs. Cruz collaborated with us on a master's-level course on literacy and assessment. Gerald and members of the research team sought to support teacher preparation students in inquiring into how various pedagogical approaches make assumptions about what it means to teach, to learn, and to be literate and in understanding how young students' potentials cannot be described fully within traditional metrics (Campano, Jacobs, & Ngo, 2014), especially among English language learners and those whose cultures and identities are often marginalized in school settings (Willis, 2008; Yoon, 2014). Our orientation to teaching stressed understanding students' learning within the broader context of their lives. The course also encouraged curriculum design that drew on students' experiences and inquiries as epistemic resources for mutual learning (Campano, 2007; Moya, 2002).

In an effort to ground teaching in the actual work of schools and the knowledge of families, we created a series of collaborations between the university course and the St. Thomas Aquinas community. As part of a relationship spanning several years, the master's students participated in the PennPal project with the Indonesian Sunday School, exchanging letters throughout the semester to learn about children's cultural backgrounds, out-of-school interests, and multimodal authoring practices; the youth in turn learned about the graduate students and university culture. Each semester culminated in a PennPal party where students from both contexts would gather to engage in shared literacy activities. We also asked Mrs. Cruz if she would be willing to host Penn students, having them work with children in her pull-out classes. We hoped to provide our students with a rich example of how one teacher was able to work within and against the current climate of high-stakes testing and provide her students with a culturally responsive learning environment. Given power asymmetries between universities and schools (Saltmarsh & Hartley, 2011), the relationship was conceived to be mutually beneficial: The master's students would gain knowledge and insights from working closely with Mrs. Cruz's class, while Mrs. Cruz and her students would have additional classroom support. Lan also volunteered in the afterschool ESOL tutoring program led by Mrs. Cruz and observed and assisted in her kindergarten and 2nd-grade classes.

Building a Reciprocal Partnership Through Intentional Planning

The master's students worked within the existing structure of the ESOL program, visiting Mrs. Cruz's classroom regularly and building a relationship with the children. The culminating assignment asked students to write a portrait of a learner that explored how the child's strengths could inform instruction. We met with Mrs. Cruz numerous times to work out the intellectual vision of the partnership as well as the logistics of scheduling visits for more than 25 university students. In an attempt to honor existing norms rather than merely superimposing our own values and expectations, we cocreated guidelines for the visits—for example, with respect to sign-in protocols and scheduling. Mrs. Cruz also invited the master's students to collaborate in preparing for the annual ESOL celebration described in the opening of the chapter, underscoring the importance of being involved in the school community beyond simply dropping in and out to complete course assignments. A calendar recording the students' planned classroom visits emphasized the notion of respecting all partners while retaining open communication should schedules need to be shifted. Attention to these ostensibly small details helped enhance trust and reciprocity.

Throughout the partnership, Mrs. Cruz modeled the importance of family involvement. It was her suggestion that we draft a joint letter to the children's caretakers explaining our presence in the classroom. The following is an excerpt from that correspondence:

> We [the university team] and Mrs. Cruz are working together to support your child's literacy development and build upon his or her strengths. Master's students from the university are visiting the ESOL classes and working with students one-on-one. The master's students will talk with your child to understand his or her strengths in reading, writing, and literacy. This work is also part of the master's students learning in a class they are taking at the university.

Mrs. Cruz's request that we make families aware of our work in her classroom and obtain their permission was not about meeting official bureaucratic requirements but instead stemmed from her ongoing effort to make her classroom practice transparent to the families. In this way and in many others, she encouraged and supported us in building relationships with the community. While research has revealed the ways immigrant families can become alienated from school, part of Mrs. Cruz's expertise was welcoming families into her classroom and thinking expansively about ways to include their knowledge in the curriculum.

Learning from Mrs. Cruz and Her Students

At an orientation for parents, Mrs. Cruz displayed a large drawing consisting of concentric hearts (see Figure 6.1) with each layer representing an essential element of the ESOL program. At the center was "family." In contrast to an individualistic model of teaching, this visual text represents how children's learning is embedded within multiple contexts and benefits from varied levels of supports, including family to community networks such as the parish, library, and local health and educational out-of-school programs. Working within conditions of economic precarity, Mrs. Cruz was incredibly innovative in procuring social and educational resources for her students beyond the walls of the classroom. She also regularly involved extended family in the classroom and valued their cultural and linguistic knowledge. Family photos and writing in multiple languages adorned the classroom walls, and students were asked to share what they were learning with their caregivers and to make connections between academic texts and out-of-school experiences. While her job description was oriented toward helping students acquire English, Mrs. Cruz was an advocate for multilingualism. She used Spanish to communicate with families, helped children value their emergent bilingualism, and encouraged students and caregivers to translate for each other at school events. During the initial meeting between the university and elementary students, Mrs. Cruz spoke with warmth and respect about her students' academic efforts, as well as their strengths and backgrounds, setting the tone for their interaction and relationship building.

Figure 6.1. Mrs. Cruz's Representation of Supporting Children

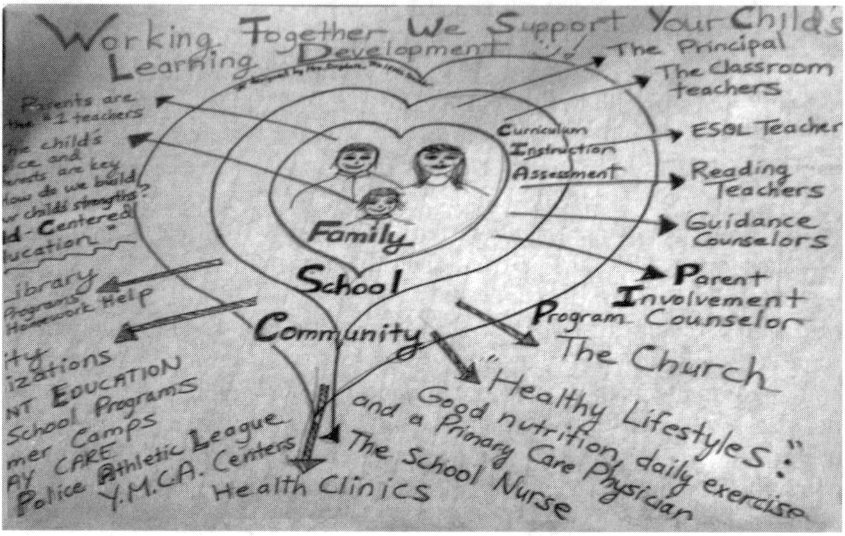

Mrs. Cruz's classroom data collection included portfolios in addition to scores from standardized exams because she was concerned that a single measure could misrepresent students' capacities. For example, after using the Dynamic Indicators of Basic Early Literacy Skills (DIBELS) to assess her students' reading level, she expressed to Lan her critique of the test—mainly that the section which tests phonemic awareness by having students read nonsense words was particularly confusing for young English language learners, a finding echoed by literacy researchers (Goodman, 2006), since without context children with multiple languages may not know which phonemic system to draw on to sound out words. Whereas test scores, such as those from the DIBELS, alone might label her students as underperforming, she used artifacts from portfolios to provide a more contextually nuanced picture of children's learning. At the same time, Mrs. Cruz noted that some students could perform well on the standardized ESL proficiency exam and test out of the program even though other evidence, including students' essays and observations of their difficulty in comprehending textbooks, indicated they could benefit from the continued academic and social supports provided by her class. Through her pedagogy as well as her counsel, Mrs. Cruz modeled for the graduate students how to cultivate a resource orientation to teaching (Campano et al., 2014) that raised questions regarding what any one measure obscured as well as revealed.

After each visit, the master's students wrote reflections and sent them to Mrs. Cruz as well as the teaching team, and whenever possible she responded either in person or over email. As the semester progressed, we saw master's students increasingly participating in Mrs. Cruz's class of their own accord, such as by sharing professional materials not tied to a specific course assignment or by continuing to volunteer there beyond the required visits. A recurring theme in their reflections was the value of learning more about the youth's lives and perspectives, as well as the ways in which Mrs. Cruz, through her pedagogical decisions, conveyed respect for the children's knowledge. Michael, for example, wrote the following about his initial meeting with one of the children:

> Once we introduced ourselves to Stella, we made nametags for each other by drawing the other person's favorite activity. My classmate's and my artistic skills clearly paled in comparison to Stella. We knew she was a talented artist based on the picture that had accompanied her narrative essay, but we gained more evidence of her ability and her passion for drawing after looking at her portfolio. She seemed to have drawn or copied pictures of anime characters, and we later found out that Mrs. Cruz encourages all students to use artwork to express themselves. Mrs. Cruz commented on Stella's "unique" style—keeping in mind the intense focus on standards and accountability in the current school climate at large, this teacher's valuing of art surprised me.

In contrast to how quantitative metrics are used as the privileged criteria from which to evaluate student learning, Michael and his peers became attuned to the multiple modes through which the children engaged in creative and intellectual production.

Another university student, Cathy, echoed similar sentiments in writing about her discussion with a young learner, Linh:

> I saw my interview with Linh not as a means to rattle off disconnected, evaluative questions about her views on reading and writing, but as a way to enter into a conversation, and as a social interaction. My goal was to position Linh as the holder of knowledge as I listened and observed . . . I used Linh's illustration [see Figure 6.2] as my main entry point. . . . Beginning with her artwork proved to be a natural gateway into obtaining information about Linh: her family, friends, first language, home language, immigration history, life in her home country, interests inside and outside of school, favorite subjects, and feelings about school both in the United States and in Vietnam.

Through the partnership with Mrs. Cruz's classroom, Cathy was able to discern a complex portrait of Linh that could not be easily captured in the label "English language learner," much less a standardized test score. She learned that Linh was a recent immigrant who was entering a longstanding Vietnamese community in the city, which provided a substantial network of support. At the same time, Linh kept active her relationships with peers and family back in Vietnam through the use of digital literacies and technologies. Written texts were her preferred mode of communication, perhaps because

Figure 6.2. Linh's Illustration, "My Last Days in Vietnam"

she had studied English in Vietnam, while she was more reticent to speak up in person. These details might have easily been lost or mischaracterized in deficit terms through a decontextualized curriculum. By partnering with a teacher who shared our values about the richness of students' linguistic and cultural resources, the focus of the university course shifted from merely assessing specific decontextualized skills to developing a much richer portrait of children's learning within the broader literate contexts of their lives.

CASE 2: YOUNG CHILDREN'S "INQUIRY INTO COLLEGE" AND VISIT TO CAMPUS

Just as preservice teachers entered the space of St. Thomas Aquinas, forging relationships and learning with and from Mrs. Cruz and her young students to better understand access to education, youth from St. Thomas Aquinas also visited the campus to research higher education. After learning that families desired greater information about college, we thought we would arrange a tour of the university but discovered that these were only available to high school students. In conversations with community leaders, we designed an Inquiry into College where children from the St. Thomas Aquinas aftercare program would research college and eventually conduct their own fieldwork through a visit to our institution that we ourselves organized (Campano, Ngo, et al., 2015). We approached this inquiry with an awareness of the barriers to university access for historically minoritized communities (e.g., Gándara, 2012).

The aftercare program was housed within the St. Thomas Aquinas School and served children from the neighborhood, only some of whom were affiliated with the parish community. The 20 children who participated in the Inquiry into College were between the ages of 5 and 10 years old and were of Southeast Asian (Vietnamese, Cambodian, and Indonesian), Latina/o, and African American backgrounds. While a visit to our university campus was the major event and midpoint of the project, the work was a sustained investigation into the children's critical sensemaking of schooling, college, and their own intellectual trajectories. We met with the children one afternoon a week for 5 months and aimed to cultivate a space in which they could draw on various semiotic resources (Kress, 2010), including photos they took and official university maps, to both participate in inquiry and represent their ideas of the university.

Negotiating Access to the University: Children's Transgressive Embodiment

We had always been aware, from the research literature and from our own experiences, of barriers to higher education access. However, it was not until navigating the logistics of the Inquiry into College Project that we gained a clearer understanding of the role of the built environment (Siebers, 2010) in regulating young children's interactions with colleges and universities. Many of the organizations and buildings we contacted told us they either were closed on the weekends or required identification cards for all visitors (unless part of an official tour through the admissions office, or, we would add, if they were children of faculty or alumni), or they simply did not return our calls. When we attempted to arrange a visit to the quadrangle that houses many of the dorms on campus, we encountered a number of challenges. For weeks before the visit, Lan and several master's students communicated with university representatives about what would be required to enter. After being told everyone would need to provide identification, and then reminding university personnel that most of the participants were young children without ID cards, an email finally came through with permission, albeit with the stipulation that we give a list of all those in attendance and the "exact time when we would be planning on going into it" (Artifact excerpt).

Echoing Bourdieu's (1986) argument that the education system is a paradigmatic mechanism of social reproduction, children from different social locations have different degrees and types of access to our university. For example, the campus bookstore is packed with gear marketed to the children of alumni, from onesies and teddy bears to kiddie-sized sports paraphernalia. Often these are the same children who can attend family alumni events and homecoming football games (a phrase which, like *alma mater*, suggests the easy homology between the university and the family milieu) or visit older siblings or relatives in the dormitories. While families mobilize social and economic capital to provide exposure to institutions of higher education, these resources are often unevenly distributed (Bourdieu, 1986; Gadsden,

1998). Access to elite universities by adolescents who do not benefit from familial points of entry is typically more tightly regulated through the official tour of the campus and formal admission procedures. The children in our study, who are not of high school age, however, were categorically denied the official tour. This barrier is compounded by well-documented imbalances in the opportunities that youth from historically minoritized communities have in attending institutions of higher education (e.g., Harper & Hurtado, 2011).

Despite our extensive preparation, when we arrived with the children and families to the quad entrance, the guard at the gate had no information about our visit. The children were left waiting for more than 45 minutes while the adults tried to resolve the situation, during which time they grew understandably restless, drawing a mix of disapproving and curious looks from passersby. For many of them, it was their first time visiting a college campus, despite it being only 2 miles from their neighborhood. While we eventually gained welcomed access, the quad's near impenetrability seemed to be sending a different message. Once allowed to enter, the children burst into the open green space with their pent-up energy, utilizing the statue of a famous alumnus as a play structure (see Figure 6.3), running around the College Green as if it were a park, and playing "Duck Duck Goose" on the lawn.

Upon reflection, we realized that far from being "unruly," the children were using play to respond reasonably and creatively to an environment that denied them entry. For young children, play is not ancillary but central to inquiry. Behaviors that initially might be read as "off task" were actually forms of agency that helped children demystify the university and make it their own, what we have come to understand—building off scholarship in early childhood literacy (e.g., Dyson, 2003; Ghiso, 2013; Vasquez, 2005; Wohlwend, 2011)—as children's critical play.

While each of the roadblocks we encountered was, as an isolated event, understandable, when taken together they point to systemic patterns of how many children are denied possible pathways to college, with financial concerns that are "frequently compounded by inadequate information about college opportunities and how to access them, cultural differences, citizenship issues, language barriers, and, too frequently, discrimination" (Baum & Flores, 2011, p. 172). Universities sometimes rebuff the presence of children on campus, particularly those from minoritized and underserved communities, except in highly structured ways. Where children are welcomed, such as through the day care or children's programming in the performing arts department, there are daunting financial barriers to supersede.

We found that we needed to address two related aspects of access to campus: first, facilitating physical access, and then creating spaces for learning within the university environment that were conducive to children's social worlds. With the social capital afforded by our university "insider"

Figure 6.3. Children Climbing a Campus Statue

status, we were able to gain entry to several areas of the campus that are typically off-limits. Katrina's husband was at the time getting his doctorate in the engineering school and helped facilitate entrance to a nanotechnology lab. He used an electron microscope to engrave an image of Sponge-Bob SquarePants onto a single human hair while the children looked on in rapt attention. The activity helped bridge the adult world of the laboratory and the children's world of mass media (Dyson, 2003), honoring children's worlds and capturing their interest without detracting from the scientific nature of the demonstration. In contrast to the frenetic energy we noticed the children exhibiting in the quad, at the laboratory they uniformly sat engrossed as they observed this technology—which the school had been very reluctant to let them near because of its exorbitant cost, even despite our insider status.

(Re)Writing the University

The children represented their inquiries about the university in playful ways, using humor and creativity to (re)construct the academic space and their roles within it. Derrick, an 8-year-old African American boy and self-professed future "spider scientist," decided to create a map of the university based on the data he collected (see Figure 6.4). His focus on the scientific world was evident during the campus visit in his photographs of squirrels and trees and his interest in the engineering laboratory.

Derrick imbued the official map of the university we had provided prior to the campus visit with his own perspectives and interpretations. As Janks (2014) notes, maps are visual texts that "shape our knowledge of the landscape" (p. 39); while considered neutral, they are actually subjective and often reveal the interests of the map's producers. Taking a central position in Derrick's map are the buildings we frequented most during the campus visit, such as the Graduate School of Education (host institution for the trip), the "Diner" where we broke for lunch, and the university library, which was often present in the background of our day. Closer to the page's margins are the science lab, a coffee shop, and the dormitories. These sites were memorable to Derrick, as he chose to adorn them with visual cues of salience and textual labels (Kress & van Leeuwen, 2006, p. 212). A number of the students had identified the Starbucks as a prominent campus landmark, and its inclusion on the map is a reminder that universities might be as much about class socialization, consumption, and leisure as they are about learning. Derrick inserts objects, people, and motifs he views as relevant to his experience there, but which are not included in the official campus map. A key example is SpongeBob, who, along with the label "microscope," serves as a visual synecdoche for the science lab. At the center of the map is Derrick himself, a stick figure climbing atop the iconic campus LOVE statue. Contrary to the university map, the physical structures are not merely decontextualized static objects but agentively interpreted and acted upon by children like Derrick.

Derrick also alters the appearance of structures that *do* appear on the university's official map, in order to imbue them with new meanings, demonstrating that once an image has been produced, it is open to remaking and transformation (Kress, 2010, p. 27). He draws the popular statue of Ben Franklin sitting on a bench but gives equal weight to the whimsical cast of a bird that shares Ben's bench, perhaps continuing to follow his interest in the natural world. Creative redesign is also evident in Derrick's drawing of the university's library, which he reinterprets to resemble a castle. Several campus buildings possess fortress-like exteriors and an overriding aura of impenetrability (Benjamin, 1936/1968), especially from the perspective of a young child visiting for the first time. The library, in particular, was a space the children were not allowed to enter on the day of our trip, an example of how the built environment regulates participation (Siebers, 2010). Derrick exaggerates the campus's Gothic collegiate style, adding turrets and a rampart, a design choice that may signal some of the historically rooted challenges of access for disenfranchised communities.

For a number of the children, redesign took the form of incorporating features of the university within popular culture iconography, which

Figure 6.4. Derrick's Map of the University

"locat[ed] new understandings within a familiar discourse" (Marsh, 2000, p. 130). Ary, a young child of Cambodian descent, used a photo of Ben Franklin taken by a peer as an opportunity to remix the historical figure into an emblem of female agency. She represented her take on how Ben Franklin discovered electricity in a comics-style drawing, crafting the founding father in the likeness of a Powerpuff Girl (see Figure 6.5), with its characteristic large head and eyes and rounded limbs. The figure now sports a beard, bow tie, and vest, accoutrements that serve to mark the figure as Franklin.

Beyond representational fidelity, the children playfully brought university icons into their worlds by utilizing familiar pop-culture tropes and circulating them throughout the social environment in which they played with and learned from each other. Throughout the campus visit, the children's carnivalesque (Bakhtin, 1984) irreverence helped democratize the space of the elite private institution. Their play also provided the children with an opportunity to explore their personal interests beyond the agenda of the visit, and to imagine for themselves future educational opportunities, especially significant for those who are members of historically disenfranchised communities and whose lives and learning are too often considered peripheral to university culture. The children's critical play employed humor to subvert authority and recontextualize the university within their own social worlds, disrupting its aura as an institution they must leave their childhoods and cultures behind in order to enter.

Figure 6.5. Ary's Rendering of Ben Franklin

CONCLUSION

In our efforts to construct a truly collaborative inquiry with the St. Thomas Aquinas community, we felt it important to acknowledge issues of access and agency across the various institutional contexts. We are concerned that preservice teachers in schools of education learn very little about students beyond generic institutional labels and where they are positioned on a bell curve according to norm-referenced evaluations. This is in large part because of the high-stakes testing and standardization paradigm that does not always honor the rich and contextualized knowledge of community and school members within teacher preparation programs (Zeichner, Payne, & Brayko, 2015). Teacher "training" has increasingly focused on mechanistically diagnosing students in order to prescribe the right remedies (Cochran-Smith & Dudley-Marling, 2012). This approach reinforces stereotypes and deficit orientations toward students and communities that have faced historical marginalization. We are equally troubled by the fact that many children, even those who live in the shadows of universities, may have very little exposure to the culture of academia. Despite a lot of good work by university members to engage in outreach, often institutions of higher education still present substantial barriers to access to those without the requisite social capital (Butin, 2003). It is of little surprise, therefore, that the chasm between universities and many communities feels as if it is only widening.

This chapter reflects our efforts to foster bidirectional inquiry and learning opportunities to close the rift between children involved in St. Thomas

Aquinas and our own Graduate School of Education. Our course encouraged master's students to situate children's learning within their rich social and cultural worlds and to understand how students' potentials cannot be contained by the categories and metrics used to explain them. The Inquiry into College supported even very young children in demystifying the university and making it their own through critical play. Both projects required tremendous attention to detail and hundreds of hours of relational labor on the part of the research team, school educators, parents, and community leaders. Unfortunately this type of care work is often dismissed as mere service in universities and not necessarily viewed as part of the rigors of research or the theoretical big ideas that have academic currency. By contrast, we would argue that these day-to-day practices are ineluctably entwined with theorizing and create the conditions for collaborative knowledge production.

Universities can acknowledge such labor by supporting it institutionally. One promising direction for bidirectional collaborations has been when methods classes are held in schools and in partnership with thoughtful teachers such as Mrs. Cruz, whose classrooms are structured around profound respect for families. On the other end, universities might invest in more explicitly welcoming families and children from nearby neighborhoods, including through infrastructure for tours designed specifically for a younger age group. We imagine that each of the respective schools on campus (e.g., engineering, education, medicine, law, and arts and sciences) could create academic play spaces similar to the one-time event we conceptualized with SpongeBob and the electron microscope. These play spaces would need to foster children's inquiry as well as be culturally and socially relevant to their own identities and experiences. Universities gear their efforts to recruiting underrepresented first-generation students, but our evidence suggests that the process might start substantially earlier. These types of shifts would communicate to young children, and their families, that the university is for them. Ideally, it would also communicate better to the university that it should be its privilege to have such creative and talented young people as part of its intellectual community.

As universities deepen their collaborations with schools and develop relationships with community organizations, an important caution is that they not reproduce deficit ideologies or view children and their families as mere victims. As Kinloch and colleagues (Kinloch, Nemeth, & Patterson, 2015) remind us, "a social justice and social awareness approach places attention on inequitable systems, moves beyond the unidirectional relationship assumed by the charity model, and embraces a dynamic network of problem-posers and problem-solvers" (p. 42). The two projects featured in this chapter demonstrate that there are multiple locations of knowledge, and that dialogue across difference is an epistemic prerequisite for equitable partnerships.

Chapter 7

Multiliteracies, the Arts, and Postcolonial Agency

David E. Low and Gerald Campano

Comics express me. When I was younger, people thought I didn't like books. My teacher said that comics aren't real books. She undermined my knowledge.

—Jamir (age 10), one of the founding members of the Comics Inquiry Community

The muralist Eliseo Art Silva timed the debut of his newest work, *Alab ng Puso: My Heart's Sole Burning Fire*, to coincide with 100 years of Filipina/o history in greater Philadelphia and to mark the centennial of the end of the Philippine–American War. At the time of its unveiling in June 2013, *Alab ng Puso* was the only public mural commemorating Filipina/o American history in the eastern United States. During an interview with David 1 month prior, Silva explained that his goal for the mural was "to create a hub of Filipino identity" at a site where people would congregate for generations (Interview, May 15, 2013). Indeed, despite the presence of over 4 million people of Filipina/o descent in the United States, major events such as the Philippine–American War (1899–1913) are often relegated to a mere footnote in American history textbooks, when they appear at all.

Many schoolchildren's experiences with their own histories do not come from textbooks, which remain Eurocentric, but from valuable family narratives, art, and literature (e.g., Low & Campano, 2013). Whereas the sanctioned histories circulated through school curricula may omit major events from the record—what E. San Juan Jr. (2005) refers to as "historical amnesia"—the arts can function as a cultural repository, historicizing subaltern experiences and imagining more inclusive futures (e.g., Campano, 2007; Ghiso & Low, 2013). The arts serve as a powerful form of memory work, particularly for experiences that have not gained wider institutional purchase (e.g., Forché, 1993; Sacco, 2012). *Alab ng Puso*, in addition to portraying scores of Filipina/os living in Philadelphia over the past century, includes notable figures from throughout Filipina/o history and employs precolonial symbols (i.e., references to architecture, sculpture, pottery, wildlife, and geometric patterns predating the Spanish conquest of 1521). Visual artists like Silva are frequently among the first to excavate and reanimate "buried histories" (Ichioka, 1974) in public venues. Muralists, in particular, often position their work as a testimonial of life within cultural borderlands—a form of "mestiza consciousness" (Anzaldúa, 1999, p. 99) designed to rally people together by interlacing multiple narratives, from various places, into a single composition within one bounded physical space (e.g., Cockcroft, Weber, & Cockcroft, 1998; Romo, 1992; Sleeter, 2014). Because these artistic goals align so closely with the day-to-day mission of the Aquinas Center in South Philadelphia, and because the St. Thomas Aquinas parish is a place where Filipina/os in the community have congregated in recent years, we were not surprised to learn that in 2013 Silva had enlisted the help of the Aquinas Center on *Alab ng Puso*.

Like many artworks that are deliberately about cultural sustenance and revitalization, Silva's mural is an example of a particular community's legacy; at the same time, it has resonances with other groups that have histories of colonization and oppression. This relationship between the particular and the universal was on display at a Community Paint Day event at the Aquinas Center, where members of the parish gathered to assist Silva in completing *Alab ng Puso*. Earlier, Silva had met with parishioners to solicit ideas for his mural, and now, late in the process, he returned with several large fabric sheets, each filled with stencil outlines and hundreds of numerals: a paint-by-numbers literally larger than life. Once the stencils were filled in, Silva affixed these parachute cloths (the Polytab nonwoven fabrics used in mural making) to a wall in Northeast Philadelphia and provided finishing touches. The individuals who came to paint reflected St. Thomas Aquinas's cultural and ethnic diversity. African American 8th-graders mingled with members of a Vietnamese youth group; Italian American seniors mixed with children from the Latina/o ministry. All participated in contributing to a mural commemorating Filipina/o American history and identity, though few themselves identified as Filipina/o. Two painters, a White man and a Vietnamese American boy, worked on coloring in a section of the mural together. Represented on the cloth was a sign held by the Filipino novelist Carlos Bulosan, reading "Positively No Filipinos Allowed" (see Figure 7.1).

Silva's image marked an instance of overt historical racism while the scene David observed revealed a multiethnic and intergenerational alliance forged in response to that history (Fieldnotes, April 13, 2013). The scene was emblematic of the Aquinas Center's critical multicultural vision and illustrative of the core question framing the work of the Community Literacies Project: How do individuals negotiate social, cultural, linguistic, and institutional boundaries to advocate for access? In the case of the Community Paint Day event, the social practices around the mural presented an opportunity to

Figure 7.1. Collaborating on the Community Mural

Top: The mural *Alab ng Puso: My Heart's Sole Burning Fire* by Eliseo Art Silva (2013, 22 x 65 ft). Bottom: Two parishioners collaborate on painting Silva's mural (April 2013).

learn from others. *Alab ng Puso* was not merely an exercise in cultural preservation but also an act of cross-cultural coalition.

There are several tensions related to the mural project that are worth exploring. As mentioned, *Alab ng Puso*'s final home is in Northeast Philadelphia, a 45-minute drive from the Aquinas Center in South Philadelphia. While a number of St. Thomas Aquinas parishioners assisted Silva in the completion of his mural in April, none were able to attend its unveiling in May (except for Gerald, who gave a keynote invoking his own Filipino identity), suggesting a divide between the production and consumption of the mural. A related tension is that Silva's vision, although informed by others, was still ultimately his creation. Finally, in spite of the fact that Silva's mural represents a buried history that links to other postcolonial experiences, murals are an inherently static medium following their completion. Once set on a wall, a mural ages and fades as the community around it evolves. What will *Alab ng Puso* mean to future residents of Northeast

Philadelphia, and how will they participate in making meaning of Silva's 2013 "hub of Filipino identity"?

The arts can become a means of mediating between the particular and the universal, between St. Thomas Aquinas's past and its present. Although the community has been changing throughout its 125-year history, the parish remains committed to its longstanding mission to "serve the immigrant and the stranger," a phrase appearing in innumerable communications and documents, including atop the parish's official website. Somewhat paradoxically, the shifting identity of the parish can leave it feeling both new and anachronistic at the same time. From the century-old nave lined with the names of bygone Italian families to common areas constructed by African Americans in an effort to desegregate the parish in the 1980s; from the still-largely-Eurocentric standardized curriculum to the robustly multicultural advocacy sponsored by the Aquinas Center, tensions between the static and the dynamic—and thus, between the parish's history and its newly arrived communities—continue to resonate.

We wondered, as educators and literacy researchers, how visual art production, which is frequently used to excavate experiences that have been buried or otherwise marginalized, might be used to reflect the ways people and communities evolve over time. Silva's mural, and the processes behind its production, point to how the arts might represent not only the experiences of who *was* here and who *is* here, but how people's identities change and evolve in collaboration with others. How might the different cultural groups at St. Thomas Aquinas assert their own specific experiences and histories while absorbing the cosmopolitan influences of the parish? What role might creativity, desire, and aesthetics play in youth's multifaceted negotiations of identity? We lacked definitive answers to these questions but found satisfying possibilities during our work at St. Thomas Aquinas, specifically in the form of young people's engagements with the popular medium of comics.

THE COMICS INQUIRY COMMUNITY

In 2011, as a contributor to the developing partnership with St. Thomas Aquinas, David began working to build relationships within several parish communities, such as the Indonesian Sunday School and the K-8 school. By attending to literacy practices across a range of parish contexts, members of the research team hoped to cultivate more complex understandings of the St. Thomas Aquinas community as a whole. David, a former classroom teacher, was particularly drawn to the parish school, which serves St. Thomas Aquinas's Asian and Latina/o worship communities, as well as many non-Catholic, predominantly Black children from the neighborhood. Early in 2012, David met Marina, an educator who, several months prior, had built the school's library in an unused storage room, filled it with donated books, and began hosting students throughout the day. In their first conversation, Marina voiced her concerns about a group of 5th-grade boys who were not using their library time to check out books, and she asked David if he had any ideas. David's interest in multimodality and popular culture led him to suggest including graphic novels or comic books. Marina responded that a number of students had requested these types of texts, and she invited David to come back to the library in several weeks with any age-appropriate comics he could get his hands on (Fieldnotes, January 25, 2012).

When David returned to the school in March, he did so with a shoebox of graphic novels and a number of questions about how the books would (or would not) be received. Upon entering the library, David sat down with the 5th-grade boys Marina had been telling him about, and his initial observations confirmed what she had prepared him for: At each other table in the library, girls and boys were thumbing through books they had selected from the shelves. At this table, five boys sat with closed books, occasionally whispering to one another. David invited the children at the table to peruse the graphic novels in the shoebox, and over the next half hour, the boys looked through the small portable library and flipped through books. A few of the boys laughed. Some showed their neighbors a particularly well-drawn action sequence. One teared up as he read the graphic novelization of Geoffrey Canada's *Fist Stick Knife Gun* (Canada & Nicholas, 2010), telling David that he felt bad for a character who was being bullied. Another boy mentioned that he "hates to read but [that he] loves comics," calling himself "a comics junkie" and a "comic book nut." David wondered how this student was defining reading and why he did not consider his engagement with comics to be legitimate reading (Fieldnotes, March 2, 2012). At the end of the session, each boy asked if he could borrow a book and when David planned to come back. They were eager to continue what they had started.

With Marina's and the school's support, the Comics Inquiry Community (CIC) began meeting regularly after school. While the group was initially composed of 5th-grade boys, it quickly expanded to include students in other grades and of both sexes. Straightaway, students began challenging David's expectations of what they wanted to do in the space. He had initially imagined a reading-intensive experience, but fairly quickly, several students formed an affinity group around comic book and manga authorship (Bitz, 2009). In it, they began collaborating on their own stories, creating new characters, negotiating roles about who would write and who would draw, and thinking about potential audiences. Codesigning became a community norm. In the first weeks of its existence, members of the group developed rituals in order to collaboratively tell stories through the multimodal medium of comics (e.g., Zimmerman, 2008).

(CO)CREATING GRAPHICA: RANDY'S LINES OF FLIGHT

During the earliest sessions of the CIC, while members discussed the sorts of comics they were interested in creating, several 5th-graders decided that if they jointly invented a character, they could tell a richer and more expansive story. In this collaborative spirit, the character of Randy was born. Randy's team of creators decided that anyone who used the character could interpret him in his own way, and this decision had an immediate impact on the breadth of stories that they crafted. Members of the group wrote about Randy's relationships with family members and his romantic interests, his goals (getting rich), his nightmares (battling the Grim Reaper outside of Taco Bell), and his daily encounters in their South Philly neighborhood. Significantly, the characteristics comprising Randy's ascriptive identity (age, race, and outward appearance) were also mutable and could be tailored to represent his creators' interests and experiences. In Jamir's Randy stories, for example, the character appeared as a Black man in his early 20s, who alternated between struggling economically (he worked minimum wage jobs) and being rich (he won the lottery). In Kevin's stories, Randy was an Asian teenager wielding katana blades and fighting demons from a skateboard (see Figure 7.2). In Chance's stories, Randy was modeled after the White teenager Jeremy from the comic strip *Zits*; these plotlines concerned generational misunderstandings between Randy and his father. In Larry's stories, Randy was used both autobiographically, to address personal issues such as health problems (see Figure 7.3), and for the purpose of social commentary (see Figure 7.4).

Each creator imagined Randy to represent his own ethnic background: Jamir and Larry are Black, Kevin is Cambodian American, and Chance was the only White student attending the school at the time. The youth used Randy as a semiotic vehicle for refracting personal experiences through a collective imaginary, and the character became a means for children to "fictionalize reality" (C. Medina & Campano, 2006) and prefigure more coalitional social spaces.

Randy's fluctuating racial identity first became evident when Kevin and Jamir produced Figure 7.2 in March 2012. This was the first composition in which differing versions of Randy, rendered by two illustrators, stood side by side for the purpose of comparison. To delineate their interpretations, Kevin included the note "Asian for my comic" while Jamir labeled his character "Randy, after rich." Both versions of Randy wear Phillies caps, shirts and ties, hoodies, branded sweatpants, and gym shoes—a chic reimagining of the school uniforms worn by Randy's creators—and they stand in nearly identical poses. Amid their many similarities, David zeroed in on Kevin's textual ethnic identifier and asked him about it. Kevin explained his version of Randy thus: "So, not to be offensive, but you know how in some Asian graphic novels, they have weapons and stuff? They fight? I'm sticking to a

Figure 7.2. Iterations of Randy

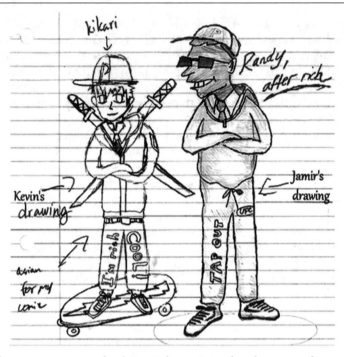

type of comic, to a type of culture. Like in Asia, they have mostly quests and stuff" (Transcript, March 23, 2012). While it is unlikely that Kevin, a Cambodian American student, could personally identify with carrying swords on his back, there was something about the prototypical quest narrative that he was drawn to and which he wanted to incorporate into his version of Randy's adventures. This impulse likely echoes the ethnic identities of many manga characters: Kevin considers them Asian rather than specifically Japanese, so as to include himself within manga's Pan-Asian cultural orbit. By coarticulating "a type of comic" with "a type of culture," Kevin is able to write himself (Cambodian American), via the Randy character (variable ethnicity), into a particular form of ethnoliterary identity: the Japanese shōnen hero (e.g., Bitz, 2009). Kevin's race bending of Randy thereby universalizes the particular (e.g., Thomas & Stornaiuolo, 2014).

Jamir was also a manga fan, perhaps even more so than Kevin. He often spoke at great length about manga he had recently read and anime films he had stayed up to watch on late-night TV. Jamir designed his version of Randy as a contemporary 20-something who looked much like himself rather than as a shōnen hero. The predominant theme in Jamir's Randy comics was socioeconomic class. He described his goal to create a character "like [the rapper] Lil Wayne," who "was broke and everything, won the lottery, spent all his money, and he can't live without his money," so he became "haunted by nightmares" (Fieldnotes, March 16, 2012). Jamir's

Figure 7.3. Randy's Health Issues

Figure 7.4. Randy and Racial Profiling

comic draws attention to a world of extremes and economic polarization, which in some ways mirrors his own gentrifying neighborhood. Although the students in the CIC had diverse cultural, linguistic, and ethnic identities, they shared a context where there was deepening economic inequality.

Of all the students who cocreated and used Randy in their comics storytelling, perhaps none was as committed to the character as Larry. In fact, Larry was the only student to use Randy, in some capacity, beyond the 2011–2012 school year. Although Larry's Randy stories eventually dwindled in number, Larry did employ the character until early 2014. During the 3 years in which Larry created stories starring Randy, he used the character for various purposes. In one story line, Randy became a father, while in another, he hit a game-winning home run as a member of the New York Yankees. Larry's stories, more so than those of other members of the CIC, often maintained a distinctly autobiographical quality. After speaking with him, it was not difficult to see how Larry used Randy as a filter for his experiences, especially those that were frustrating or exciting him at a given moment. Larry's version of Randy, like Larry himself, made frequent hospital visits due to various health problems. In Figure 7.3, for example, Randy is involved in a car accident, followed by the media announcement that "We can see that Randy [is] hurt [and] will not play this year." Larry created this page the same week he was informed that he was not healthy enough to participate in sports.

Larry's Randy stories also bore elements of social critique. For instance, Larry created one sketch, in April 2012, about racial profiling in his Philadelphia neighborhood. In this single-page story, Randy is harassed and detained by four officers (depicted as a faceless monolithic block) who construe his very existence as a criminal act (see Figure 7.4). Randy is not the instigator of this exchange; rather, he is confronted by the officers, who provoke him into making oppositional but typically teenager-like comments and then imprison him. Drawing on the historical ties between slavery and imprisonment (e.g., Alexander, 2010; Hedges & Sacco, 2012), Larry's inclusion of the word "cuff" in the center of the page becomes a symbol for the relationship between African American youth and the criminal justice system. As Larry explained to David about the genesis of his graphic narrative, "I was watching a cop show . . . and this guy, he was just sitting on a curb and smoking, and the cops just came up and started, like, they got racist with him. So that's what made me think of that."

Larry's comic satirizes injustices in the criminal justice system, specifically with respect to the racist profiling of young Black males. Through Randy, Larry critiques an America in which "mass incarceration defines the meaning of blackness" (Alexander, 2010, p. 192) by exposing racial discrimination at the core of its institutions. In Larry's hands, Randy is able to function multiply, as an instrument of voiced dissent, as a means of representing his personal and community knowledge, and as a creative way of situating himself—and by extension, all of Randy's cocreators—within longstanding activist traditions. Larry's multimodal authorship suggests a "theory of literacy located on the edges of hope, where young Black males are finally heard as members in the long chorus of justice that defines our humanity" (Kirkland, 2013, p. 12).

CONCLUSION

In the world of mainstream comic books, few characters are illustrated by the same artist for very long. In fact, iconic characters such as Batman and Spider-Man have been depicted by hundreds of artists across many decades, each of whom left her or his unique stamp on the character. By embracing the mutability of the comics medium and its history of shifting representation, several young members of the CIC were able to represent their own interests and experiences through a single character. Indeed, they went further than many mainstream comics artists, designing Randy's age and race to be as fluid as any other characteristic. In a school and parish made up of diverse students with a range of cultural experiences, Randy was cocreated as an inherently transcultural figure. While the children's Randy stories were not necessarily intended to surface buried histories in quite the same way as Silva's mural, the boys did use the character to articulate aspects of their identities that are marginalized both in the context of school and in society at large (e.g., Low, 2015). Randy possessed immediacy due to his customizability, and because he was born out of the students' own inquiries. Each creator used Randy to say something about himself and the world around him; once the message was made, the character was free to evolve into his next form. Whereas Silva designed *Alab ng Puso* to be a cultural repository and relied on a cross-cultural coalition to breathe life into it, Randy was temporary, transient, designed to tell a story in the moment and then morph into a new identity, always in the act of becoming yet bearing the traces of its previous iterations. The character gained power by being unfixed and limitless, a series of fragments much like the medium of comics itself (Postema, 2013). Because of this, Randy was able to function at the level of the particular (used to tell stories about his individual cocreators' concerns) while also representing the community that collaboratively brought him into the world.

The mural *Alab ng Puso* and the CIC reflect two different manifestations of postcolonial agency (Bignall, 2010) through the arts. The first is to assert the dense particularity of a group's experiences that have been largely erased in dominant narratives. The promise of such an approach is that it reveals the history and logic of colonizations (Rodríguez, 2010), such as the genocide of the Philippine–American War, that continue to impact the lives of communities of color. The problem may be that these subaltern histories can become assimilated into a larger master narrative of redemption and progress (Bignall, 2010) that does not necessarily address youth's contemporary realities, struggles, and interests. A second form of agency would involve honoring students' intellectual desire to represent and (re) imagine their own world, as the youth in the CIC did. As educators of young people, we are concerned that critique should be coupled with hope (Duncan-Andrade, 2009). By infusing pop cultural sensibilities and experiential knowledge into their group storytelling, the youth in the CIC were, as Simon (2012) writes, emblematic of so many young people "for whom literacy and identity are coextensive...claim[ing] an identity counter to the one[s] ascribed to [them]" (p. 516). Through artistic narratives the youth could pursue their own creative desires, in the process both analyzing the current social world and actualizing new possibilities. Ultimately, it was a group of children interested in comics who co-constructed the archetypal citizen of one world to encompass many. The figure of Randy was less about representing one particular experience and more about the proliferation of multiple experiences and creative lines of flight. We found both forms of agency, embodied by the mural and the CIC, respectively, to be invaluable, helping to reveal histories that have been buried as well as actualize new possibilities for identity and sociality.

Chapter 8

The Community Researchers Project
The Role of Care in Critical Work

Grace Player, Lan Ngo, Gerald Campano, and María Paula Ghiso

The bad thing is that they are closing many schools and they make it more difficult because we have to get up earlier, go farther away, and there are more children in one classroom. So these are barriers that exist sometimes, and also for college where also [students] cannot study, they put up more barriers. Sometimes there are students who really want to study, who have that desire, that gift to study and they no longer can, so also for them it's a frustration because one cannot give them what they need or what they want.

—Latina mother, discussing educational opportunities (translated from Spanish)

Seven Indonesian and Latina/o middle and high school students gathered at the front of a large room at the University of Pennsylvania Ethnography in Research Education Forum before an audience of academics, educators, and parents to discuss their participation in the Community Researchers Project (CRP), an out-of-school program designed for supporting youth in investigating issues that mattered to them. Neatly coiffed and bespectacled, Martin, a 15-year-old Indonesian youth, stood among his peers to present the opus to his inquiry-based research project—a documentary he cowrote and directed with another student from his high school. He spoke with confidence, explaining,

> I chose to do a documentary about the Doomsday Budget Cuts that were passed in 2014, affecting many public schools in the Philadelphia area. . . . It affected my life, teachers' lives, and parents' lives. And it impacted the community of Philadelphia as a whole because it united students together from all these different schools to stand up for something they believed in. (Transcript, February 28, 2015)

Martin demonstrated solidarity with peers, teachers, and family members as he spoke about the severe budget cuts that undermined the public

education system in his city. In this chapter, we explore the activist stance
Martin cultivated as he investigated educational equity within the context
of the CRP. This stance was rooted, we believe, in an ethics of care that enabled him to learn from multiple perspectives and propelled him to share
his wisdom with younger generations.

BACKGROUND AND ORIENTATION OF THE PROJECT

The CRP was designed to center the knowledge and experiences of Martin
and his peers in a nonfiction literacy curriculum. The project was conceived
in response to community input regarding educational opportunities for
their children. Parents had expressed a desire for the university to support
middle school students with nonfiction reading and writing, as this had
become a focus in their schools through the Common Core State Standards
(CCSS). While the research team had critiques of the CCSS, including how
certain iterations of the policy devalued personal narratives (see Campano,
Ngo, & Player, 2015), we believed the request provided an opportunity to
have youth transact with rich nonfiction texts in ways that were culturally responsive and that addressed issues they perceived as affecting their
communities. Through a microgiving initiative directed at Penn faculty,
staff, and alumni, Gerald raised money to purchase dozens of high-quality,
award-winning young adult books, many chosen by St. Thomas Aquinas
community leaders, from the list of Notable Books for a Global Society
from the International Literacy Association. All the texts addressed issues
of social justice and transnationalism, which we hoped would provide the-
matic cues for the immigrant youth and authorize them to investigate topics that may be invisible in the mandated school curriculum.

The 14 youth (ages 10–14) who participated in the CRP brought with
them and built upon a wealth of knowledge that arose from their own experiences, some shared, some unique. All of the students came from immigrant backgrounds: 12 identified as Indonesian, and two were of Mexican
descent. The CRP youth met every other weekend in the Aquinas Center
from Fall 2013 to Spring 2014. They began by exploring the nonfiction
books as mentor texts, which, in conjunction with reflections about their
communities, inspired them to develop their own research projects. They
also studied qualitative research methodology, such as developing a question, reviewing relevant literature, and making a case for the significance of
one's interests. The youth then pursued their research questions using various methods, including interviewing and engaging in participant observa-
tion, and ultimately created multimodal representations of their findings.
In a celebratory event at the end of the project, the students shared their
work with families, friends, and community members. They also presented their research at the Ethnography Forum conference described in this
chapter's opening.

OUR STANCE ON CRITICAL LITERACY: BEGINNING WITH CARE

The CRP was not designed to remediate, which is too often the thrust of educational programming aimed at historically disenfranchised communities. The goal of the project was to "build on rather than tear down what students bring" (Nieto, 2000, p. 356). We made efforts to recognize and validate students as cosmopolitan intellectuals (Campano & Ghiso, 2011) who have knowledge derived from their own transnational and transcultural experiences that is often unutilized in traditional educational settings. We believed youth's complex identities could be mobilized in the literacy curriculum and serve as interpretive lenses through which to develop their own conceptual understandings of the world, including how power operates to sustain inequality (e.g., Campano, 2007; Moya, 2002). Their lived experiences were a profound intellectual resource, fostering organic forms of critical literacy (Campano, Ghiso, & Sánchez, 2013), where criticality derives not solely from the teacher or official curriculum but from students' daily struggles and community legacies as well. Each student's identity—a constellation of intersectionalities shaped by race, ethnicity, gender, immigration, and class—informed his or her research interests.

The CRP reminded us that care and love are the foundations for critical work. One of the most humbling validations of our partnership came from the fact that parents were even willing to give up their children's time in their normal Sunday School schedule—which plays an invaluable role in cultural and community sustenance—to allow them to work with us. Bethany speculated that this was because we had spent years demonstrating our care for the children through initiatives such as the PennPal project, Family Literacy Night, and the parents' action research project around high school admissions. Additionally, the project's roots in parents' desire to address the CCSS also weighed in on their decision. As we hope will become clear as we share Martin's example, the youth showed care for each other, their elders, their teachers, and the larger community. We believe this commitment to one another is why they decided to spend a large portion of their Sundays engaged in research.

Patricia Hill Collins (2000) argues that an "ethic of caring" often serves to validate knowledge and to spark coalitional strength. Expressiveness, emotion, and empathy are key to equitable relationships as they cultivate the trust required to share difficult, often silenced, stories. Philosopher María Lugones (2003) has argued that it is through traversing and negotiating multiple social worlds, or what she calls "'world'-traveling," that individuals from minoritized backgrounds may better understand shared experiences of oppression and thus more effectively work in coalition against injustices. For Lugones, loving perception is cultivated through embracing a multiplicity of identities and experiences. Genuine solidarity does not try to subsume or homogenize difference but is rather forged through difference. As Lugones (1992) discusses, when we see care in everyday actions and relationships as anti-oppressive work, we can break from dominant discourses that frame people as helplessly enmeshed in oppression and, instead, view them as agents of change. By sharing their insights in congress with one another, communities may be able to see their cumulative power and their potential for coalitional action.

Researchers have also highlighted the role of care in children's education, beginning by deconstructing romanticized notions of affection and emphasizing the "political and ideological dimensions of caring and love" (Bartolomé, 2008, p. 2). When care for students is undergirded by deficit assumptions about their capacities, it can result in subtractive schooling; conversely, within culturally responsive contexts, care is an essential dimension of more liberatory pedagogies (Beauboeuf-Lafontant, 2002; Valenzuela, 1999). Immigrant families and youth may already bring notions of care into classrooms as part of their own funds of knowledge (González et al., 2005). For example, in Latina cultures, the concept of education itself is entwined with *cariño* (care, affection) and *respeto* (respect) (Valdés, 1996). These cultural values are reflected in, and inform, students' language and literacy practices. Ghiso (2016) describes how young Latina/o children engaged in care work to support their families in out-of-school contexts such as the Laundromat, and once in school extended this ethos to their teachers and peers. This participation across neighborhood spaces and the classroom context was mediated by transactions with (and creation of) multilingual, multimodal texts. In out-of-school spaces like St. Thomas Aquinas, literacies can be coalitional:

> critical social practices whereby community members use language and literacy across cultural boundaries in order to learn from others, be reflective of one's own social location, foster empathy, cultivate affective bonds, and promote inclusion in the service of progressive change. (Campano et al., 2013, p. 315)

The work of these feminist scholars and many others is a reminder of the various forms of social cooperation and activism already present in communities. Resistance and care need not be thought of in opposition; rather, care and love are the foundation on which diverse people make common cause. In design and in action, the CRP invited youth to engage in intellectual inquiry in a noncompetitive and nurturing environment.

RESEARCHING FROM THE REALITIES OF THEIR LIVES

Though we brought a critical orientation to our teaching, throughout the CRP we tried to avoid striking a high-pitched rhetoric. We were wary of telling the youth what to think and, following Juan Guerra's (2004) caution, reproducing a transmission model of criticality. We were also sensitive to the fact that many of the immigrant and refugee parents at St. Thomas Aquinas might be skeptical about overly strident language, given many of their own experiences with violence, war, and even genocide. We hoped that the books we chose would increase the pool of hermeneutical resources (Fricker, 2007) through which the youth might name and research topics that mattered to them. We followed students' leads, and our inquiry stance attuned us to moments when we could pursue critical questions.

As our own relationships with the students deepened, their inquiries began to reflect the realities of their lives: For example, one student examined the lack of healthy food options in her neighborhood; two students researched friendships and how to navigate the social dynamic of school; and two others scrutinized the effects of illness and problems with accessing adequate health care in their families (see Campano, Ngo, & Player, 2015). By making themselves a bit vulnerable, the youth connected their own subjective experiences to the objective social conditions that produce social stratification. These research topics began to reveal inequities. We sought to provide a space where care and sociality were valued as intellectually and politically important. This caring ethos became the foundation for learning from each other and engaging in critique. In the sections that follow, we describe how Martin, motivated by an ethics of care, mined the curricular invitations of the CRP to examine the educational crisis in city schools. Looking closely at Martin's story provides a rich example of how students researched their communities and engaged in care-based social action.

"A WOUND ON OUR EDUCATION SYSTEM": MARTIN'S DOCUMENTARY INQUIRY

Martin, as a high school sophomore, was the oldest student in the CRP and the one who most clearly adopted an activist identity. He joined our group having already been involved in youth organizing to protest what he and many of his peers had characterized as an assault on public education. One project Martin was in the midst of was a documentary he was producing and directing with a friend on the "Doomsday Budget Cuts" in Philadelphia. The CRP provided a space for Martin to learn about research methodology, receive feedback on his ideas, and eventually facilitate a series of conversations about the state of education in his city to a range of audiences. In the process, Martin began to more fully realize his role as an organic and public intellectual (Gramsci, 1971), speaking truth to power on behalf of his community, which he defined expansively as "your surroundings, your city, your neighbors . . . the people you live with, the people you interact with and the people who you go to work with on a daily basis or go to school with" (Interview, June 15, 2014). Martin mobilized his and others' perspectives in a collective statement about the importance of education in a participatory democracy.

Martin's documentary came during a particularly contentious period in the politics of education in Philadelphia, and in the CRP the youth expressed their ongoing grievances about the educational injustices they perceived, citing examples such as overcrowded classrooms and overemphasis on testing over substantive learning. In 2001, the district had been placed under state control (Rieser, 2003), and a Declaration of Distress signed by the education secretary led to "the formation of a School Reform Commission [SRC] to oversee the troubled public school system" (Clowes, 2002). Many educators were concerned about the lack of a locally elected school board, given that three of the five members of the SRC were appointed by the governor and the other two were appointed by the mayor. In the summer of 2013, just before the official start of the CRP, 4,000 layoff notices were sent to district staff members, including teachers and counselors (Jablow, 2013). During the spring semester of the CRP, the SRC voted to close 24 schools, which, as mentioned in Chapter 4, affected numerous families at St. Thomas Aquinas. The district "lost" $300 million in state funding (the *Notebook*, Jablow, 2013)—a fact that led Martin to name his documentary "The Doomsday Budget Cuts in Philadelphia."

Martin's film powerfully critiqued this undermining of the public school system. He eloquently explained the purpose of his project:

I just want to express how these cuts really drastically hurt these schools, and I want to show to the SRC and Superintendent [name redacted], and [the governor], that what they did, it left a wound on our education system in Philadelphia. (Interview, June 26, 2014)

Martin is explicit about his social justice stance and is not shy about placing blame. His poster for his research presentation (see Figure 8.1) depicts planes, engraved with the names of various politicians, bombing the beleaguered city school district. In his representation, he identifies the human cost obscured by euphemistic policy abstractions such as "budget cuts" and labels specific school communities that were directly impacted. The image calls to mind Ralph Ellison's quote, "Hey Man, there's real people down here" (cited in Long, 1986, p. 183), people impacted by these top-down political decisions too often made by those in power who most likely do not send their own children to city public schools, much less the ones that are being closed down. Martin's research privileges the perspectives of the actual people "down here"—parents, youth, children, and educators—whose lives were upended by a neoliberal educational agenda.

In the concluding segment of the documentary, Martin begins to discern the underlying logic that subtends various injustices, as well as how the situation might be remedied:

Figure 8.1. Martin's Representation of the "Doomsday Budget Cuts"

[My] high school and other Philadelphia public schools currently re-main proud and resilient although put in a serious disadvantage in comparison to other schools. Many battles have been and are being fought to get public schools in Philadelphia the money that they need. The students and faculty in the district have united in the fight against the School Reform Commission and [the governor]. We have come a long way, but much more needs to be done. The school district needs a fair funding formula. Citizens of Philadelphia should be able to elect members of the SRC and not have them chosen. The state should pri-oritize education over the construction of prisons, like the planned $400 million super prison. We need to balance the financial backing for all schools, which will in turn let the education and students of public schools prosper. (Documentary excerpt)

Martin calls attention to the collective efforts that characterize the fight for educational equity and provides a concrete vision for reform. He displays an emerging understanding of how a coalition is forged through identifying the links between various forms of social subordination. Mar-tin juxtaposes the attenuation of public education with the windfall in-vestment in criminal (in)justice. It is not conspiratorial to suggest that the miseducation of youth provides the human fodder for the Prison Industrial Complex (Alexander, 2010), a profit-making enterprise whose explosive growth, exemplified by a "$400 million super prison," exists in an inverse relationship to the prosperity of public schools and students.

Through an ethics of care, Martin highlights the ways these financial constraints affected teachers' lives and livelihood, their ability to do their jobs, and by extension the opportunities afforded to students:

> About 3,700 teachers lost their jobs, both teachers and faculty. They lost their jobs. Students are now working in overcrowded classes. Teachers can't have a one-to-one talk to another student without affecting all the other students, and it's piling in a lot in one classroom, and the teacher can't really single out activities to like modify certain students because he or she will have to accommodate all now. . . . And teachers have less time to prep . . . I feel like students, they can't have that quality of education that they had in their middle school years or during their elementary school years because now, like at for example [my school], we only have two counselors. Then they're always busy with seniors, and so anyone else who wants to talk to them can't really talk. They got to wait their turn in line. (Interview, June 26, 2014)

Martin's comments add nuance to the research literature on youth oppositional identities in education (e.g., Ogbu, 1987). Martin and his peers are not oppositional to schools and teachers per se. Instead, they resisted a system that dehumanizes both educators and students and, through multimodal projects like the film, worked toward fostering empathy across these roles, acknowledging solidarity and mutual care as an essential element of resistance. Martin's analysis of systemic inequities moves beyond symptomatic personal dramas that are too often the focus of "urban education." His statements depict the ways in which teachers' and students' experiences are interwoven—teachers feel the impact of overcrowded classes and diminished time for preparation as much as the youth who are trying to learn in these under-resourced contexts. Martin also underscores the importance of counselors who might talk to students—the relational and nurturing dimension of education that is gendered as "soft," a frill that might easily be downsized or eliminated in schools.

The production of the documentary itself also embodied care and solidarity. Martin cowrote and codirected the documentary with another student; several teachers from his high school were interviewed and filmed; he incorporated knowledge that arose from his conversations with others; he worked alongside members of the CRP to produce an illustrated interpretation of the budget cuts (see Figure 8.1); and he shared the documentary with different audiences, such as schoolmates, teachers, families involved in the CRP, the broader St. Thomas Aquinas community, and the audience at the Penn Ethnography Forum, which included families, academics, teachers, and graduate students. These varied spectators engaged Martin in dialogue about the findings he presented and expressed their own concerns about the state of education. At the Ethnography Forum, several university faculty and students voiced appreciation for his work. One attendee noted the overlaps between the students' inquiries and research being carried out in the academy, while another commented on the importance of student perspectives, noting, "So often we come to events like this and people talk *about* youth, and we don't really get to hear from you. But to hear from you in such a way and see all the complicated questions that you are developing in your research means a lot to us" (Transcript, February 28, 2015).

In discussing the rationale for this documentary, Martin noted, "I feel that my voice is too small to impact, but together as a community . . . together as a school, collaborated and spread out a word that we could have more impact there" (Interview, June 26, 2014). Martin expresses a humility that challenges notions of the individual leader in activist movements and of the individual academic carrying out research and instead connects social change to working alongside others toward a common cause. Freire (1998) writes,

> Humility requires courage, self-confidence, self-respect, and respect for others. Humility helps us to understand this obvious truth: No one knows it all; no one is ignorant of everything. We all know something; we are all ignorant of something. (p. 39)

Martin's research is animated by multiple voices, all of which carry important knowledge about educational conditions in his city. He adopts a sense of humility that entails, following Freire, both "self-respect" for what one knows as well as "respect for others" and what they might have to teach us.

Martin orchestrates various viewpoints—those of teachers, students, and parents—which are often framed in opposition to one another in public discourse. The testimonials and collective efforts he showcases provide reason for hope and evidence that teachers and students show concern and empathy for one another amid the fiscal violence done to schools. Martin himself was a high-performing student attending a well-regarded institution, and he had less to gain than others from critiquing a system that he had been able to navigate successfully. Learning from the experiences of those he interviewed through his research, however, helped Martin cultivate a critical stance. Martin's care for others expanded his breadth of inquiry and resulted in a comprehensive and humanizing picture of public education in his city, including how it might be changed for the better.

INTERGENERATIONAL CARE

While the multimodal products created as part of the CRP explicitly illustrate Martin's social justice stance, there were also more subtle ways in which Martin embodied this ideal. Against the backdrop of a high-stakes testing paradigm informed by individualistic ideologies and meritocratic ideologies, the CRP provided a space for youth to engage in mutually supportive practices. Martin was one of the quiet leaders in building and sustaining this caring community.

One of Martin's primary networks was the Indonesian parishoners at St. Thomas Aquinas, whose members have seen it as their duty to work with one another to help young people access educational opportunities. As described in Chapter 3, the Indonesian parents created processes for sharing information about the various hurdles within the education system and pooled resources for overcoming them. Martin played a valuable role in this web of support. Through his involvement with Indonesian elders, he was attuned to the reasons the families left their previous country as well as their current struggles surviving in the United States. At the same time, Martin himself is a product of the city's public schools. This enabled to him to serve as an intergenerational cultural broker between the Indonesian parents and the younger generations, just one more example of his "world"-traveling (Lugones, 2003) and facility for thinking across social boundaries. Martin heard about the CRP from the Indonesian parents and families. Although he was not initially invited to join us because he was older than the other students, he nonetheless approached the research team to request permission to participate. By availing himself of connections from the Indonesian community, Martin found a supportive environment in which to pursue and deepen his interest in educational justice, gaining additional skills (such as qualitative research methodologies) he could add to his intellectual and activist repertoires.

As Martin benefited from the support of community elders, he, in turn, carried on this legacy of care in his relationships with the younger students. Martin became a mentor or older brother figure in the group; students looked to him for guidance in their research as well as in their lives more generally. In informal conversations while working on their projects, the younger students expressed their anxieties about high schools and the looming admissions process. As someone who had already made this transition, the youth turned to Martin for advice. He shared anecdotes of his experiences, from the practical to the philosophical, helping to demystify a complex system, providing insights on how to navigate it, and affirming the younger students' feelings. Because of the nature of Martin's research in the CRP, the other members of the group were privy to the difficult conditions of the school district. At the same time, Martin's caring mentorship helped mitigate these realities, keeping them from feeling deterministic. Alongside gaining critical consciousness about the problems of the system, the youth became aware of the myriad of caring people, from older peers like Martin to community elders to the teachers he featured in his documentary, who were working daily to make things better.

MOVING FORWARD TOGETHER

Coalitional work is neither straightforward nor easy, and over the course of the CRP, we noticed dissonances that would go on to inform our future work. For instance, although all students shared immigrant backgrounds, two came from Latina/o families while the rest were of Indonesian descent. The relationships between the Latina/o and Indonesian students did not become as close as the bonds that already existed within each of the cultural groups. Additionally, age and gender at times resulted in subgroupings within the CRP. Cherríe Moraga (1983) stresses that a coalition across difference is not automatic; it is something that builds over time and requires trust. We stress here that *time* is crucial to this trust building. The Indonesian youth had spent years together in Sunday School, and the Latina/o children, who had grown up together because their parents were friends and neighbors, were new to the larger group. Thus, it was not surprising that the youth felt most comfortable turning to members of their own cultural communities for insights on their research. The culminating event of the Ethnography Forum, however, seemed to strengthen cross-cultural bonds as parents and children from the different groups met one another, younger siblings played together, and the community researchers presented topics with which nearly everyone could relate. As we continue with the partnership, we hope to provide time and space for fostering new relationships and strengthening emergent ones. We must also be mindful that there are times when being in the company of those who share a particular background can lead to inquiries that may not occur in heterogeneous contexts. For example, the observations about gendered groupings in the CRP and the concerns and issues raised by the young women is informing a new girls-of-color writing group facilitated by Grace, where female students might feel more at ease inquiring into gender dynamics.

The day of the Ethnography Forum, we were delighted by the turnout of families who came to show support for their children's work. With 15 caregivers and siblings, as well as university students, Philadelphia teachers, and out-of-town conference attendees, the room was packed. The CRP youth took turns presenting their research and findings. During the question-and-answer session following the viewing of Martin's film, his documentary partner indicated their plans to continue the work:

> One thing that we'd like to do is update it, because, I mean, this documentary we made last year. And clearly things have changed. So certain things have changed and we'd argue are on the up and up. Our documentary certainly had a rather negative connotation. And we think if we were to update it, it'd have a more positive connotation. And let people know how things have been going. (Transcript, February 28, 2015)

This comment reminds us that critical projects need not stop at documenting injustices and oppressions, of which there are many, but should also focus on community agency. The film both captured and, in its production, helped cultivate solidarity among teachers and students as they united against public school budget cuts. While the struggle is by no means over, significant coalitional organizing has been taking place, with educators, youth, and families joining together to protest closings and agitate for change, and a turnover in city leadership focusing on fair funding and on restoring financial supports to public schools. Duncan-Andrade (2009) makes the case that teaching should be hopeful as well as critical, "connect[ing] the moral outrage of young people to actions that relieve the undeserved suffering in their communities" (p. 182). Martin and his documentary partner remind us that nurturing such "long-term, sustainable, critical hope" (Duncan-Andrade, 2009, p. 182) is a bidirectional process—just as educators inspire students to channel their rightful indignation into projects for change, so too can they learn from youth and community members about hopeful actions already taking root in local soil.

Once the conference presentation was over, the families all wanted to come upstairs to visit Gerald's office and to meet his and María Paula's infant daughter. They knew it had been a difficult pregnancy and had been asking for frequent updates about the baby's health. Each parent posed for pictures with the family, and they brought a gift for Gabriela—a snuggly outfit to keep her warm in the long months of an especially frigid winter. The more than 100 photos they took at the event reminded us that care, too, is a reciprocal commitment in university–community partnerships that nourishes sustained collective projects for change.

Chapter 9

Ethical and Professional Norms in Community-Based Research

Thank you for the help, support, *cariño* [care, affection], time, and much teaching that you have brought us. I have learned a lot about all the experiences that each person has shared. Hopefully this can continue for a long time because we all need each other and if the communication continues we can better our future and of course give a better education to our children. (Translated from Spanish)

—A Latina leader, commenting on the partnership

Throughout our partnership with St. Thomas Aquinas, we have been grappling with how to create more egalitarian research processes that honor the questions, forms of knowledge, and interests of participants. Power asymmetries between universities and community contexts have been well documented, and these are especially exacerbated when universities work with groups whose knowledge and experiences have historically been devalued (Harkavy & Hartley, 2009, 2012; Warren, 2005). But it is also important to note that the community and the university are not homogenous entities with unified perspectives themselves. For example, members of our research team have been from a range of culturally and linguistically minoritized backgrounds and have families that share affinities with a lot of the parishioners. The leadership of both the Aquinas center and the church, who have been on the ground cultivating relationships and working in solidarity with community members, are European Americans serving predominantly parishioners of color. The Church as an institution has a history of both supporting colonized communities but also perpetuating missionary ideologies. Although few of the parishioners are affluent, they come from a range of class backgrounds and also have important differences with respect to immigration status. Across their varied positionings, everyone has agency, power, knowledge, and expertise. Despite the multiplicity of identities and experiences, which could at times be a source of tension, participants in the research collaboration have attempted to live by the ideal articulated by Michael Hames-García (2011) that "one's people are those with whom we make common cause" (p. xv).

Given the complexity of research relationships and in order to build a foundation for collaborative work, it has been important to establish certain ethical and professional norms for the partnership. The norms, which we describe in this chapter, are not meant to be prescriptive. They may serve as a reminder that all school and community-based educational research is governed by assumptions regarding how we view and engage others, whether or not they are made visible. We hope that by articulating ethical and professional norms in our own community-based research we will inspire others who are thinking through what it means to create collaborative knowledge projects geared toward shared visions of social justice in their own contexts, including university partnerships with schools, neighborhood centers, activist organizations, and faith communities. These local inquiries may collectively contribute to broader intellectual conversations that seek to (re)imagine education for a participatory and pluralistic democracy.

DEVELOPING NORMS:
WORKING THE DIALECTIC OF THEORY AND PRACTICE

Although we had been thinking about the nuances of conducting respectful and ethical research for some time, our norms emerged from the partnership itself. We found that even among the university-based faculty and graduate students there was a range of understandings about what constitutes community-based research. There were different perspectives on what community involvement entailed (from participating in predesigned research to being involved in formulating the research process throughout), which became apparent when explaining our collaboration to community members. There was also a sense that the research process was being rushed without having established adequate trust. At times, team members expressed views that positioned minoritized and immigrant communities as lacking critical awareness or interpretive agency about their own lives and experiences. These varying assumptions manifested themselves in our day-to-day engagements at St. Thomas Aquinas, conveying contradictory messages regarding our vision for the research.

What surfaced as a dissonance in our practice of partnering became an opportunity to articulate, within a community of inquiry, a stance and working ideal toward community-based research in the form of the norms we share in this chapter. The development of the norms took shape from "working the dialectic" of theory and practice, which Cochran-Smith and Lytle (2007) characterize as "the reciprocal, recursive, and symbiotic relationships of research and practice, analysis and action, inquiry and experience, theorizing and doing" (p. 31). We grounded the construction of these norms in problems of practice and our situated interpretive lenses, including the theoretical traditions that have informed our scholarship. We drew on these influences in reciprocal and recursive ways to help us better understand and respond to the complexities and dissonances we were encountering at St. Thomas Aquinas.

By *norms* we mean to make explicit a set of guidelines that affirm our shared vision of a university–community research partnership. They serve as a touchstone that guides collaboration through specific practices and policies that become normalized. Norms, of course, may change or be revised, ideally through ongoing participatory inquiry that takes into account new experiences and the evolving input of interested parties, in particular from those most directly impacted by or invested in the research. *Professional* signals that community-based research and community organizing, sometimes overlapping endeavors, require a specialized theoretical and practical knowledge base that informs "responsible, wise, and selfless" judgment for the betterment of a greater good in the face of "the ubiquitous condition of uncertainty, novelty, and unpredictability" (Gardner & Shulman, 2005, pp. 14–15).

Our use of *ethical* follows recent trends in critical theory that make a distinction between ethics and morality. As Culler (2011) notes, "Moral principles lay claim to universality but can often be shown to be a result of class interest, historical circumstances, cultural tradition, and even self-interest" (p. 122). *Ethics,* by contrast, emphasize the situated nature of deliberation and evaluative judgment and concerns one's relationship to and engagement with others (Levinas, 1969), often across social boundaries. An ethical orientation to research therefore strives to build in a self-reflexive component throughout every stage of the inquiry process, which entails participants considering how they may be superimposing and universalizing their own principles and interests onto others. With this awareness also comes the need to take seriously others' perspectives, concerns, and well-being. Centering ethics in research collaborations prioritizes how we engage with, learn from, and coexist with others.

We believe that the relational labor involved in fostering empathy and inclusivity is compatible with the scholarly virtue of knowledge production and supports, rather than compromises, our roles as researchers. A number of scholars have cogently argued that a diversity of perspectives is an epistemic precondition for inquiry into human good and a deeper understanding of our shared social worlds (e.g., J. Medina, 2013; S. Mohanty, 1997; Nussbaum, 2008). An acknowledgment of our interdependence and sociality corrects dominant ideologies of the neutral individual researcher who imposes a singular interpretation. Rather than seeing ourselves as dispassionate outside critics and explicators, we recognize that we invariably bring our own identities into our research sites (e.g., Lather, 1986) and that we are constantly engaged in the hermeneutics of learning from and alongside differentially situated others whose own cultural and experiential horizons inform our interpretive processes (Alcoff, 2006).

CURRENT ETHICAL AND PROFESSIONAL RESEARCH NORMS

The norms developed through the ongoing dialogue among the university research team and community members. They are not the result of a linear and bounded process (the way, e.g., a mission statement might be forged) and are always open to revision and refinement. As new projects take shape, we ask community members for their perspectives about university involvement, both in formal meetings and through informal conversations. We also wanted the norms to be theoretically grounded and part of, not ancillary to, our research methodology. Informed by our data, we began putting these down on paper and bringing them to several leadership committees at St. Thomas Aquinas and to individual community members, all of whom commented on, revised, and added to the norms.

We share the ethical and professional norms of our research with the caveat that they represent a work in progress, an attempt to capture our current thinking. As the research project evolves, with new perspectives included and new tensions identified, our inquiry into the norms will continue and, hopefully, deepen. While we detail them below as distinct, we have found that the norms mutually reinforce one another.

Norm 1: View Equality As the Starting Point, Not the End Point

The phrase "equality is the starting point, not the endpoint," borrowed from the philosopher Jacques Rancière (2004), has at least two relevant valences. First is the presumption that equality ought to be an "initial axiom" (Rancière, 2004, p. 223) in our relationships with all members of the community. This means, for example, that just because a person may be struggling economically, may be an English language learner, or may have little formal education, in the larger picture this should not compromise his or her capacity to be or become a theorist, teacher, leader, or researcher. We strive to view everyone as equally intelligent and remain vigilant against the impulse to circumscribe others' capacities. The second related valence is that this type of equality is not merely a goal for some nebulous future once injustices are remedied but a day-to-day social practice that might govern every aspect of our methodological approach.

One way we have tried to enact the presumption of equality was through the formation of a committee called the Education and Research Group (EaR), composed of ourselves and volunteers from the various cultural and linguistic communities at St. Thomas Aquinas. The formation of the EaR group resulted from a problem of practice. We desired a systematic and transparent way to relay what we were doing in order to remain attentive to the concerns and insights of community members, solicit feedback on ongoing projects, and prevent ourselves from imposing a preconceived agenda.

After our initial meetings, we noted that too much of our time together was devoted to university-based researchers reporting what we were doing, which reproduced existing hierarchies of knowledge. We realized that we needed to change the nature of the EaR group to treat members as intellectual equals—so that everyone on the committee helped conceptualize the research, germinate new ideas for the partnership, and provide critical feedback. Members of the EaR group communicated with other parish members about the collaboration and solicited their insights, such as through meetings of the various cultural groups or digital communications like electronic mailing lists or Facebook pages.

Another way we understand the norm of equality is as a form of horizontalism, or *horizontalidad*, a concept that is linked to the resistance movements that formed in Argentina after the economic collapse of 2001 (Sitrin, 2006). In the absence of a functional government, people organized into neighborhood assemblies and recuperated workplaces to adopt processes of direct democracy that eschewed hierarchical, or more vertical, forms of political participation and authority. In a similar way, St. Thomas Aquinas community members and university partners come together in a repurposed church space to address issues that affect them and aspire to more egalitarian relationships. There are many examples of horizontal practices at St. Thomas Aquinas. One is the way in which community members rotate leadership positions; a person may be in charge of a Sunday School program one year and the next year join the EaR committee, relinquishing previous responsibilities to a young adult in the youth group. Through sharing their findings on inquiries relevant to their lives, Indonesian and Latina/o middle school students in the Community Researchers Project educated parish elders and university students about problems impacting the neighborhood. Members of the university research team, in turn, have joined numerous parish committees, helped organize events (e.g., a health fair), and assisted local leaders and students in creating a community garden.

The roles participants take on are, to some degree, fluid and not exhaustively determined by job and educational background, enabling opportunities for individuals to cultivate new intellectual, creative, and leadership capacities. Engaging in horizontal processes, however, does not presuppose leveling everyone into the same fungible categories or eliding differences. As Alcoff (2012) observes, "Aiming merely to neutralize all differences, rather than acknowledge them, means that we cannot take advantage of the positive epistemic possibilities that differences can sometimes provide" (p. 270). As our next norm indicates, equality also necessitates honoring and learning from the range of individuals' experiences and expertise.

Norm 2: Take Seriously Community Members' Knowledge and Perspectives

The presumption of equality as the starting point is particularly important when working with members of historically disenfranchised communities who may experience what Fricker (2007) has characterized as "systematic identity prejudice," whereby someone is discredited in their capacity as a knowledge generator "owing to some feature of their social identity" (p. 28). Because of the intersections of race, social class, language difference, gender, and immigration status that exist in contemporary society, many community members at St. Thomas Aquinas may be likely to experience identity prejudice and thus be more vulnerable to research and service relationships that discount their perspectives.

Our second norm suggests that it may not be sufficient to merely neutralize bias and identity prejudice. Educational research committed to social justice ought to go a step further and recognize that many community members are in a unique position to analyze inequality because of their minoritized identities and experiences, which constitutes an epistemic privilege (Moya, 2002). Alcoff (2006) makes the case that "social identity is relevant to epistemic judgment . . . not because identity determines judgment but because identity can in some instances yield access to perceptual facts that themselves may be relevant to the formulation of various knowledge claims or theoretical analyses" (p. 43). At St. Thomas Aquinas, many of the community members live in social precarity, and they face poverty, lack of adequate health care, deportations, linguistic stigma, and school closings. A number of them also have knowledge derived from their roles as local organizers, activists, leaders, and educators who are dedicated to changing the conditions that produce precarity. Their judgment with respect to these inequalities is an invaluable intellectual resource. For example, like many Latina/o youth and families at St. Thomas Aquinas, Francisco, the middle school student featured in Chapter 5, has firsthand knowledge about being undocumented and consequently about the importance of human rights that are not tethered to national citizenship. These are issues that many middle-class Americans born in the country may never have to consider. Francisco also has knowledge derived from attending a religious school and serving as a parish altar boy. He is able to pair these experiences to discern and take action around social issues, joining a long-standing American intellectual legacy, perhaps going back to Frederick Douglass, of invoking the Bible to argue for human equality and liberation.

Unfortunately, the very perspectives that are germane to social justice inquiries are often excluded in traditional research approaches. Part of what makes our partnership so edifying is that the diverse participants potentially supply many vantage points from which to interpret social inequality and imagine alternatives. Learning from community members' knowledge and recognizing their epistemic privilege is a stance we strive to uphold throughout every aspect of our partnership. Within a multiethnic, multilingual context, this ideal requires ongoing reflection about whose perspectives are being included and whose are being left out. Such contemplation occurs through a range of processes, including respectfully soliciting the viewpoints of community members who may feel apprehension about speaking up, deliberately incorporating opportunities to elicit differences of opinion into research meetings, and being attuned to how what we hear and observe at St. Thomas Aquinas may (or may not) be reflected in the research process.

An example of how we have attempted to take into account the perspectives of community members is our involvement with the Concerned Black Catholics. One prevalent church narrative highlights the role of progressive priests in creating a welcoming atmosphere for new immigrants, and much of our own research has involved inquiries about the immigration experience as related to the church's mission and discursive practices. The president of the CBC made us aware that this focus on immigration left out the perspectives of the Black community, and so Bethany and students from a service learning course at a local college launched the South Philly Story Project to address this omission. Through this research initiative, undergraduate university students worked with the CBC to design interviews and collect oral histories of its group members. Bethany facilitated this inquiry and arranged for the students to meet CBC members at one of their homes over a meal, where the African American women shared their experiences of growing up and raising families in the neighborhood. This initial gathering led to a more systematic documentation and inclusion of CBC members' perspectives.

Through the South Philly Story Project we gained insights into the role that African American women in the neighborhood played in making St. Thomas Aquinas a more integrated and pluralistic environment. By helping to desegregate the parish, they also contributed to creating an atmosphere that would make St. Thomas Aquinas more welcoming to refugee and immigrant families of color. These narratives may have been missing in some accounts of the church's history and its stance of inclusivity. The epistemic privilege of CBC members aids in historicizing the struggle for inclusion within local legacies of activism and provides a more comprehensive understanding of the factors that have contributed to the parish's mission to promote diversity and intercultural cooperation. We first witnessed cooperation and expressions of solidarity across cultural groups at the Know Your Rights workshop described in Chapter 1, when members of the Indonesian immigrant community commented on the human rights links between their situation and those of African Americans and Latina/os. While our research supports the ideals of solidarity and learning from others' experiences, it is worth noting that parishioners at St. Thomas Aquinas have been drawing on the multiple perspectives of the neighborhood—long before our involvement—to better understand the complex social space they share.

Recognizing community members' knowledge counters dominant tendencies in some research traditions to treat them merely as informants, data sources, or deliverable constituencies who provide details to be interpreted by others—what Fricker (2007) characterizes as a form of "epistemic objectification." These instrumental framings can position community members as the raw material for theorizing rather than as epistemic agents and partners in research and activism. It has become clear to us that a necessary component of building trust and solidarity in community-based research involves everyone feeling as if the authority of their experiences is being honored and that each person has something to teach, as well as learn from, others.

Norm 3: Codesign Specific Research Foci and Questions with Community Members

As researchers, we invariably bring to St. Thomas Aquinas our own broad interests, including a desire to understand how families cooperate across social boundaries to advocate for their children's education and immigrant rights. We shared our interests with community members from the very beginning, such as in Parish Council meetings. Before initiating any research, however, members of the university research team spent 9 months at St. Thomas Aquinas developing relationships and supporting the community with its own projects, including sponsoring a picnic for the Indonesian and Vietnamese youth and a Family Literacy Night. Throughout this period and continuing to the present, we have engaged in innumerable conversations with community members and learned about educational issues that matter to them and their own desires for the research partnership. It is the ongoing creative alchemy between the interests and resources we university researchers bring to St. Thomas Aquinas and those of the community participants that shapes the design of our research collaborations and the questions we investigate together.

At St. Thomas Aquinas, the codesign of research has taken different forms. For example, as detailed in Chapter 3, Mary and Karim from the university research team and a group of Indonesian parents have been investigating how immigrant and refugee families can support their children's education, with a particular focus on high school admissions. The inquiry focus was collectively determined, and families gathered data, distilled themes and insights, and shared findings with the larger Aquinas community. One aforementioned challenge of the participatory research design was the deference to authority that some community members conveyed to university students and faculty. Mary and Karim resisted tendencies to position themselves and be positioned as the ones possessing all the knowledge, and eventually a number of parents took a leadership role in the research process and in conceptualizing its direction.

Another example of how this norm was enacted involved our collaboration with members of St. Thomas Aquinas's Latina/o community. María Paula and Alicia, both native Spanish speakers, reached out to families and leaders regarding their goals for a possible collaboration, and based on their input co-constructed the language and literacy class described in Chapter 4. They conducted the class bilingually so that Latina/o families could together determine the topics to be explored and the nature of the curricular activities. For both the Indonesian and Latina/o parents, codesigning the research proved to be beneficial in that the synergy of interests, desires, and resources helped propel it forward and, in the process, nurtured trust.

Norm 4: Have Research Benefit the Community

Debates about the nature, role, and quality of research are prevalent in the educational literature. Hostetler (2005) argues that determining what "good" research is requires a consideration of the ethical as well as the methodological: "Education research is a matter not only of sound procedures but also of beneficial aims and results" with the "ultimate aim . . . to serve people's well-being—the well-being of students, teachers, communities, and others" (p. 17). These concerns, Hostetler argues, are not typically foregrounded in institutions of higher education. For instance, academic contexts place emphasis on explications of methodological rigor for processes of research approval, publication, and performance review. Similarly, community-based organizations may rely on funding sources that require particular types of measurable "outcomes." However, a number of alternative theoretical and methodological traditions have striven to enact research practices that not only benefit the field in an abstract sense but also positively impact the lived experiences of community members as they themselves see it (e.g., Lather, 1986). These orientations include, but are not limited to, practitioner research (Cochran-Smith & Lytle, 1999, 2009) and participatory action research (Cahill, 2007; Cammarota & Fine, 2008; Kemmis & McTaggart, 2005; Morrell, 2006), which aim to situate inquiry within processes that honor the needs and interests of all involved.

There is a range of ways that our research has contributed to the St. Thomas Aquinas community. Some benefits involved joint research where community members identify questions to be answered and then carry out these investigations through data collection, analysis, dissemination, and action, a participatory process we have engaged in with both youth and adults, such as the inquiry with Indonesian parents (Chapter 3) and the Community Researchers Project (Chapter 8). Another type of benefit, which is exemplified in the Comics Inquiry Community described in Chapter 7, may entail providing spaces for children to participate in reading and writing practices that tap into their multiple literacies and out-of-school interests. We have also documented in our fieldnotes some benefits of research that may have been less tangible, such as community members adopting new roles, building connections with individuals from different cultural groups, enjoying the company of others, or cultivating new intellectual or creative potentials. For example, Pamela, one of the Latina mothers shared with us how the family ESOL class (Chapter 4) provided a respite, a place where she could connect with others and have fun despite the duress she was feeling due to immigration policies, racism, and financial constraints. By drawing on her bilingual knowledge and her experiences of living in the area for more than 10 years, Pamela was also able to take on a leadership role in the class, helping recently arrived mothers navigate the educational system, teaching them specific language structures to accomplish this, and encouraging her peers to advocate for their rights.

Irrespective of the aspirations of the various collaborative projects we undertook at St. Thomas Aquinas, we agreed that they all needed to have a sense from the start of how research can contribute to the well-being of the community and its individual members. Doctoral students who plan to engage in dissertation research at St. Thomas Aquinas propose their ideas at our EaR group and articulate what they envision to be the benefits of their particular project. This dialogical process—a community-based comple-ment to the university review board—provides structured opportunities for community members to ask questions, weigh in on possible benefits and risks of the research, and offer suggestions for changes. In preparation, doc-toral students create a handout describing the background of a project and its benefits, which pushes them to condense lengthy dissertation proposals into key points. Presenting to the EaR group allows students to discuss their plans directly with community members at the site, thereby prevent-ing the objectification of participants and counteracting the academic ten-dency to think about abstract scholarly contributions to the exclusion of more immediate benefits to those involved in a study.

According to David, speaking with the EaR group encouraged him to ask critical questions, such as how he may have been obscuring his ideas with jargon that might alienate families. Robert received invaluable advice about talking with a respected Vietnamese elder in the community before he proceeded with his research. Gerald and María Paula were reminded that community members' schedules do not conform to the academic cal-endar. Such processes of transparency and dialogue become opportunities to think alongside one another, be self-reflexive about our respective social locations, and build shared investments. These feedback mechanisms help ensure that our approach to research considers the ethics of who benefits and how and sets a foundation of dialogue so that if concerns arise they can be addressed respectfully, directly, and collaboratively.

Norm 5: Make Research Public in Transparent, Collaborative, and Creative Ways

Research is often shared through conventional academic products, such as journal articles or conference presentations. In our attempts to enact a mutual partnership, we have tried to make these venues more inclusive and participatory while also expanding ways of going public with research in-sights so that community members' intellectual and creative contributions are not solely mediated by academic practices.

We have become aware of how our desire to involve community mem-bers in our scholarship could be an anxiety-producing imposition that keeps our own agenda at the center. Many parents at St. Thomas Aquinas work long hours in multiple jobs, and their time is a limited and valuable resource, often leading members of our research team to be the ones representing the research to other academic audiences. We have therefore tried to make such presentations more collective and transparent by seeking consultation from community members and the EaR group prior to introducing our research at conferences or in publications. We are also mindful of which scholarly venues are most receptive to community-based research. For example, Practitioner Research Day at the University of Pennsylvania, where the youth from the Community Researchers Project presented their work, has a long tradition of including the voices of teachers, students, parents, and activists. This conference encourages sharing of in-progress research rather than polished findings, allows for alternative formats such as Readers Theater and small-group discussions, and is relatively free of esoteric language. Thus, when community members do join us in academic settings, these can be fruitful engagements where their knowledge will be valued and the time it takes to prepare feels worthwhile.

We have also attempted to create more varied opportunities for sharing the collaborative work taking place at St. Thomas Aquinas, both for transparency and so that the insights resulting from particular inquiries reach a wider audience. We are in the process of instituting a recurring partnership newsletter that will spotlight specific projects and, with the help of community leaders, be translated into the five languages of the parish. In some cases, the research itself has a public dimension, such as the workshop conducted by Indonesian parents for other families at the church. Research may also go public in small ways that can nonetheless have concrete effects—for instance, talking with the pastor or members of the Parish Council to put on the table issues that then can be addressed more readily.

Presenting research may include opportunities for intellectual expression broadly defined—such as the arts—that engage community members' talents and interests. There are multiple ways of knowing and representing knowledge that do not need to be constrained by traditional academic conventions. For example, as described in Chapter 2, the Aquinas Center partnered with the city's Mural Arts Program and a local neighborhood organization to engage in a shared inquiry into the histories of the various linguistic and cultural groups of the parish and then artistically represent these braided legacies on one of the walls facing the public street. The youth in the Community Researchers' Project represented their inquiries by composing multimodal nonfiction texts, including a film. The products of their research were unveiled in a poster presentation and screening at the Aquinas Center, where the public—families, community leaders, and university representatives—had the opportunity to engage with their findings. These varied intellectual projects are expanding and democratizing the location of knowledge production and the forms through which it might be shared.

CONCLUSION

The ethical and professional norms shape our own aspirations to create a robust, long-term, and, perhaps most importantly, trusting university–community partnership that honors the dignity and knowledge of all individuals involved. Developing trust between the university research team and the St. Thomas Aquinas parishioners is the goal of the norms, and, in turn, creating and refining them has strengthened the trust among members of the partnership. Trustworthiness in community-based research, we have found, is a relational endeavor and is achieved collectively through the types of interrelated methodological considerations described in the five norms.

Trust is also premised on intellectual respect and requires that all individuals be respected in their capacities as knowers, leaders, and creators. If those engaged in a university–community partnership do not believe that they have something to learn from one another, then there is really no genuine partnership, and trust may erode. This type of cooperation across social boundaries does not deny conflict or imply that partners will always reach consensus. In fact, contrasting perspectives and a certain level of disagreement can fuel inquiry and may be necessary to challenge received assumptions and practices, including ones that unnecessarily reproduce hierarchies or scapegoat individuals or communities. However, as J. Medina (2013) suggests, the choice in democratic engagement need not involve a false dichotomy between, on one hand, a facile consensus that suppresses conflicting perspectives or, on the other, a privileging of agonism and dissensus; an alternative may be that the "coexistence of different perspectives could be regulated by something deeper: being accountable and responsive to one another" (p. 276). The ethical and professional norms regarding the presumption of equality, the acknowledgment of community members' privileged insights, the co-construction of the research design and reflection on its benefit to participants, and the imperative to share the fruits of the research in transparent and inclusive ways are all conceived to be accountable and responsive to others throughout the research process.

Chapter 10

Collaboration and Advocacy in a Cosmopolitan Counterpublic

We're part of a community, and if one part of the community is suffering, we're
suffering, and if one part of the community is hungry, we're hungry, and if one part of
the community is discriminated against, we're discriminated against . . . we all have the
responsibility not to leave it to the other person but to [work for] systemic changes.

— Fr. Shields

After our 5-year participatory immersion with families at St. Thomas Aquinas—what we expect to be the midpoint to a 10-year project—we have
discerned several themes that will inform our work as we move forward
and that we believe will resonate with educational and community-based
researchers invested in the lives and learning of youth in diverse 21st-cen-
tury classrooms and neighborhoods.

EDUCATIONAL ADVOCACY

It would be difficult to underestimate the profound emotional investments
that families at St. Thomas Aquinas place in education. They have often
made tremendous sacrifices and have traveled, across oceans and borders,
to bring their children to the school door where many of our own current
and former university students teach. It is through education that parents
project their aspirations for their own children and for future generations
of their communities. Education, recalling the Indonesian priest in Chapter
1 who initially invited our collaboration, is what gives hope. The ineluc-
table twinning of hope and education has been expressed in words and
actions by every cultural and linguistic group at St. Thomas Aquinas. It is
exemplified in the initiatives of the CBC, who, for decades, have been raising money—turning water into wine, we joke—in order to provide extra-
curricular enrichment for neighborhood children in both under-resourced
public and parish schools. Sometimes the hope is expressed loudly and
righteously, as when parents across cultures and in a unified voice protest

the state of education in the city. It is also conveyed in subtle ways, as when Indonesian parents give up hours from their children's Sunday School to allow them to learn about research methods with university graduate students or when Latina mothers rehearse parent–teacher meetings in a Saturday family ESOL class. There are innumerable day-to-day examples of educational advocacy that may be invisible to educators, especially if they have little genuine exposure to the neighborhoods and communities of their students. While we might have expected the parish to be a world apart from schooling, we have found quite the opposite to be true. Discussions about and organizing around education permeate almost every aspect of daily congress at St. Thomas Aquinas.

In many ways, the families at St. Thomas Aquinas are not that different from many families who view education as one of the last avenues for economic stability and possible entry into the middle class. However, we also believe there is something more than economic incentives at work in the role that education plays in the imaginations of families and youth. We wonder if, for many who are ascribed as perpetual foreigners, second-class citizens, or "exceptions" (Agamben, 2005) in whatever borders they may find themselves in, education may be conceived as a cosmopolitan state, a more universal intellectual community that may help transcend the contingencies of history and provide new opportunities for self-determination.

EDUCATIONAL PRECARITY

Unfortunately, the imagined potential of education contrasts sharply with its realities in our city and many other districts across the country. While the idea of social precarity, a governing concept in this book, calls attention to a general condition of human fragility and vulnerability, we believe it may be worth teasing out *educational precarity* as a particular strand of this condition that contributes to families' and students' feelings of duress and instability. The theme of educational precarity—the attenuation of the public education sector—manifests itself in families' daily struggles, including the following: the sudden closing of a school that severed children from a nurturing learning environment and teacher; a middle school student's anxiety about applying to and getting into an adequate high school; an undocumented student's despair when she realizes that, despite her hunger for knowledge, she might be denied a higher education; the criminalization of an eager student as truant because he fears going to school and being bullied (Campano, Ghiso, et al., 2013); the racism and linguistic stigma a mother feels when trying to advocate for adequate ESOL services for her child; a student falling through the cracks in an overcrowded classroom in a school that resembles, and in some ways functions, as a prison; an exasperated mother who is trying to find a way to get her child across the city, where she is pinning her hopes on a new charter school; a high-stakes testing paradigm that inappropriately tracks an emergent bilingual student; a teenager with an expansive intellectual curiosity who has become disenchanted with a curriculum primarily focused on test-taking. These, and many other incidences and testimonials, were shared with us over the years at St. Thomas Aquinas by those who are most directly impacted by urban educational policies. They paint a challenging picture of how we are failing the aspirations of so many families and students.

RETURNING TO OUR CONCEPTUAL MODEL: NOURISHING HOPE THROUGH COLLABORATIVE RESEARCH AND PRACTICE

Throughout this book, we have documented the ways individuals at St. Thomas Aquinas work across discourse communities to advocate for education and immigrant rights, a conceptual model we laid out in Chapter 1. The model reflects a pluriversal (Mignolo, 2011) conception of the location of knowledge and suggests that inquiry and change are best thought of as collective endeavors. As ethnographers, we have been attentive to various ways of speaking, writing, and transacting with texts entailed in each discourse community's "work in the world," as instantiated in our fieldnotes, interviews with leaders, and the documents we have collected. As practitioner researchers, our goal has been more pragmatic: to support thoughtful and informed action based on the generation of local knowledge. Our understanding of the various communities at St. Thomas Aquinas has been deepened by adopting an inquiry stance into the dissonances we have encountered throughout our practice of partnering. What we have been identifying as tensions in many cases may have been a result of competing values and assumptions regarding how to move forward, as participants, including ourselves, attempt to cooperate across community boundaries. We attempt to work through these assumptions in order to "better" (Lytle, 2008) engage our practice by honoring the multiple perspectives and knowledge traditions at St. Thomas Aquinas.

The discourse communities—religious, activist, cultural, service, legal, and educational research—all use language and literacy in specific ways, including through particular terminology, genre, and tone. Although never homogenous, they reflect general centers of gravity and tendencies regarding the ways in which their participants enact individual and collective agency. The discourse communities may be thought of as interdependent, linked together by the recurring tropes of a human rights and social justice metanarrative. They do not map onto individuals, much less cultural or linguistic groups, in any essentializing manner. People engage numerous discourse communities, often simultaneously, although they may nurture primary affiliations. Grassroots inquiry entails collaboratively drawing on diverse discursive and epistemic resources in order to advocate for community interests. The boundaries between discourse communities at St. Thomas Aquinas are also porous, hybrid, and shifting. This is not to suggest that they dissolve into one another. During moments of tension they may certainly become more rigid and exclusionary. Conflict is an inevitable aspect of community-based work, but it may also be a vehicle for growth and solidarity. The interactive sum of the respective discourse communities is more insightful and effective than they would be if they were operating solely on their own terms.

This potential is never fully realized, and there are certainly contradictions and impasses. Nevertheless, as the work featured in this book exemplifies, many people are willing to think across discourse communities to participate in collective knowledge and advocacy projects. There is an unabashedly utopian, or more specifically heterotopian (Foucault, 1986), dimension to community-based research. Together members of a partnership can build upon the cosmopolitan impulses already present in spaces such as St. Thomas Aquinas in order to prefigure alternative, more socially just worlds.

CONGREGATION: A PRECONDITION FOR SOLIDARITY

Social precarity is not an abstract economic or political concept. It is a lived reality experienced and understood most directly by people on the ground. Therefore, a response to precarity also comes from everyday people organizing, often in the shadows of official political parties and institutions. Cooperating to advocate for social change, in heterogeneous contexts and across multiple identities and experiences, requires first and foremost that people be with and learn from one another. A moment early on in our partnership reminds us of the visceral power of congregation as a precondition for solidarity. During a Parish Council meeting, Fr. Shields asked parish leaders to pray for a neighborhood family enduring a neighborhood tragedy related to mental health issues by reciting the Our Father "in the language closest to your heart." The room filled with the sounds of Indonesian, Spanish, Tagalog, Vietnamese, and English harmonizing to a common cadence. Community members joined together to participate in a shared religious literacy event but did so while retaining, and drawing on, their specific cultural and linguistic resources—a focus on universal well-being that at the same time does not erase the particular. The family to which the prayer was directed was Buddhist and thus not part of the St. Thomas Aquinas congregation. The parish ethos of radical hospitality extended beyond bounded delineations of belonging, such as who is or is not a registered member of the church. There was rather a cosmopolitan commitment to support, as one of the Sisters put it, "human dignity" and "protect the vulnerable . . . to protect the human person" (Interview, February 2012).

In his call to prayer for the Cambodian family, the Father referenced the difficulties experienced by immigrant communities and the inadequate mental health services available to them, comments that interpret individual tragedy within larger social inequities. The prayer itself made a claim to a common humanity through the particularities of people's diverse language practices. By recognizing that we are all interconnected through a shared vulnerability, it helped foster compassion for a family that might otherwise have been shunned. Those of us who were there can testify to the immediate emotional, maybe even spiritual, impact it had on us, and we walked away with a renewed commitment to our neighbors and to addressing health disparities in the neighborhood.

We share the example of the multilingual prayer because it does not choose between embracing human commonality and honoring cultural and linguistic difference, or shy away from naming how social precarity is unevenly distributed across identities. Attention to the relationships between difference, commonality, and power—"how specifying difference allow us to theorize universal concerns more fully" (C. T. Mohanty, 2003, p. 505)— is necessary, Chandra Mohanty argues, for a decolonial feminist solidarity. The prayer event was one instance of many we have witnessed and been part of at St. Thomas Aquinas where people have gathered to think across their experiences and engage in social critique. This process of coming together is also an affective one that can entail conflict, grief, and anger, but, just as importantly, "joyful relation" (Bignall, 2010, p. 236), often simultaneously. The bonds that come with working and learning in a collective project for change can motivate individuals in the intersecting discourse communities to seek further relations with each other across boundaries. The moments of joyful sociality that congregation fosters in turn create fertile soil on which to address issues that negatively impact community members' lives, such as inadequate mental health services. Some gatherings, like the prayer, emerge from the cosmopolitan energy of the context, where people mingle across boundaries daily. Others are designed to build on this ethos of radical hospitality and interdependence, such as the projects we have shared throughout this book. Together, they nurture ever-widening and overlapping circles of solidarity. We identify three circles of solidarity that can animate educational advocacy efforts: solidarity with other educators, with community organizations, and with youth. When these circles of solidarity are anchored "in relations of mutuality, coresponsibility, and common interests" (C. T. Mohanty, 2003, p. 24), interests such as advocating for immigrant rights and educational justice through "decolonial practices" (Gaztambide-Fernández, 2012, p. 60), they offer generative ways to move forward in collaborative efforts for educational change.

FIRST CIRCLE OF SOLIDARITY: COMMUNITIES OF INQUIRY WITH EDUCATORS

The first expanding circle of solidarity that gives us hope is when educators see themselves as cultural workers (Freire, 2005) by pooling their expertise, talents, and knowledge together in communities of inquiry in order to collaboratively investigate more equitable educational practices and arrangements. An emphasis on the collective nature of knowledge production goes against the grain of individualistic ideologies in both academia and in the teaching profession and has important implications for graduate student mentoring as well as university–school partnerships. When Gerald took a new position at the university, he soon had the good fortune to mentor, eventually alongside María Paula and Bethany, a dedicated group of graduate students who arrived to the program with a rich array of experiences as teachers, community organizers, activists, writers, and artists. Members of the research team had worked with students across the educational life span—from pre-K to adults—in both in- and out-of-school contexts. They had diverse cultural, linguistic, and class backgrounds and degrees in a range of disciplines, including critical theory, Latin American studies, postcolonial studies, and economics. This opportunity, however, also brought with it certain challenges that come with what Cochran-Smith and Lytle (2009) characterize as the "constructive disruption" (p. 86) of university culture.

Although all members of the research team participate in several discourse communities, one message that academia sometimes sends students is that they have to shed their previous identities—as practitioners, organizers, and cultural/gendered/classed beings—in order to properly acquire the dispositions of a scholar. This often happens through a process whereby graduate students apprentice into the profession by supporting their advisors' research projects and questions until they have learned the skills to distinguish themselves and carve out their own professional identities. In the alternative model of mentorship represented by this book, we have created a shared research context where graduate students could collaboratively support the overall project of which Gerald and María Paula were the principal investigators while simultaneously cultivating their own intellectual interests and social commitments. Members of the research team, individually and collectively, are not removed from the conceptual model, analyzing it from a neutral distance. We are all located in it and navigate between its various communities at St. Thomas Aquinas and within a larger counterpublic that advocates for families' education. It is therefore important for us to be self-reflexive about our dynamics as a research team. Our variously situated perspectives have made the research stronger and also, as we hope the chapters have demonstrated, helped to engender rich educational opportunities that would not have blossomed were the research team merely collecting data on a narrowly defined question predetermined by the principal investigators. The comics club, ESOL teaching, Inquiry into College, investigation into religious literacies, and participatory action research on high school admissions were all the result of a creative alchemy between the intellectual passions of the university researchers and the interests of community members.

While we worked hard to create a collaborative space that honors the diverse knowledge and interests of all members of the research team, this ethos of interdependence exists in tension with academia's competitive culture. Many scholars feel pressures to individuate themselves by rushing to publish in order to claim authorship of ideas, engaging in self-branding, being entrepreneurial, and generally pursuing self-interest and recognition—what feminist scholars have identified as characteristics of the neoliberal academic subject (e.g., Archer, 2008). These pressures are understandable and perhaps have intensified given the precarious realities of the academic job market, student debt, and the proliferation of contingent faculty. Over the years, the research team has experienced conflicts, rifts, and rivalries. While we have certainly shared many moments of joyful solidarity, there have also been hurt feelings. For example, individuals at times did not seek one another's academic expertise or cultural knowledge and sometimes downplayed the collaborative nature of the work.

One of the tensions of action research is that, in the urgency to get things done, educators may not always take time to nurture their own relationships. We have therefore found it important to slow down the research process (e.g., Mountz et al., 2015) and return to the core dynamic of congregation ourselves, inspired by the sense of collective well-being and interdependence of so many of the youth and families at St. Thomas Aquinas. This has occurred in a number of ways, including through a yearly research retreat where members of the research team have shared their own familial narratives of immigration, a group activity that revealed how our own histories are intertwined with, rather than separate from, the experiences of parishioners. We planned activities to deepen our collective knowledge of the neighborhood, such as a tour of local landmarks, and juxtaposed media representations of the area with community members' testimonials about neighborhood riches as well as the detrimental effects of gentrification. We have also made more efforts to implement collaborative data analysis procedures, such as descriptive review protocols (Himley & Carini, 2000), in order to leverage the diverse perspectives of the research team as well as interpret the data across the respective projects. Through the retreat and ongoing opportunities for collaborative analysis, we have fostered discussions about the direction of our work at St. Thomas Aquinas and reaffirmed the shared social justice orientation and the ethical and professional norms (Chapter 9) that guide our work together. We have found that being immersed in the community and doing participatory projects together has bonded individuals through a sense of shared purpose.

The communities of inquiry that give us hope extend beyond our immediate university research team. The collaboration described in Chapter

6, for example, brought together differently located educators to think together about how to support immigrant students: an elementary ESOL teacher, Mrs. Cruz, who adopted an activist stance to her practice; master's students with a range of education experiences in school and community-based settings; and university researchers with social justice commitments who had taught diverse students. The family ESOL class featured in Chapter 4 involved parents as teachers of their children who are uniquely positioned to understand the impact of social precarity on schooling, as well as offer alternative visions of educational flourishing that are antiracist, culturally relevant, and linguistically inclusive. The Aquinas Center itself has many educators involved in its programs, from youth who teach visitors about the neighborhood and the parish community, as Francisco did in Chapter 5, to volunteers from a range of organizations who share their talents with youth and families, to employees who run a variety of classes. Constantly under financial pressure to stay afloat, the Aquinas Center tries to creatively assemble resources, such as volunteers, to attend to pressing community needs. An inquiry stance provides a mechanism for uncovering and negotiating contesting perspectives. For example, in coplanning a class, a volunteer educator brought to our inquiry group a popular program for addressing children in poverty that has been discredited as deficit-oriented and racist. Working collaboratively with one another provided opportunities for making different pedagogical frameworks visible, discussing racism and classism explicitly, and productively addressing conflict around educational issues.

Communities of inquiry involve difficult relational intellectual labor. They are time-consuming, in contradiction to the premium placed on efficiency in educational settings, and they require that individuals make themselves vulnerable in order to better learn from and alongside others. Yet they are also one of our best hopes and vehicles through which to forge solidarity across social boundaries. We have noticed that during the period of this research inquiry communities of educators have been sprouting across our city as a response to the defunding of public education, documented by Martin and his peers in Chapter 8, joining longstanding educational justice networks such as the Philadelphia Writing Project (Lytle, Portnoy, Waff, & Buckley, 2009). These collective efforts have brought teachers—and academics—out of their individual classrooms and reenergized educational activism and research in the service of local concerns.

SECOND CIRCLE OF SOLIDARITY: COMMUNITY NETWORKS AND GROUPS

The second circle of solidarity involves educators partnering with community networks and groups to advocate for social change, as illustrated in projects like the Pennsylvania Fight for Drivers Licenses. Bethany was approached 2 years ago about providing a space at Aquinas Center to congregate around advocating for licenses to be issued through a taxpayer identification number rather than a social security number, a practice that had been in place in the state prior to 2002. The issue of driver's licenses is one that many ESOL educators (e.g., Chapter 4) have identified as stymieing their abilities to forge consistent and meaningful relationships with parents. Members of the Latina/o community began meeting monthly, and then weekly, to discuss the issue and plan for possible action, and it quickly became evident that this topic also directly impacted Asian Americans at the parish. A joint information session was planned to discuss the cause and garnered an impressive turnout. Community members from the different cultural groups gave testimonials of their experiences, uncovering shared struggles as well as how not all communities are experiencing undocumented immigration status in the same way. Their racialized identities as Latina/os and Asians differentially shaped their relationship to law enforcement. The movement began to have outward reach, with parishioners traveling to Harrisburg to petition for the legislative bill, community leaders taking action and mobilizing their respective cultural groups in support of the issue, and a multilingual letter-writing campaign to legislators being publicized through the parish Masses and through social media.

The different discourse communities all uniquely contribute to this cause. The Fight for Drivers Licenses is a coalition involving different activist organizations, including the Media Mobilizing Project and the New Sanctuary Movement of Philadelphia, which help craft a targeted political message and take concrete action. The service discourse community provides opportunities for regular congregation and ongoing discussion, as well as services directed toward identified needs, such as an education session outlining U.S. legislative processes. Members of the diverse cultural groups at St. Thomas Aquinas have direct knowledge of how the lack of driver's licenses, and the policing of documentation as related to immigration, impacts their lives, including their abilities to get their children to school, which could easily be across the city. The specifics of the legislative bill and the contents of the letter-writing campaign benefit from the technical expertise of volunteer lawyers, who provide pointed interventions and rebuttals to common counterarguments. The focus on dignity has resonances with religious teachings, and the Mass itself becomes a platform for organizing. A research lens situates this specific cause within the intersecting social and political issues that impact immigrant communities. The Fight for Drivers Licenses draws on the metanarrative of a universal humanity, arguing that "the right to mobility, to move freely, is inscribed in the Universal Declaration of Human Rights. Many other fundamental needs—to work, to education, and to human dignity—are only accessible via valid identification and adequate transportation" (Artifact, May 2015). This is just one of many possible examples of how the various discourse communities can function in a productively interdependent and synergistic manner to advocate for immigrants in what might accurately be characterized as a cosmopolitan counterpublic. Educators in Pre-K–12 and university settings would do well to learn from and link with these multifaceted community efforts.

One promising avenue is to foster more reciprocal school–community–university partnerships, including with organizations such as St. Thomas Aquinas, the New Sanctuary Movement, and the Media Mobilizing Project, where all members are recognized as knowledge generators who can teach each other about the education of diverse students (Zeichner, 2015). By learning from community organizations, current and future teachers might begin to situate teaching and learning within the broader cultural and political contexts of students' lives, beyond institutional labels such as "English language learner." Understanding a coalitional effort such as the Fight for Drivers Licenses might foster a deeper appreciation for the collective knowledge and agency in communities and challenge deficit and savior ideologies that too often frame the education of immigrant and minoritized youth.

THIRD CIRCLE OF SOLIDARITY: OUR YOUTH

Another source of hope are the youth themselves, who in their daily lives are already navigating multiple discourse communities. Martin, who we featured in Chapter 8, is currently applying to universities. As an undergraduate, he will not need to participate in a study abroad program in order to cultivate global citizenship because he has been developing a comparative transnational lens simply by stepping out of his front door into one of the most culturally and linguistically diverse areas of Philadelphia.

Martin's comparative lens is not just a matter of weighing the pros and cons of a homogenous Indonesian culture against a homogenous American one. Martin's family was from a minoritized population in their home country, and he is being raised in a diverse neighborhood and going to a school with peers who embrace a plurality of intersecting identities. For example, early in our partnership Martin attended a picnic that brought together the Indonesian and Vietnamese youth groups at St. Thomas Aquinas. One group included the grandchildren of individuals who had fled a communist regime; the other was composed of the grandchildren of individuals who, because of their ethnicity, were labeled and terrorized for being potential Communists. Their experiences reflect legacies of colonization, imperialism, and the Cold War, which was perhaps the prime mover of both their respective group migrations. Within the context of their South Philadelphia neighborhood, however, the youth share an identity as Asian Americans growing up in an economically and racially stratified city with a severely under-resourced public school system.

One of the promises of the intermingling of such diverse identities is that youth might learn about their overlapping histories. Just as importantly, they may envision better futures together by drawing on multiple perspectives. Leaders in the Indonesian and Latina/o communities, for example, have taken inspiration from African American history in their own efforts to forge a coalitional movement for immigrant rights through groups such as the interfaith activist organization the New Sanctuary Movement. When Martin himself joined the Community Researchers Project, he had already been involved in youth organizing against what he and many of his peers had characterized as the assault on public education.

Another member of the CRP was Pablo, a Mexican American boy just entering middle school. Unlike Martin, Pablo was initially more hesitant to share his experiences with the group, and his quiet demeanor could be interpreted as disengagement. Throughout his schooling, Pablo had been ascribed a number of deficit labels—"limited English Proficient," "struggling student"—and had been prescribed related educational interventions. However, he had a rich intellectual identity that was not necessarily visible to his teachers. We would come to learn that Pablo already had a passion for research because of an ethnography that had been done about his indigenous grandmother in Mexico. The academic book was a treasured artifact that had been passed down to Pablo in the United States as an emblem of his family's history and culture and a way to connect with a relative he was not able to visit in person. In the CRP, Pablo would participate in research much like his grandmother had done.

We had gotten to know Pablo through his mother, Ángela, because she had participated in the ESOL research project (Chapter 4). Ángela described her son's introduction to school as a young child as "traumatic." He was coming from a Spanish-speaking home into an English-only environment, and he simply stopped speaking. Searching for answers to help her child adjust and learn, and feeling that she had failed him as a mother because she could not speak English herself, Ángela began visiting the school. She would go to the classroom as a volunteer, from 8:30 in the morning until dismissal, starting in preschool and continuing through 3rd grade, helping teachers by prepping materials, escorting young children to the bathroom, and communicating with other Spanish-speaking students. At the school, Ángela experienced pushback and racism, people who would tell her she did not belong there and who admonished her to stay away from the children, and others who chastised her for giving away her labor for free as a volunteer. She was lucky, though, to find an ally in the principal and teachers, who recognized her investment in her child's learning and offered her ways to become part of the school.

The hard work on his mother's part set the foundation for Pablo's learning within and outside of school, as he hones his understandings of particular group histories and also develops cross-cultural links. Pablo participates in a local immigrant rights organization, where he has learned from testimonials of individuals with undocumented immigration status about the experiences of many in the Latina/o community, including some of his family members, while recognizing the privileges he has from being born in the United States. In public, Pablo has nonetheless been the target of xenophobic threats aimed at "illegals." After such incidents, Pablo and his mother talk about why these aggressions occur, and she reminds him, "You have to study because that will be the best way to demonstrate who you are and that despite these treatments, with your studies you will be able to defend yourself" (Interview, July 2015). For his own part, Pablo also encourages his mother to study, to learn English for a time when he will no longer be able to act as a translator and cultural broker.

In reflecting on his work as part of the CRP, Pablo noted, "I thought it was something small, but when I presented it I thought that now it was really something bigger for me, something better, that can serve me for my future too. . . . I feel that the things they give me in school, the projects, become a bit easier for me now that I already know what it means to investigate" (Interview, July 2015). For Pablo, education is one way to "defend" oneself from oppression and "investigate" a broader world beyond nativist and parochial sentiments.

It has become commonplace in the mission statements of schools to say they are preparing students for world citizenship. This cosmopolitanism would involve creating a less ethnocentric curriculum, valuing difference and human variety, and thinking comparatively across cultures. If indeed we are serious about cultivating world citizenship beyond the need to prepare students to compete globally, and if we conceive of our educational mission as a genuine scholarly and ethical investigation into our shared humanity, then perhaps there is no greater intellectual resource and source of hope than the youth—youth such as Martin, Pablo, Ary, Linh, Derrick, Larry, Jamir, Kevin, Chance, and Francisco—and the rich cosmopolitan neighborhoods they navigate daily.

TOWARD A VISION OF SOCIAL AND EDUCATIONAL JUSTICE

When educators participate in ever-widening and overlapping circles of solidarity—solidarity with one another, with community networks and organizations, and with youth—there is the potential to transform how we think about teaching and learning in diverse 21st-century classrooms. Students might both examine what is particular to a group while simultaneously looking for connections between communities, such as common experiences of colonization, war, globalization, and migration. To get past rigid "us" and "them" dichotomies, they would explore how peoples' histories are intertwined and the political and economic reasons why individuals from vastly different areas of the world find themselves sitting alongside one another in the same classroom. There would be hard conversations about power and equity, on local, national, and transnational scales. Some students, and educators, might have to decenter their own experiences in order to make room for the insights of those who have been silenced. Everyone would have to adopt a stance of listening and learning from others, yet the reward would be the exhilarating potential of transforming one's own identity and self-understanding through dialogue with others.

Coming together around a shared vision of social and educational justice, especially when there is such a multiplicity of perspectives in our neighborhoods and classrooms, is not easy. We believe the human rights metanarrative we found so prevalent at St. Thomas Aquinas is one anchor for coalitional work, as members of diverse discourse communities use language and literacy to agitate for change in small and big ways. Recently the idea of human rights and the liberal humanist ideals that undergird them have been subjected to trenchant critique. The category of the human is historically variable and "carries 18th Century baggage" (Siebers, 2007) that has been invoked to justify colonization, patriarchy, and enslavement of those others who were viewed as somehow less rational or capable and therefore less than human. One of the most revealing observations about "human rights" is quoted in the chilling documentary *The Act of Killing* (Herzog et al., 2012), about the genocide in Indonesia, by one of the perpetrators, who has been growing old with the status of a national hero: "Take me to the Hague," he provokes, "War Crimes"—and the human rights foundation on which they are based, we can presume—"are defined by the winners, and we're winners." Nevertheless, the various advocacy discourse communities at St. Thomas Aquinas all invoke human rights tropes, and it is still hard for us to think beyond human rights and a universalism that transcends nationhood, especially in our work and partnership with immigrant, migrant, stateless, and refugee communities. If human rights, what the historian Samuel Moyn (2014) refers to as a last Utopia, are to be retained, we believe they can be reimagined to be more radically inclusive and attentive to issues of power—a concept continually interrogated rather than taken for granted, but a working ideal nonetheless.

In a world of mass migration and increasing refugee and stateless populations, it is important to reaffirm human rights not tethered to citizenship, including the right to an education, without prejudice or exclusion. This would require educators to become sensitized to how many youth and families—such as those who are labeled undocumented—experience discrimination and fear in the larger public sphere that might affect their relationships to school, and to intentionally work to create safer and more caring learning environments. A human rights orientation would also acknowledge both local and global injustices as well as the suffering of many immigrants, migrants, and refugees by providing adequate social supports and services. However, it is equally important to not view youth and their families as merely victims, which would reproduce savior ideologies in schools. As the chapters in this book have emphasized, the communities at St. Thomas Aquinas demonstrate their agency in appealing to human rights ideals to transform their situation and work toward change. Educators and researchers need to be better aware of the human rights and social justice activism already present in the neighborhoods within which they teach and to link with existing networks to support student flourishing in the most expansive sense.

We conclude with one recent inspiration that comes from the youth community researchers, described in Chapter 8, who investigated topics that they felt were relevant to their own lives and communities. We thought that the young people would focus on immigration, but instead many researched health care issues and cited as the motivation for their scholarship the inadequately treated ailments, both physical and mental, endured by loved ones and, in some cases, themselves. The middle school students were highly attuned to bodily fragility and believed this acknowledgment of common human vulnerability to be the starting place from which to envision a more just world. Their insights resonated with the disability studies scholar Tobin Siebers (2007), who argues for "establishing the fragility of the human mind and body as the foundation for a universal human rights" (para. 8). Using this "thin standard as common denominator of humanity," Siebers argues, has a number of advantages. Most crucially "it locates the activation of human rights at the point of greatest need, requiring the recognition of humanity to those people at the greatest risk of losing their place in the world" (para. 8). The implications for such a universalism on educational research, policy, and practice are far-reaching. It would require that our educational priorities and resources were, by rule and not exception, directed toward the point of greatest need and always in the service of recognizing the full humanity of those most disenfranchised. Educators dedicated to such a vision would do well to take inspiration from the ethos of interdependence and solidarity of cosmopolitan counterpublics evident in places such as St. Thomas Aquinas.

References

Agamben, G. (1998). *Homo sacre: Sovereign power and bare life* (D. Heller-Roazen, Trans.). Stanford, CA: Stanford University Press.

Agamben, G. (2005). *State of exception* (K. Attell, Trans.). Chicago, IL: University of Chicago Press.

Agamben, G. (2013). *The highest poverty: Monastic rules and form-of-life* (A. Kotsko, Trans.). Stanford, CA: Stanford University Press.

Alcoff, L. M. (2006). *Visible identities: Race, gender, and the self.* Oxford, UK: Oxford University Press.

Alcoff, L. M. (2012). Then and now. *Journal of Speculative Philosophy, 26*(2), 268–278.

Alexander, M. (2010). *The new Jim Crow: Mass incarceration in the age of colorblindness.* New York, NY: The New Press.

Anzaldúa, G. (1999). *Borderlands/la frontera: The new mestiza* (2nd ed.). San Francisco, CA: Aunt Lute Books.

Appadurai, A. (2011). Cosmopolitanism from below: Some ethical lessons from the slums of Mumbai. *The Johannesburg Salon, 4*, 32–43.

Archdiocese of Philadelphia. (2007). Catholic healthcare services announces construction of St. John Neumann Place in South Philadelphia. Available at archphila.org/press%20releases/pr001185.php

Archer, L. (2008). The new neoliberal subjects? Young/er academics' constructions of professional identity. *Journal of Education Policy, 23*(3), 265–285.

Arendt, H. (1976). *The origins of totalitarianism.* New York, NY: Harcourt.

Asen, R. (2000). Seeking the "counter" in counterpublics. *Communication Theory, 10*(4), 424–446.

Auerbach, E. (1995). Deconstructing the discourse of strengths in family literacy. *Journal of Reading Behavior, 27*, 643–661.

Auerbach, E. (1997). *Making meaning, making change: Participatory curriculum development for adult ESL literacy.* Washington, DC: Center for Applied Linguistics.

Bakhtin, M. (1984). *Rabelais and his world* (H. Iswolksy, Trans.). Bloomington, IN: Indiana University Press.

Banki, S. (2013). The paradoxical power of precarity: Refugees and homeland activism. *Refugee Review: Social Movement, 1*(1), 1–20.

Bankston, C. L. (2004). Social capital, cultural values, immigration, and academic achievement: The host country context and contradictory consequences. *Sociology of Education, 77*(2), 176–179.

Bankston, C. L. & Zhou, M. (2002). Being well vs. doing well: Self-esteem and school performance among immigrant and non-immigrant racial and ethnic groups. *International Migration Review, 36*, 389–415.

Bartolomé, L. I. (2008). Authentic cariño and respect in minority education: The political and ideological dimensions of love. *International Journal of Critical Pedagogy, 1*(1), 1–17.

Barton, D., & Hamilton, M. (1998). *Local literacies: Reading and writing in one community.* London, UK: Routledge.

Baum, S., & Flores, S. M. (2011). Higher education and children in immigrant families. *The Future of Children, 21*(1), 171–193.

Baynham, M. J. (2009): "Just one day like today": Scale and the analysis of space/time orientation in narratives of displacement. In J. Collins, S. Slembrouck, & M. Baynham (Eds.), *Globalization and language in contact: Scale, migration and communicative practices* (pp. 130–147). London, UK: Continuum.

Bazerman, C. (2009). Issue brief: Discourse communities. *National Council of Teachers of English.* Available at www.ncte.org/college/briefs/dc

Beach, R., Campano, G., Edmiston, B., & Borgmann, M. (2010). *Literacy tools in the classroom: Teaching through critical inquiry, grades 5–12.* New York, NY: Teachers College Press.

Beauboeuf-Lafontant, T. (2002). A womanist experience of caring: Understanding the pedagogy of exemplary Black women teachers. *Urban Review, 34*, 71–86.

Benhabib, S. (1996). Toward a deliberative model of democratic legitimacy. In. S. Behnabib (Ed.), *Democracy and difference: Contesting the boundaries of the political* (pp. 67–94). Princeton, NJ: Princeton University Press.

Benjamin, W. (1936/1968). The work of art in the age of mechanical reproduction. In H. Arendt (Ed.), *Illuminations* (pp. 217–242). New York, NY: Schocken Books.

Bignall, S. (2010). *Postcolonial agency: Critique and constructivism.* Edinburgh, UK: Edinburgh University Press.

Bitz, M. (2009). *Manga high: Literacy, identity, and coming of age in an urban high school.* Cambridge, MA: Harvard Education Press.

Blommaert, J. (2007). Sociolinguistic scales. *Intercultural Pragmatics, 4*(1), 1–19.

Bloome, D., Beierle, M., Grigorenko, M., & Goldman, S. (2009). Learning over time: Uses of intercontextuality, collective memories, and classroom chronotopes in the construction of learning opportunities in a ninth-grade language arts classroom. *Language and Education, 23*(4), 313–334.

Bloome, D., & Katz, L. (1997). Literacy as social practice and classroom chronotopes. *Reading & Writing Quarterly, 13*(3), 205–225.

Bourdieu, P. (1986). The forms of capital. In J. Richardson (Ed.), *Handbook of theory and research for the sociology of education* (pp. 241–258). New York, NY: Greenwood.

Bourdieu, P. (1990). *The logic of practice.* Cambridge, UK: Polity Press.

Bourdieu, P., & Thompson, J. B. (1991). *Language and symbolic power.* Cambridge, MA: Harvard University Press.

Brandt, D. (2001). *Literacy in American lives.* New York, NY: Cambridge University Press.

Buff, R. I. (2008). *Immigrant rights in the shadows of citizenship.* New York, NY: New York University Press.

Butin, D. (2003). Of what use is it? Multiple conceptualizations of service learning within education. *The Teachers College Record, 105*(9), 1674–1692.

Butler, J. (2009). *Frames of war: When is life grievable?* London, UK: Verso.

Butler, J. (2011, May 24). The precarious life: The obligations of proximity (potentiality of intercultural spaces). Lecture at Nobel Museum, *Svenska Akademiens Börssal.* Available at www.youtube.com/watch?v=KJT69AQtDtg

Cahill, C. (2007). Repositioning ethical commitments: Participatory action research as a relational praxis of social change. *ACME: An International Journal of Critical Geographies, 6*(3), 360–373.

Cammarota, J., & Fine, M. (Eds.). (2008). *Revolutionizing education: Youth participatory action research in motion.* New York, NY: Routledge.

Campano, G. (2007). *Immigrant students and literacy: Reading, writing, and remembering.* New York, NY: Teachers College Press.

Campano, G., & Ghiso, M. P. (2011). Immigrant students as cosmopolitan intellectuals. In S. Wolf, P. Coates, P. Enciso, & C. Jenkins (Eds.), *Handbook on research on children's and young adult literature* (pp. 164–176). Mahwah, NJ: Lawrence Erlbaum.

Campano, G., Ghiso, M. P., & Sánchez, L. (2013). "No one knows the . . . amount of a person": Elementary students critiquing dehumanization through organic critical literacies. *Research in the Teaching of English, 48*(1), 98–125.

Campano, G., Ghiso, M. P., & Welch, B. (2015). Ethical and professional norms in community-based research. *Harvard Educational Review, 85*(1), 29–49.

Campano, G., Ghiso, M. P., Yee, M., & Pantoja, A. (2013). Toward community research and coalitional literacy practices for educational justice. *Language Arts, 90*(5), 314–326.

Campano, G., Honeyford, M. A., Sánchez, L., & Vander Zanden, S. (2010). Ends in themselves: Theorizing the practice of university–school partnering through horizontalidad. *Language Arts, 87*(4), 277–286.

Campano, G., Jacobs, K. B., & Ngo, L. (2014). A critical orientation to literacy assessment: Learning from others through a stance of solidarity. In J. Brass & A. Webb (Eds.), *Reclaiming English language arts methods courses: Critical issues and challenges for teacher educators in top-down times* (pp. 97–108). New York, NY: Routledge.

Campano, G., Ngo, L., Low, D. E., & Jacobs, K. B. (2015). Young children demystifying and remaking the university through critical play. *Journal of Early Childhood Literacy.* Published online first, April 7, 2015. doi:10.1177/1468798415577875.

Campano, G., Ngo, L., & Player, G. (2015).Researching from buried experiences: Collaborative inquiry with Asian American youth. *LEARNing Landscapes, 8*(2), 77–94.

Canada, G., & Nicholas, J. (2010). *Fist stick knife gun: A personal history of violence (a true story in Black and White).* Boston, MA: Beacon Press.

Castro-Gómez, S. (2005). *La hybris del punto cero: Ciencia, raza e ilustración en la Nueva Granada (1750–1816)*. Bogotá, Colombia: Editorial Pontifica Universidad Javeriana.

Castro-Salazar, R., & Bagley, C. (2010). "Ni de aquí ni from there": Navigating between contexts: Counter-narratives of undocumented Mexican students in the United States. *Race Ethnicity and Education, 13*(1), 23–40.

Chávez, L. R. (2008). *The Latino threat: Constructing immigrants, citizens and the nation*. Stanford, CA: Stanford University Press.

Clowes, G. A. (2002). State takes over Philadelphia's failing schools. *Heartland*. Available at news.heartland.org/newspaper-article/2002/02/01/state-takes-over-philadelphias-failing-schools

Cochran-Smith, M., & Dudley-Marling, C. (2012). Diversity in teacher education and special education: The issues that divide. *Journal of Teacher Education, 63*(4), 237–244.

Cochran-Smith, M., & Lytle, S. L. (1999). Relationships of knowledge and practice: Teacher learning in communities. *Review of Research in Education, 24*(1), 249–305.

Cochran-Smith, M., & Lytle, S. L. (2007). Everything's ethics: Practitioner inquiry and university culture. In A. Campbell & S. Groundwater-Smith (Eds.), *An ethical approach to practitioner research* (pp. 24–41). London, UK: Routledge.

Cochran-Smith, M., & Lytle, S. L. (2009). *Inquiry as stance: Practitioner inquiry for the next generation*. New York, NY: Teachers College Press.

Cockcroft, E., Weber, J. P., & Cockcroft, J. (1998). *Toward a people's art: The Contemporary mural movement*. Albuquerque, NM: University of New Mexico Press.

Coleman, J. S. (1988). Social capital in the creation of human capital. *American Journal of Sociology, 94*, S95–S120.

Collins, P. H. (2000). *Black feminist thought: Knowledge, consciousness, and the politics of empowerment* (2nd ed.). New York, NY: Routledge.

Culler, J. (2011). *Literary theory: A very short introduction*. Oxford, UK: Oxford University Press.

Cushman, E. (1999). Critical literacy and institutional language. *Research in the Teaching of English, 33*, 245–274.

De Genova, N. (2005). Impossible subjects: Illegal aliens and the making of modern America. *Latino Studies, 3*(1), 153–155.

Delgado Bernal, D., Alemán, E., & Carmona, J. F. (2008). Transnational and transgenerational Latina/o cultural citizenship among kindergarteners, their parents, and university students in Utah. *Social Justice, 35*(1), 28–49.

Delgado-Gaitán, C. (1991). Involving parents in schools: A process of empowerment. *American Journal of Education, 100*, 20–46.

Derrida, J. (1999). *Adieu to Emmanuel Levinas* (P. Brault & M. Naas, Trans.). Stanford, CA: Stanford University Press.

Doucet, F. (2011). Parent involvement as ritualized practice. *Anthropology & Education Quarterly, 42*(4), 404–421.

Duncan-Andrade, J. (2009). Note to educators: Hope required when growing roses in concrete. *Harvard Educational Review, 79*(2), 181–194.

Dutro, E., & Selland, M. (2012). "I like to read, but I know I'm not good at it": Children's perspectives on high-stakes testing in a high-poverty school. *Curriculum Inquiry, 42*(3), 340–367.

Dyson, A. H. (2003). *The brothers and sisters learn to write: Popular literacies in childhood and school cultures.* New York, NY: Teachers College Press.

Ebaugh, H., & Chafetz, J. (2000). *Religion and the new immigrants: Continuities and adaptation in immigrant congregations.* Walnut Creek, CA: Alta Mira.

Epstein, J. L. & Dauber, S. L. (1991). School programs and teacher practices of parent involvement in inner-city elementary and middle schools. *The Elementary School Journal, 91*(3), 289–305.

Erickson, F. (1986). Qualitative methods in research on teaching. In M. C. Wittrock (Ed.), *Handbook of research on teaching* (3rd ed., pp. 119–161). Thousand Oaks, CA: Sage.

Fairclough, N. (2003). *Analyzing discourse: Textual analysis for social research.* New York, NY: Routledge.

Fine, M. (1993). Parent involvement: Reflections on parents, power and urban schools. *Teachers College Record, 94*(4), 682–710.

Flores, W. (2003). New citizens, new rights: Undocumented immigrants and Latino cultural citizenship. *Latin American Perspectives, 30*(2), 87–100.

Flores, W., & Benmayor, R. (Eds.) (1997). *Latino cultural citizenship: Claiming identity, space, and rights.* Boston, MA: Beacon Press.

Forché, C. (Ed.). (1993). *Against forgetting: Twentieth century poetry of witness.* New York, NY: Norton.

Foucault, M. (1986). Of other spaces (J. Miskowiec, Trans.). *Diacritics, 16*(1), 22–27.

Foucault, M. (1990). *The history of sexuality: An introduction* (R. Hurley, Trans.). New York, NY: Penguin Books.

Fránquiz, M. E., & Brochin-Ceballos, C. (2006). Cultural citizenship and visual literacy: U.S.–Mexican children constructing cultural identities along the U.S.–Mexico border. *Multicultural Perspectives, 8*(1), 5–12.

Fraser, N. (1992). Rethinking the public sphere: A contribution to the critique of actually existing democracy. In C. Calhoun (Ed.), *Habermas and the public sphere* (pp. 109–142). Cambridge, MA: MIT Press.

Freire, P. (1970). *Pedagogy of the oppressed.* New York, NY: Continuum.

Freire, P. (Ed.). (1998). Fourth letter: On the indispensable qualities of progressive teachers for their better performance. In *Teachers as cultural workers: Letters to those who dare teach* (pp. 39–46). Boulder, CO: Westview Press.

Freire, P. (2005). *Teachers as cultural workers: Letters to those who dare teach* (D. Macedo & D. Koike, Trans.). Boulder, CO: Westview Press.

Fricker, M. (2007). *Epistemic injustice: Power and the ethics of knowing.* Oxford, UK: Oxford University Press.

Gadsden, V. L. (1998). Family cultures and literacy learning. In J. Osborn & F. Lehr (Eds.), *Literacy for all: Issues in teaching and learning* (pp. 32–50). New York, NY: Guilford Press.

Gándara, P. (2012). *Expanding opportunity in higher education: Leveraging promise.* Albany, NY: State University of New York Press.

Gándara, P., & Hopkins, M. (2010). *Forbidden language: English learners and restrictive language policies.* New York, NY: Teachers College Press.

Garcia, F. C, & Sanchez, G. (2008). *Hispanics and the US political system: Moving into the mainstream.* Upper Saddle River, NJ: Prentice Hall.

Gardner, H., & Shulman, L. S. (2005). The professions in America today: Crucial but fragile. *Daedalus, 134*(3), 13–18.

Gaztambide-Fernández, R. (2012). Decolonization and the pedagogy of solidarity. *Decolonization: Indigeneity, Education & Society, 1*(1), 41–67.

Genishi, C., & Dyson, A. H. (2009). *Children, language, and literacy: Diverse learners in diverse times.* New York, NY: Teachers College Press.

Ghiso, M. P. (2013). Playing with/through non-fiction texts: Young children authoring their relationships with history. *Journal of Early Childhood Literacy, 13*(1), 26–51.

Ghiso, M. P. (2016). The Laundromat as the transnational local: Young children's literacies of interdependence. *Teachers College Record, 118*(1).

Ghiso, M. P., & Campano, G. (2013). Coloniality and education: Negotiating discourses of immigration in schools and communities through border thinking. *Equity and Excellence in Education, 46*(2), 252–269.

Ghiso, M. P., & Low, D. E. (2013). Students using multimodal literacies to surface micronarratives of United States immigration. *Literacy, 47*(1), 26–34.

Girard, R. (1986). *The scapegoat* (Y. Freccero, Trans.). Baltimore, MD: Johns Hopkins University Press.

Goffman, E. (1979). Footing. *Semiotica, 25*(1–2), 1–30.

González, N., Moll, L. C., & Amanti, C. (2005). *Funds of knowledge: Theorizing practices in households, communities, and classrooms.* Mahwah, NJ: Lawrence Erlbaum.

Goodman, K. S. (2006). *The truth about DIBELS: What it is, what it does.* Portsmouth, NH: Heinemann.

Gramsci, A. (1971). *Selections from the prison notebooks.* New York, NY: International.

Guerra, J. (2004). Putting literacy in its place: Nomadic consciousness and the practice of transcultural repositioning. In C. Gutiérrez-Jones, *Rebellious reading: The dynamics of Chicana/o cultural literacy* (pp. 19–37). Santa Barbara, CA: University of California, Santa Barbara, Chicano Studies Institute.

Gutiérrez, K. (2008). Developing a sociocritical literacy in the third space. *Reading Research Quarterly, 43*(2), 148–164.

Gutiérrez, K., & Orellana, M. F. (2006). The "problem" of English language learners: Constructing genres of difference. *Research in the Teaching of English, 40*(4), 502–507.

Habermas, J. (1991). *The structural transformation of the public sphere: An inquiry into a category of bourgeois society* (T. Burger & F. Lawrence, Trans.). Cambridge, MA: MIT Press.

Hames-García, M. (2011). *Identity complex: Making the case for multiplicity.* Minneapolis: University of Minnesota Press.

Harkavy, I., & Hartley, M. (2009). University–school–community partnerships for youth development and democratic renewal. *New Directions for Youth Development, 2009*(122), 7–18.

Harkavy, I., & Hartley, M. (2012). Integrating a commitment to the public good into the institutional fabric: Further lessons from the field. *Journal of Higher Education Outreach and Engagement, 16*(4), 17–36.

Harker, C. (2012). Precariousness, precarity and family: Notes from Palestine. *Environment and Planning A, 44*(4), 849–865.

Harper, S. R., & Hurtado, S. (Eds.). (2011). *Racial and ethnic diversity in higher education* (3rd ed.). Boston, MA: Pearson.

Heath, S. B. (1982). What no bedtime story means. *Language in Society, 11*(1), 49–76.

Hedges, C., & Sacco, J. (2012). *Days of destruction, days of revolt.* New York, NY: Nation Books.

Herzog, W., Morris, E. (Executive Producers), Sorensen, S. B., Singer, A., Kohncke, A., Brink, J. T., Grude, T. (Producers), Oppenheimer, J., Cynn, C., & Anonymous (Directors). (2012). *The act of killing* [Motion picture]. Copenhagen, Denmark: Final Cut for Real.

Himley, M., & Carini, P. F. (Eds.). (2000). *From another angle: Children's strengths and school standards: The Prospect Center's descriptive review of the child.* New York, NY: Teachers College Press.

Hirschman, C. (2004). The role of religion in the origins and adaptation of immigrant groups in the United States. *International Migration Review 38*(3), 1206–1233.

Honeyford, M. A. (2013). Critical projects of Latino cultural citizenship: Literacy and immigrant activism. *Pedagogies: An International Journal, 8*(1), 60–76.

Hostetler, K. (2005). What is "good" education research? *Educational Researcher, 34*(6), 16–21.

Ichioka, Y. (Ed.). (1974). *A buried past: An annotated bibliography of the Japanese Research Project collection.* Oakland, CA: University of California Press.

Jablow, P. (2013). Previous cuts were bad enough, staffers say. *The Notebook.* Available at thenotebook.org/october-2013/136414/previous-cuts-were-bad-enough-staffers-say

Jacobs, J. (1961). *Death and life of great American cities.* New York, NY: Vintage Books.

Janks, H. (2014). The importance of critical literacy. In J. Z. Pandya & J. Ávila (Eds.), *Moving critical literacies forward: A new look at praxis across contexts* (p. 32–44). London, UK: Routledge.

Juzwik, M., & McKenzie, C. (2015). Writing, religious faith, and cosmopolitan dialogue: Portraits of two American Evangelical men in a public school English classroom. *Written Communication, 32*(2), 121–149.

Kase, A. (2010, June 15). Hiding in plain sight: S. Philly Indonesians fear deportation: Reports of ethnic profiling underscore immigration issues here. *Philadelphia Weekly.* Available at www.philadelphiaweekly.com/news-and-opinion/hiding-in-plain-sight-s-philly-indonesians-fear-deportation.html

Kell, C. (2009). Weighing the scales: Recontextualization as horizontal scaling. In J. Collins, S. Slembrouck, & M. Baynham (Eds.), *Globalization and language* in contact: Scale, migration, and communicative practices (pp. 252–274). New York, NY: Continuum.

Kell, C. (2011). Inequalities and crossings: Literacy and the spaces-in-between. *International Journal of Educational Development, 31,* 606–613.

Kemmis, S., & McTaggart, R. (2005). Participatory action research. In N. K. Denzin & Y. S. Lincoln (Eds.), *The SAGE handbook of qualitative research* (3rd ed., pp. 559–603). Thousand Oaks, CA: Sage

Kirkland, D. (2013). *A search past silence: The literacy of young Black men.* New York, NY: Teachers College Press.

Kinloch, V., Nemeth, E., & Patterson, A. (2015). Reframing service-learning as learning and participation with urban youth. *Theory into Practice, 54*(1), 39–46.

Kress, G. (2010). *Multimodality: A social semiotic approach to contemporary communication.* London, UK: Routledge.

Kress, G., & van Leeuwen, T. (2006). *Reading images: The grammar of visual design* (2nd ed.). London, UK: Routledge.

Lather, P. (1986). Research as praxis. *Harvard Educational Review, 56*(3), 257–278.

Latour, B. (2005). *Reassembling the social: An introduction to Actor-Network-Theory.* New York, NY: Oxford University Press.

Lefebvre, H. (1970). *The urban revolution.* Minneapolis: University of Minnesota Press.

Leonardo, Z., & Porter, R. K. (2010). Pedagogy of fear: Toward a Fanonian theory of "safety" in race dialogue. *Race Ethnicity and Education, 13*(2), 139–157.

Levinas, E. (1969). *Totality and infinity: An essay on exteriority* (A. Lingis, Trans.). Pittsburgh, PA: Duquesne University Press.

Levitt, P. (2003). "You know, Abraham was really the first immigrant": Religion and transnational migration. *International Migration Review, 37*(3), 847–873.

Lewis, C., Enciso, P., & Moje, E. (2007). *Reframing sociocultural research on literacy: Identity, agency, and power.* Mahwah, NJ: Lawrence Erlbaum.

Long, C. (1986). *Significations: Signs, symbols, and images in the interpretation of religion.* Minneapolis, MN: Fortress Press.

Lopez, M. P. (2006). The intersection of immigration law and civil rights law: Noncitizen workers and the international human rights paradigm. *Brandeis Law Journal, 44,* 611–635.

Lorde, A. (1984). The master's tools will never dismantle the master's house. In *Sister outsider: Essays and speeches* (pp. 110–114). Berkeley, CA: Crossing Press.

Low, D. E. (2015). *Comics as a medium for inquiry: Urban students (re-)designing critical social worlds* (Unpublished doctoral dissertation). University of Pennsylvania, Philadelphia.

Low, D. E., & Campano, G. (2013). The image becomes the weapon: New literacies and canonical legacies. *Voices from the Middle, 21*(1), 26–31.

Lugones, M. (1992). On Borderlands/La Frontera: An interpretive essay. *Hypatia, 7*(4), 31–37.

Lugones, M. (2003). *Pilgrimages/peregrinajes: Theorizing coalition against multiple oppressions.* Lanham, MD: Rowman & Littlefield.

Lytle, S. L. (2008). At last: Practitioner inquiry and the practice of teaching: Some thoughts on *Better*. *Research in the Teaching of English, 42*(3), 373–379.

Lytle, S. L., Portnoy, D., Waff, D., & Buckley, M. (2009). Teacher research in urban Philadelphia: Twenty years of working within, against, and beyond the system. *Educational Action Research, 17*(1), 23–42.

Lytle, S. L. (2013). Foreword: The critical literacies of teaching. In C. Kosnik, J. Rowsell, P. Williamson, R. Simon, & C. Beck (Eds.), *Literacy teacher educators: Preparing teachers for a changing world* (pp. xv–xix). Rotterdam, The Netherlands: Sense.

Mangual Figueroa, A. (2012). "I have papers so I can go anywhere!" Everyday talk about citizenship in a mixed-status Mexican family. *Journal of Language, Identity and Education, 11*(5), 291–311.

Marsh, J. (2000). Teletubby tales: Popular culture in the early years language and literacy curriculum. *Contemporary Issues in Early Childhood, 1*(2), 119–133.

McCann, E. (2002) The cultural politics of local economic development: Meaning-making, place-making, and the urban policy process. *Geoforum, 33*, 385–398. DOI:10.1016/S0016-7185(02)00007-6

Medina, C., & Campano, G. (2006). Performing identities through drama and teatro practices in multilingual classrooms. *Language Arts, 83*(4), 332–341.

Medina, J. (2013). *The epistemology of resistance: Gender and racial oppression, epistemic injustice, and resistant imaginations.* Oxford, UK: Oxford University Press.

Menken, K. (2008). *English learners left behind: Standardized testing as language policy.* Clevedon, UK: Multilingual Matters.

Mezzacappa, D. (September 2012). Choosing a high school keeps getting more complicated. *The Philadelphia Public School Notebook, Looking ahead to high school: Fall guide, 20*(1), p. 3.

Mignolo, W. (2000). *Local histories/global designs: Coloniality, subaltern knowledges, and border thinking.* Princeton, NJ: Princeton University Press.

Mignolo, W. (2011). *The darker side of Western modernity: Global futures, decolonial options.* Durham, NC: Duke University Press.

Mirra, N., Garcia, A., & Morrell, E. (2015). *Doing youth participatory action research: Transforming inquiry with researchers, educators, and students.* London, UK; Routledge.

Mohanty, C. T. (2003). *Feminism without borders: Decolonizing theory, practicing solidarity.* Durham, NC: Duke University Press.

Mohanty, S. (1997). *Literary history and the claims of history: Postmodernism, objectivity, multicultural politics.* Ithaca, NY: Cornell University Press.

Mora, G. C. (2013). Religion and the organizational context of immigrant civic engagement: Mexican Catholicism in the USA. *Ethnic and Racial Studies, 36*(11), 1647–1665.

Moraga, C. (1983). Refugees of a world on fire: Forward to the second edition. In C. Moraga & G. Anzaldúa (Eds.) *This bridge called my back: Writings by radical women of color* (2nd ed.). New York, NY: Kitchen Table: Women of Color Press.

Morrell, E. (2006). Critical participatory action research and the literacy achievement of ethnic minority groups. In J. V. Hoffman, D. L. Schallert, C. M. Fairbanks, J. Worthy, & B. Maloch (Eds.), *55th yearbook of the National Reading Conference* (pp. 60–77). Oak Creek, WI: National Reading Conference.

Mountz, A., Bonds, A., Mansfield, B., Loyd, J., Hyndman, J., Walton-Roberts, M., . . . Curran, W. (2015). For slow scholarship: A feminist politics of resistance through collective action in the neoliberal university. *ACME: An International E-Journal for Critical Geographies, 14*(4), 1235–1259.

Moya, P. (2002). *Learning from experience: Minority identities, multicultural struggles.* Los Angeles, CA: University of California Press.

Moyn, S. (2014). *Human rights and the uses of history.* London, UK: Verso.

Nakagawa, K. (2000). Unthreading the ties that bind: Questioning the discourse of parent involvement. *Educational Policy, 14*(3), 443–472.

Ngai, M. M. (2004). *Impossible subjects: Illegal aliens and the making of modern America.* Princeton, NJ: Princeton University Press.

Nieto, S. (2000). Lessons from students on creating a change to dream. In B. M. Brizuela, J. P. Stewart, R. G. Garrillo, & J. G. Berger (Eds.), *Acts of inquiry in qualitative research* (pp. 355–387). Cambridge, MA: Harvard Educational Review.

Nussbaum, M. (2008). Toward a globally sensitive patriotism. *Daedalus, 137*(3), 78–93.

Ogbu, J. (1987). Variability in minority school performance: A problem in search of an explanation. *Anthropology & Education Quarterly, 18*(4), 312–334.

Ortega, M., & Alcoff, L. M. (2009). *Constructing the nation: A race and nationalism reader.* Albany, NY: State University of New York Press.

Owens, M. L., & Smith, R. D. (2005). Congregations in low-income neighborhoods and the implications for social welfare policy research. *Nonprofit and Voluntary Sector Quarterly, 34*, 316–339.

Patel, L. (2012). *Youth held at the border: Immigration, education, and the politics of inclusion.* New York, NY: Teachers College Press.

Paris, D., & Winn, M. T. (2013). *Humanizing research: Decolonizing qualitative inquiry with youth and communities.* London, UK: Sage.

Perea, J. F. (1997). *Immigrants out! The new nativism and the anti-immigrant impulse in the United States.* New York, NY: New York University Press.

Pérez Huber, L. (2009). Challenging racist nativist framing: Acknowledging the community cultural wealth of Chicana college students to reframe the immigration debate. *Harvard Educational Review, 79*(4), 704–729.

Postema, B. (2013). *Narrative structure in comics: Making sense of fragments.* Rochester, NY: RIT Press.

Putnam, R. (2000). *Bowling alone: The collapse and revival of American community.* New York, NY: Simon & Schuster.

Rancière, J. (2004). *The philosopher and his poor.* Durham, NC: Duke University Press.

Rieser, L. (2003). Analysis: Do Philadelphians still have a voice at the school district? Understanding the state takeover of Philadelphia's schools. *Perspectives on Urban Education, 2*(2). Available at www.urbanedjournal.org/archive/volume-2-issue-2-fall-2003/analysis-do-philadelphians-still-have-voice-school-district-under

Rivera, L., & Lavan, N. (2012). Family literacy practices and parental involvement of Latin American immigrant mothers. *Journal of Latinos and Education, 11*(4), 247–259.

Rodríguez, D. (2010). *Suspended apocalypse: White supremacy, genocide, and the Filipino condition.* Minneapolis, MN: University of Minnesota Press.

Rohr, M. (2001, February 5). A nation's turmoil prompts a new beginning: Philadelphia's Indonesian community may number 6,000. More arrive weekly. *Philadelphia Inquirer.* Available at articles.philly.com/2001-02-05/news/25319209_1_indonesian-students-indonesian-churches-indonesian-immigrants

Romo, R. (1992–1996). Borderland murals: Chicano artifacts in transition. *Aztlán, 21*(1–2), 125–154.

Rosaldo, R. (1987). *Cultural citizenship concept paper.* Inter-University Program for Latino Research (IUP) Latino Cultural Studies Working Group, Stanford, CA: Stanford University.

Rymes, B. (2010). Classroom discourse analysis: A focus on communicative repertoires. In N. Hornberger & S. McKay (Eds.) *Sociolinguistics and language education* (pp. 528–546). Buffalo, NY: Multilingual Matters.

Sacco, J. (2012). *Journalism.* New York, NY: Metropolitan Books.

Said, E. (1985). Orientalism reconsidered. *Cultural Critique, 1,* 89–107.

Saldívar, J. D. (2012). *Trans-americanity: Subaltern modernities, global coloniality, and the cultures of greater Mexico.* Durham, NC: Duke University Press.

Saltmarsh, J., & Hartley, M. (2011). Democratic engagement. In J. Saltmarsh & M. Hartley (Eds.), *To serve a larger purpose: Engagement for democracy and transformation of higher education* (pp. 14–26). Philadelphia, PA: Temple University Press.

Sánchez, L. (2011). Building on young children's cultural histories through placemaking in the classroom. *Contemporary Issues in Early Childhood, 12*(4), 332–342.

San Juan Jr., E. (2005, February 27–March 5). U.S. genocide in the Philippines and the new armed intervention. *Bulatat, 5*(4). Available at www.bulatlat.com/news/5-4/5-4-genocide.html

School District of Philadelphia. (2013). 2013 High school directory. Available at March 5, 2013 from http://webgui.phila.k12.pa.us/uploads/Gz/IK/GzIKF3AOBKzZ28C9l4IXTA/HS-Directory-2013.pdf

Segura, D. A., & Facio, E. (2007). Adelante, mujer: Latina activism, feminism, and empowerment. In H. Rodríguez, R. Sáenz, & C. Menjívar (Eds.), *Latina/os in the United States: Changing the face of America* (pp. 294–307). New York, NY: Springer.

Siebers, T. (2007). Disability and the right to have rights. *Disability Studies Quarterly,* 27(1–2). Available at dsq-sds.org/article/view/13/13

Siebers, T. (2010). *Disability aesthetics.* Ann Arbor: University of Michigan Press.

Silverman, R. (2013). *Schools and urban revitalization: Rethinking institutions and community development.* New York, NY: Routledge.

Simon, R. (2011). On the human challenges of multiliteracies pedagogy. *Contemporary Issues in Early Childhood, 12*(4), 362–366.

Simon, R. (2012). "Without comic books, there would be no me": Teachers as connoisseurs of adolescents' literate lives. *Journal of Adolescent & Adult Literacy, 55*(6), 516–526.

Sitrin, M. (2006). *Horizontalism: Voices of popular power in Argentina.* Oakland, CA: AK Press.

Sleeter, C. (2014). Public art and marginalized communities. *Ubiquity: The Journal of Literature, Literacy, and the Arts, 1*(1), 9–17.

Spolan, S. (2011, June 14). International Philly: Indonesians quietly forge strong bond with city. *Flying Kite.* Available at www.flyingkitemedia.com/features/indonesiansphilly0614.aspx

Standing, G. (2013). Defining the precariat: A class in the making. *Eurozine.* Available at www.eurozine.com/articles/2013-04-19-standing-en.html

Stepick, A., Rey, T., & Mahler, S. J. (2009). *Churches and charity in the immigrant city: Religion, immigration, and civic engagement in Miami.* New Brunswick, NJ: Rutgers University Press.

Street, B. V. (1995). *Social literacies: Critical approaches to literacy in development, ethnography, and education.* Harlow, UK: Pearson Education.

Suárez-Orozco, M., Suárez-Orozco, C., & Todorova, I. (2008). *Learning a new land.* Cambridge, MA: Harvard University Press.

Thomas, E. E., & Stornaiuolo, A. (2014, December). *Reading the self into existence: Transgressive textual readings in a digital age.* Paper presentation at the annual meeting of the Literacy Research Association, Marco Island, Florida.

Thomson, P. (2008). Field. In M. Grenfell (Ed.), *Pierre Bourdieu: Key concepts* (pp. 67–81). Durham, UK: Acumen.

Tocqueville, A. de. (2000/1835). *Democracy in America* (H. C. Mansfield & D. Winthrop, Eds. & Trans.). Chicago, IL: University of Chicago Press.

Tuck, E., & Yang, W. (Eds.). (2014). *Youth resistant research and theories of change.* New York, NY: Routledge.

Vagle, M., & Jones, S. (2012). The precarious nature of social class sensitivity in literacy: A social, autobiographic, and pedagogical project. *Curriculum Inquiry, 42*(3), 318–339.

Valdés, G. (1996). *Con respeto: Bridging the distance between culturally different families and school.* New York, NY: Teachers College Press.

Valenzuela, A. (1999). *Subtractive schooling: U.S.–Mexican youth and the politics of caring.* Albany, NY: State University of New York Press.

Vasquez, V. (2005). Creating opportunities for critical literacy with young children: Using everyday issues and everyday text. In, J. Evans (Ed.) *Literacy moves on: Popular culture, new technologies, and critical literacy in the elementary classroom* (pp. 83–105). Portsmouth, NH: Heinemann.

Vatican Radio. (2015, May 31). *Pope: The Holy Trinity exhorts us to live "one with the other."* Available at http://www.news.va/en/news/pope-the-holy-trinity-exhorts-us-to-live-one-with

Vieira, K. (2011). Undocumented in a documentary society: Textual borders and transnational religious literacies. *Written Communication, 28*(4), 436–461.

Walia, H. (2013). *Undoing border imperialism.* Oakland, CA: AK Press and the Institute for Anarchist Studies.

Warner, M. (2002). Publics and counterpublics. *Public Culture, 14*(1), 49–90.

Warren, M. R. (2005). Communities and schools: A new view of urban education reform. *Harvard Educational Review, 75*(2), 133–173.

Warriner, D. S. (2013). "It's better life here than there": Elasticity and ambivalence in narratives of personal experience. *International Multilingual Research Journal, 7*(1), 15–32.

Welch, B. (2009). Sustainable urban infrastructure: How feasible is the adaptive reuse of parochial schools to house charter schools? Paper presented at the 39th annual meeting of the Urban Affairs Association, Chicago, IL.

Welch, B. (2012). A dual nature: The archdiocesan community development corporation. *Community Development, 43*(4), 451–463.

Whelan, A. (2012, October 12). Former South Philadelphia Catholic school will become upscale apartments. *Philadelphia Inquirer.* Available at http://articles.philly.com/2012-10-13/news/34413789_1_new-development-nice-apartments-annunciation

Willis, A. (2008). *Reading comprehension research and testing in the U.S.: Undercurrents of race, class, and power in the struggle for meaning.* New York, NY: Lawrence Erlbaum.

Wohlwend, K. E. (2011). *Playing their way into literacies: Reading, writing, and belonging in the early childhood classroom.* New York, NY: Teachers College Press.

Wortham, S. (2006). *Learning identity: The joint emergence of social identification and academic learning.* New York, NY: Cambridge University Press.

Wuthnow, R. (2004). *Saving America? Faith-based services and the future of civil society.* Princeton, NJ: Princeton University Press.

Wuthnow, R., & Offutt, S. (2008). Transnational religious connections. *Sociology of Religion, 69*(2), 209–232.

Yazzie-Mintz, T. (2007). From a place deep inside: Culturally appropriate curriculum as the embodiment of Navajo-ness in classroom pedagogy. *Journal of American Indian Education, 46*(3), 72–93.

Yoon, H. S. (2014). Assessing children in kindergarten: The narrowing of language, culture and identity in the testing era. *Journal of Early Childhood Literacy.* doi:10.1177/1468798414548778.

Young, I. M. (2000). *Inclusion and democracy.* New York, NY: Oxford University Press.

Zeichner, K. (2010). Rethinking the connections between campus courses and field experiences in college- and university-based teacher education. *Journal of Teacher Education, 61*(1–2), 89–99.

Zeichner, K. (2015). A candid look at teacher research and teacher education today. *LEARNing Landscapes, 8*(2), 49–57.

Zeichner, K., Payne, K. A., & Brayko, K. (2015). Democratizing teacher education. *Journal of Teacher Education, 66*(2), 122–135.

Zimmerman, B. (2008). Creating comics fosters reading, writing, and creativity. *Education Digest,* 55–57.

Index

Activist discourse community, 18, 20, 129–130

Advocacy. *See also* Discourse communities
  collective, in family ESOL class, 58–65
  in cosmopolitan counterpublic, 127–140
  for education/education rights, 54–65, 127–128
  health care, 59–62

Agamben, G., 13, 128

Alab ng Puso: My Heart's Sole Burning Fire (Silva), 92–95, 93, 94

Alcoff, L. M., 4, 117, 119, 120

Alemán, E., 56

Alexander, M., 100, 109

Amanti, C., 8, 58, 79, 106

Anzaldúa, G., 7, 93

Appadurai, A., 9

Aquinas Center, 16–17, 27–38
  aesthetics of, 31–33
  community input and goals for, 33–37, 57–62, 119–123
  history of, 28–29
  planning for, 30–31
  promoting literacy engagement within, 66–77

Archer, L., 133

Arendt, H., 8

Arts
  community building through, 95–96
  learning through, 92–95, 125

Asen, R., 55

Auerbach, E., 57

Bagley, C., 56

Bakhtin, M., 89

Banki, S., 10, 11, 59, 62, 63

Bankston, C. L., 45, 46

Bartolomé, L. I., 106

Barton, D., 19

Baum, S., 86

Baynham, M. J., 71, 73

Bazerman, C., 18

Beach, R., 68

Beauboeuf-Lafontant, T., 106

Beierle, M., 70, 73

Benhabib, S., 55

Benjamin, W., 88

Benmayor, R., 56

Bignall, S., 101, 102, 131

Bitz, M., 98

Blommaert, J., 67, 75

Bloome, D., 70, 71, 73

Bonds, A., 133

Borders
  child migrant "crisis" and, 5–6
  postcolonial perspective on, 7

Borgmann, M., 68

Bourdieu, P., 23, 44, 47, 85, 86

Brandt, D., 68

Brayko, K., 90

Brink, J. T., 139

Brochin-Ceballos, C., 8

Buckley, M., 134

Buff, R. I., 10, 56

Butin, D., 90

Butler, J., 11

Cahill, C., 2, 123
Cammarota, J., 123
Campano, G., 3, 8, 9, 10, 11, 16, 24, 63, 68, 79, 80, 82, 84, 92, 97, 104, 105, 106, 107, 128
Canada, G., 96
Care
  duty of, 105–106
  intergenerational, 111–112
Carini, P. F., 133
Carmona, J. F., 56
Castro-Gómez, S., 17
Castro-Salazar, R., 56
Catholic Campaign for Human Development (CCHD), 34
Catholic Charities USA, 70
Chafetz, J., 68
Chávez, L. R., 56
Child migration crisis, 5–6
Civic engagement, meaning-making and, 69–75
"Class News," 58–61
  curricular inquiries based on, 61–63
Clowes, G. A., 108
Cochran-Smith, M., 2, 4, 64, 79, 90, 116, 123, 132
Cockcroft, E., 93
Cockcroft, J., 93
Coleman, J. S., 46
Collaboration
  between community and Indonesian immigrants, 40–42, 52–53
  in cosmopolitan counterpublic, 127–140
  within discourse communities, 129–130, 134–136
Collective advocacy, in family ESOL class, 58–65
Collins, P. H., 105
Colonialism
  legacies of, 10
  postcolonial theorists and, 6–7

Comic books, multicultural, 97–101
Comics Inquiry Community (CIC), 96–101
Community Literacies Project
  benefits of, 123–124
  community input and perspectives, 119–122
  equality and, 118–119
  overview, 22–26
  presentation of, 124–126
  research interdependence in, fostering, 12–16
  research questions, 1, 122–123
  research team, 2–3, 15–16
  theory and practices for, 115–126, 129–130
Community networks, educators and, 134–136
Community Researchers Project (CRP)
  educational conditions/budgets cuts, 107–111
  goals of, 105–106
  learning from real life experiences, 106–107, 136–138
  overview, 103–104
  support within, 111–114
Community(ies)
  of discourse. See Discourse communities
  immigrant. See Immigrant communities
  of inquiry, educators and, 132–134
  research based in. See Community Literacies Project; Community Researchers Project (CRP)
Compassion, and hospitality, 6
Concerned Black Catholics (CBC), 14, 20, 21, 121
Conflict, discourse communities and, 130
Congregation, St. Thomas Aquinas
  characteristics, 1–2
  human rights narrative, 19, 21–22

solidarity within, 130–131
"Constructive disruption," 132
Cosmopolitan counterpublic, 19
  collaboration and advocacy in,
    127–140
"cosmopolitan intellectuals," 8
"cosmopolitanism from below," 9
Counterpublic(s), 4
  concepts of, 55–56
  cosmopolitan, 19, 127–140
  immigrant rights workshop and,
    4–5
Critical literacy, 105–106
Culler, J., 117
Cultural capital, 44, 46–48
Cultural discourse communities, 18,
    20, 129–130
Cultural mismatch theories, 9
Curran, W., 133
Cushman, E., 3

Dauber, S. L., 42
De Genova, N., 56
Deferred Action for Childhood
    Arrivals, 20
Delgado Bernal, D., 56
Delgado-Gaitán, C., 42
Derrida, J., 6
Discourse communities, 18–22
  collaboration and research within,
    129–130, 134–136
  conflict and, 130
  cross-pollination between, 21–22
  defined, 18
  diverse identities and, 136–138
  human rights metanarrative of,
    21–22
  Latina/o immigrants and, 56–63
  synergistic relationship of, 19–21
  types of, 18
Doomsday Budget Cuts
    (documentary), 103, 107–112
Doucet, F., 42, 50
Dudley-Marling, C., 90

Duncan-Andrade, J., 102, 114, x
Dutro, E., 10
Duty of care, 105–106
Dyson, A. H., 9, 86, 87

Ebaugh, H., 68
Edmiston, B., 68
Education
  advocating for, 127–128
  budget cuts within, 107–111
  critical literacy and, 105–106
  educators, circle of solidarity for,
    132–134
  ESOL students and, 54–65, 78–91,
    137
  funding cuts, 107–111
  learning through diversity and,
    136–138
  parental support for, 40–53
  precarity relevance to, 10–12,
    128–129
Education and Research Group
    (EaR), 16, 118–119, 124
Educational justice, working toward,
    138–140
Educational precarity, 10–12, 128–
    129
Educational research discourse
    community, 18, 19–20, 129–130
Encisom P., 4
English as a second language (ESOL)
  class for families, 54–65
  School–University Partnership and,
    78–91, 137
Epstein, J. L., 42
Equality, community-based research
    and, 118–122
Erickson, F., 2
ESOL. See English as a second
    language (ESOL)
Ethical norms, in community-based
    research, 118–126
Ethnography Forum, 113

Facio, E., 57
Fairclough, N., 69, 73
Family ESOL class, 54–65
Fight for Drivers Licenses, 134–136
Fine, M., 42, 123
Fist Stick Knife Gun (Canada &
    Nicholas), 96
Flores, S. M., 86
Flores, W., 56
Forché, C., 92
Foucault, M., 13, 37, 130
Franciscan social movement, 13–14
Fránquiz, M. E., 8
Fraser, N., 55
Freire, P., 11, 57, 64, 111, 132
Fricker, M., 35, 36, 107, 120, 121

Gadsden, V. L., 86
Gándara, P., 8, 85
Garcia, A., 22
Garcia, F. C., 67
Gardner, H., 117
Gaztambide-Fernández, R., 131
Genishi, C., 9
Ghiso, M. P., 3, 8, 9, 10, 11, 12, 14,
    16, 24, 57, 67, 86, 92, 105, 106,
    128
Girad, R., 21
Goffman, E., 51
Goldman, S., 70, 73
González, N., 8, 58, 79, 106
Goodman, K. S., 82
Gramsci, A., 107
Grigorenko, M., 70, 73
Grude, T., 139
Guerra, J., 18, 106
Gutiérrez, K., 8, 9, 47

Habermas, J., 55
Habitus, literacy and, 46–48
Hames-García, M., 115
Hamilton, M., 19
Harkavy, I., 115
Harker, C., 10
Harper, S. R., 86

Hartley, M., 80, 115
"Hay racismo" (there is racism),
    62–63
Health, advocating for, 59–62
Heath, S. B., 4
Hedges, C., 100
Herzog, W., 139
Himley, M., 133
Hirschman, C., 10, 25
Homo sacer, 13
Honeyford, M. A., 3, 56
Hopkins, M., 8
Hospitality
    and compassion, 6
    radical. *See* Radical hospitality
Hostetler, K., 123
Human rights, metanarrative in
    discourse communities, 19,
    21–22, 138–140
Hurtado, S., 86
Hyndman, J., 133

Ichioka, Y., 93
Immigrant children/youth, 6, 136–
    138
    diverse identities of, 136–138
    Inquiry into College Project, 78–90
    literacies of, 8–10, 46–48
Immigrant communities
    developing civic engagement for,
        69–75
    research partnerships with, 3
    self-representation of (vignettes),
        3–8
    working with parents within,
        39–53, 137
Immigrants/Immigration
    Indonesian, community
        collaboration with, 40–42,
        52–53
    Know Your Rights workshop, 4–5,
        16, 121
    Latina/o, discourse communities
        and, 54–63
    scapegoating of, 5–8

viewpoints on, 6–8, 56, 138
Inquiry into College Project, 78–91
Intergenerational care, 111–112
Intergenerational learning/learning
    space, 15, 57

Jablow, P., 108
Jacobs, J., 30
Jacobs, K. B., 16, 24, 79, 82, 84, 104,
    107
Janks, H., 88
Jones, S., 10
Juzwik, M., 72

Kase, A., 41
Katz, L., 71
Kell, C., 69, 72
Kemmis, S., 123
The Killing Act (documentary), 139
Kinloch, V., 91
Kirkland, D., 101
Know Your Rights workshop, 4–5,
    16, 121
Kohncke, A., 139
Kress, G., 85, 88

Lather, P., 117, 123
Latour, B., 72, 73
Lavan, N., 57
Learning
    bidirectional, in School–University
        Partnership, 78–91
    intergenerational, 15, 57
    through diversity, 136–138
    through the arts, 92–95
Lefebvre, H., 30
Legal discourse community, 18, 20,
    129–130
Leonardo, Z., 36
Levinas, E., 117
Levitt, P., 68
Lewis, C., 4
Linguistic capital, 47–48
Linguistic habitus, 47–48
Linguistic stigma, 62–63

Literacy(ies)
    arts and, 92–102
    civic engagement through, 66–77
    critical, 105–106
    of immigrant youth and families,
        8–10, 46–48
    of interdependence, 12
Long, C., 108
Lopez, M. P., 59
Lorde, A., 15
Low, D. E., 16, 24, 84, 92, 101, 104,
    107
Loyd, J., 133
Lugones, M., 105, 112
Lytle, S. L., 2, 4, 21, 64, 79, 116, 123,
    128, 132, 134

Mahler, S. J., 68
Mangual Figueroa, A., 56
Mansfield, B., 133
Marsh, J., 88
McCann, E., 30
McKenzie, C., 72
McTaggart, R., 123
Meaning-making, civic engagement
    and, 69–75
Media Mobilizing Project, 135, 136
Medina, C., 97
Medina, J., 117, 126
Menken, K., 10
Mestiza consciousness, 7
Mezzacappa, D., 49
Mignolo, W., 7, 17, 53, 128
Mirra, N., 22
Mohanty, C. T., 131
Mohanty, S., 9, 117
Moje, E., 4
Moll, L. C., 8, 58, 79, 106
Mora, G. C., 67, 68
Moraga, C., 113
Morrell, E., 22, 123
Morris, E., 139
Mountz, A., 133
Moya, P., 9, 18, 63, 80, 105, 120
Moyn, S., 21, 139

Multicultural comics, creating,
97–101
Mural Arts Program, 92–95, 125

Nakagawa, K., 42, 43
Nemeth, E., 91
New Sanctuary Movement, 4, 135,
136
Ngai, M. M., 10
Ngo, L., 16, 24, 79, 82, 84, 104, 107
Nicholas, J., 96
Nieto, S., 105
Norms, ethical and professional,
115–126
North American Free Trade
Agreement, 7
"Nosotras te ayudamos" (we will help
you), 61–62
Notebook (Jablow), 108
Nussbaum, M., 117

Offutt, S., 71
Ogbu, J., 110
Oppression
future impact of, 11–12
postcolonial theorists and, 6–7
Orellana, M. F., 9, 47
Ortega, M., 4
Owens, M. L., 27

Pantoja, A., 11
Parental involvement
community building and, 39–53,
137
family ESOL class and, 54, 57–58
Paris, D., 62
Patel, L., 67
Patterson, A., 91
Payne, K. A., 90
Perea, J. F., 56
Pérez Huber, L., 56
Philadelphia, Archdiocese of, 38
Placemaking, for radical hospitality,
27–38. See also Aquinas Center

Pluriversality
conceptual model, 18–22
defined, 7
Porter, R. K., 36
Portnoy, D., 134
Postcolonial agency, manifestations
of, 92–102
Postcolonial theorists, 6–7
Postema, B., 101
Precarity of place, 11
Aquinas Center and, 17
education and, 10–12, 128–129
ontological, 11–12
self-efficacy and, 62
Prison Industrial Complex, 109
Professional norms, in community-
based research, 118–126
Property development, problems
caused by, 37–38
Public sphere/publics, scapegoating
in, 5–8
Putnam, R., 68

Racial stigma, 62–63
Radical hospitality, 8, 13, 14–15, 21
placemaking for, 27–38. See also
Aquinas Center
Ranciére, J., 118
Religious discourse community, 18,
20, 21, 70–75, 129–130
Religious engagement, literacy and,
67–68
Research, community-based. See
Community Literacies Project;
Community Researchers Project
(CRP)
Rey, T., 68
Rieser, L., 108
Rivera, L., 57
Rodríguez, D., 21, 101
Rohr, M., 41
Romo, R., 93
Rosaldo, R., 56
Rymes, B., 47

Sacco, J., 92, 100
Said, E., 6
St. Thomas Aquinas. *See also* Aquinas
    Center; Shields, Fr. Hugh J.
    as "shared parish," 15
    social justice education and, 1–26
Saldívar, J. D., 67
Saltmarsh, J., 80
San Juan, Jr., E., 92
Sanchez, G., 67
Sánchez, L., 3, 30, 105, 106, 128
Sanctuary, 2, 14–15
Scapegoating, of immigrants, 5–8
Schools
    funding cuts, 107–111
    resources and admissions process
        of, navigating, 48–51, 137
School–University Partnership,
    bidirectional learning in, 78–91
Segura, D. A., 57
Selland, M., 10
Service discourse community, 18, 20,
    21, 129–130
Shields, Fr. Hugh J.
    quotes of, 2, 10, 27, 66, 70, 71, 74,
        127
    role of, 29, 30, 70, 71, 130
Shulman, L. S., 117
Siebers, T., 28, 85, 88, 139, 140
Silva, Eliseo Art (muralist), 92–95,
    101
Silverman, R., 27
Simon, R., 102
Singer, A., 139
Sitrin, M., 119
Sleeter, C., 93
Smith, R. D., 27
Social capital, 44–48
Social justice, working toward, 119–
    122, 138–140
Social justice education
    budget cuts within, 107–111
    cross-cultural interaction and, 1–26
    support for, 111–112, 138–140

Solidarity
    circles of, 132–138
    community networks and, 134–136
    congregation and, 130–131
    educational equality through,
        132–134
    precarity of place and, 62
    working with young people and,
        136–138
Sorensen, S. B., 139
South Philly Story Project, 121
Spolan, S., 41
Standing, G., 10
Stepick, A., 68
Stigmas, racial and linguistic, 62–63
Stornaiuolo, A., 98
Street, B. V., 9
Suárez-Orozco, C., 42, 45
Suárez-Orozco, M., 42, 45

Teachers, unemployment of, 110
Thomas, E. E., 98
Thompson, J. B., 47
Thompson, P., 44
Tocqueville, A. de., 68
Todorova, I., 42, 45
Tuck, E., 22

U. S. Immigration and Customs
    Enforcement (ICE), 4
Universal Declaration of Human
    Rights, 8, 135

Vagle, M., 10
Valdés, G., 57, 106
Valenzuela, A., 106
Van Leeuwen, T., 88
Vander Zanden, S., 3
Vasquez, V., 86
Vatican Radio., 38
Vieira, K., 67, 68

Waff, D., 134
Walia, H., 8, 11

Walton-Roberts, M., 133
Warner, M., 56
Warren, M. R., 115
Warriner, D. S., 71
Weber, J. P., 93
Welch, B., 16, 27, 38
Whelan, A., 38
Willis, A., 79
Winn, M. T., 62
Wohlwend, K. E., 86
Workshops(s)
    for building community strength,
        35–37
    for immigrants rights, 4–5, 16, 121
World citizenship, striving towards,
    138

Wortham, S., 71
Wuthnow, R., 68, 71

Yang, W., 22
Yazzie-Mintz, T., 8
Yee, M., 11
Yoon, H. S., 79
Young, I. M., 55
Youth. *See* Immigrant children/youth
Youth Voices program, 35–36

Zeichner, K., 24, 79, 90, 136
Zhou, M., 45, 46
Zimmerman, B., 96

About the Authors

Gerald Campano, University of Pennsylvania, is associate professor and chair of the Reading/Writing/Literacy Division at University of Pennsylvania's Graduate School of Education. His scholarship focuses on practitioner research, critical literacy, identity, and university–community partnerships. Previously, Gerald was a full-time classroom teacher in Texas, Puerto Rico, and California. He has garnered numerous teaching awards at the elementary and university level. Gerald is a Carnegie Scholar and the recipient of the David H. Russell Award for Distinguished Research in the Teaching of English from the National Council of Teachers of English for his book *Immigrant Students and Literacy: Reading, Writing, and Remembering*.

María Paula Ghiso, Teachers College, Columbia University, is an assistant professor in the Department of Curriculum and Teaching at Teachers College, Columbia University. Her scholarly interests include early childhood literacy in multilingual and transnational contexts. María Paula is a former New York City dual language teacher and has facilitated professional development on language and literacy learning in a range of contexts. She has published in venues such as *Journal of Literacy Research, Equity and Excellence in Education, Research in the Teaching of English*, and *Teachers College Record*.

Bethany J. Welch, Aquinas Center, is the founding director of Aquinas Center and a nonprofit management consultant. Her research on the Catholic Church and urban revitalization prompted Philadelphia's St. Thomas Aquinas parish to invite her to help repurpose a former convent into a space that builds unity in diversity, supports learning, and inspires thoughtful action. In 2014, she was recognized by the U.S. Conference of Catholic Bishops with the Cardinal Bernardin New Leadership Award for her work on the effects of poverty and injustice. A VISTA volunteer in 2003–2004, she also received a Spirit of Service Award in 2006 from the Corporation for National and Community Service for advancing transformational change in urban communities through research, planning, and capacity building.